Archaeology into History I

GREEKS, CELTS AND ROMANS

ARCHAEOLOGY INTO HISTORY I

Greeks, Celts and Romans

Studies in Venture and Resistance

Edited by
Christopher and Sonia Hawkes

ROWMAN AND LITTLEFIELD
Totowa, New Jersey

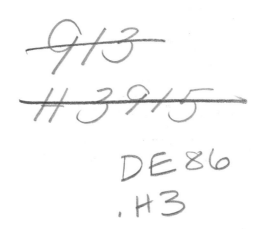

Library of Congress Cataloging in Publication Data

Hawkes, Charles Francis Christopher, 1905–
    Greeks, Celts and Romans.

    (Archaeology into history, 1)
    Includes bibliographies.
        1. Greece—History—Addresses, essays, lectures.
    2. Rome—History—Addresses, essays, lectures.
    3. Iron age—Europe—Addresses, essays, lectures.
    4. Bronze age—Europe—Addresses, essays, lectures.
    I. Hawkes, Sonia Chadwick, joint author. II. Title.
    III. Series.
    DE86.H3   938   73-1223
    ISBN 0-87471-176-2

PRINTED IN GREAT BRITAIN

Contents

List of Illustrations in the Text

List of Plates

Foreword

We are introducing in this series a new kind of archaeological book. Single-author and single-subject books, if they aim at an exhaustive treatment, are more prone today than ever before to erosion by newer work; and the wider their field and the more parts it covers, the more so. This may be true even where each part has its own author, for the speed of a convoy is the speed of its slowest ship. And if the books aim at a treatment less exhaustive than brightly attractive, they lose the value of all the parts this leads them to omit, and therefore tend to cover the omissions up, leaving most readers unaware of what may be serious concealments. As for books of separate studies or essays, where their subjects are diverse they naturally have to lose the value of unity. Yet such essays, being short or of medium length, do suit archaeology's novelty and freshness, as a field that owes its charm so much to new discovery. What is more, they suit authors who themselves are new: who have fresh work and thought in them because they are young. Conventionally, these are expected to give their writings to the learned journals. Yet not only are the journals now in archaeology too few—other than those serving limited regions, like the English counties—but their subscribers are only a portion of its modern reading public. The size of this is shown by the popularity of existing books. There should be room for a new kind, then, combining advantages that till now have not been very readily brought together.

The first advantage will be authors who have something new to say: fresh work and thought, such as the journals are not sufficient for and existing kinds of book do not always suit. The second concerns their subjects. Though these may appear diverse, in any one volume in the series they will have been brought together purposely to show a broader sort of unity: a unity of theme, expressed in the volume's title, which each distinct study will share without any loss to itself. The means used for bringing this out will be editorially written commentaries, introducing each study and linking it up with those before it. The third advantage, certainly novel enough (we believe) today, will be that readers will find a breaking down of conventional subject barriers, and a pleasure in thus discovering new interests across them, extending their more familiar ones and lighting these up by resemblances possibly unexpected. For there really is no denying that archaeology, at present, has an all too obvious part in the fate that attends all growths of knowledge, of splitting away into specialisms which tend to be ever more constricted, so that development, itself so enlivening, ends in dullness. Submission to that fate could ruin the subject for the public, by making most archaeologists bores whom only bores will read or listen to, and also destroy its own inner development, by losing it all unity of intelligence. How appalling.

Lastly, then, and arising straight from that, we turn to the series as a whole, and the title we have deliberately given it: Archaeology into History. It means exactly what it says. Just as exactly for what may be termed the prehistoric, as for Greek, Etruscan, Roman, Early Christian, medieval or anything later or farther out. For just when historians, out of the darkness of old suspicion, have been coming more and more to realize that archaeologists may be human, and seeing even prehistoric ones as fiends at least in human shape, there are quarters in archaeology now where to talk in terms of history is to court derision. Only thirty and twenty-five years ago, Vere Gordon Childe, the archaeologist sage and a professed prehistorian, took *What Happened in History* and simply *History* as titles for books which he started each time with the Palaeolithic. The later one's opening chapter, true, he called 'Society, Science and History', and before its last, 'History as a Creative Process', he had one on 'History as a Comparative Science'. He was of course using 'science' as in 'political science', or 'social science': such were just then acquiring their modern name of 'the human sciences'. But it is with these that prehistoric and protohistoric archaeology, just like history, have their place.

Their laws are not exactly mathematical, any more than their general scheme is static or fixed. Their work, on the history of man as continually seeking for control of nature and for social organization, is work done throughout in a human-scientific manner, impartially using concrete or physical remains, art and words and documentary texts and all writing. The fact that mathematics or physics will aid their study of remains, as also that of art and of writing itself, can open no breach between archaeology and history, nor give them grounds for mutual suspicion or derision in the name of science. But since time is irreversible, and we cannot read writing until after the time when all mankind was palaeolithic, written history has got to have a prehistory before it; so too in various regions, of which Europe is only one, there are intermediate phases for which some knowledge derived from writing, or probabilities or conjectures extrapolated out from it, can affect what would otherwise be prehistory more strictly. Both in this and in any such protohistoric phase, and in what is history more strictly, archaeology is always a factor. The less written record there is, the more we have to look to it; yet the converse, though broadly and for the most part also true, does not operate in quite the same way in practice. This is because judgement, of ancient writings' acceptability, uses a range of skills that stretches away from those employed to interpret relics, and because scholars skilled with texts, and knowing the languages they are written in, work in an old and refined tradition; while archaeology's is young, and may be professed by people innocent of any language but their own. So there are tendencies to pull and keep the two sides apart. Yet history, in a Gordon Childe's sense, is always one. Our series aims at helping to keep the two together within it: against the pull, it will gently push. Archaeology into History; archaeology becoming history.

In this first of our volumes, with its title *Greeks, Celts and Romans*, the gentle push is from the margins of prehistory into ancient history: that history of the classical Greek and Roman world, which education used to make more widely familiar than it now does, but which still lies self-illumined behind the history of Europe as such, beside and in front of remoter studies, prehistoric or Oriental. It attained its primary extent on the map through the Greeks' foundation of colonies, most on Mediterranean, some as far as on Black Sea, coasts, but nowhere more momentously than in southern Italy and Sicily. Bringing archaeology into its very beginning and before, our first contributor shows it ensuing on a movement of trade, by sea. New as it was in itself, this was in general just of the kind which prehistorians see in their maps of distributions, and argue about as an agency of diffusion amongst their cultures. And of peoples in inland Europe to whom Greek trade went on to spread, the same ancient history gives us the name that in the West we employ now more widely, that of the Celts. Our employing this as we do opens the door through protohistory to questions which to linguistic scholars are Indo-European, but to archaeologists mostly appear as entirely prehistoric. So our second contributor here, to balance the first one's graves and vases, can discuss the forms that excavators find in the plans of houses, as a question of prehistoric as much as of later archaeology, without any real removal of his subject from the book's main theme.

This theme, as appears from our sub-title, *Studies in Venture and Resistance*, is that of ancient initiative or venture or enterprise, as something that archaeology can bring alive as a force in history, and equally use its historical side for instructing prehistorians. 'Human wills,' as Sir John Myres once said, 'sometimes get the better of circumstances': not by trying to ignore the control they exert but through taking what advantages they offer. This is as true of prehistoric or later invasions in the British Isles, delicately though one needs to go in inferring these from archaeology, as it is of the venturing of early Greeks discerned likewise in Italy. And when in Italy that protohistoric age had passed, to leave us facing the history of Rome, the enterprise that is shown by this is that of organized advances, or aggressions, that led to empire. Roman venture into various parts of Europe found Celts as spirited resisters; and so we are led to the Roman venture into Britain, and the organized military placing of its forts, those instruments of conquest that archaeology can explore, and expound with modern precision, nowhere better than in our country, and notably in the north of it.

Here is the opportunity for our third contributor. Yet what she shows, from older excavations in the heart of the city of Manchester, is that the earlier phases, matched at Templebrough on the Yorkshire side of the hills, were succeeded by one that endured through much of Late Roman times. Then, what it represents is no longer venture but resistance, against forces that had remained outside these imperial frontiers, and were reasserting the barbarian or protohistoric order across them. And finally, just as the old population living inside them, for so long resistant to Rome, now outlasted her own resistance, so we are able to see from the whole of the volume's last portion, guided by our Austrian fourth contributor, how resistance met barbarian reassertion along the Danube. That archaeology can be more intimate with written history there, past the time of fully recorded Roman organization, is due to the very human will of a Christian saint, Severin, who for long got the better of circumstance and received a written record. But each of the four contributions offers aspects of the same one theme, which is that of action and response in history studied with archaeological aid.

Commentary *1*

The Greek Venture and Archaeology

Between the fall of Mycenae and the rise of Persia, the most decisive event for Europe was its opening, from the Mediterranean, to the enterprise of maritime states and towns then newly rising. Possession of iron for serving industries which must have included shipbuilding, and of alphabetic script for advancing literacy and numeracy, made the Mediterranean's eastern or Levantine coast, past 1000 B.C. and through to the ninth and eighth centuries, a zone where the prosperous Orient fell into fresh relations westward. Opposite Cyprus and to south, between the shore and the Lebanon mountains, were the cities of the Phoenicians led by Sidon and Tyre; through ancient links with Egypt, commercial and political, they were turned to venturing on towards a coast again African, where their focus grew to be Carthage, and so to a zone that stretched to Spain. Cyprus too, through the extending of their power there, obtained some share in that farther-western zone. But Cyprus had also Greeks; and its own seaborne metal trade, traditionally in copper but now with an extension into iron, can be discerned already in Crete and anyhow southern Greece. Not only that: it can be glimpsed, indirectly at least, in Sicily. Italy, moreover, with its toe stretched alongside, had in its heel people probably still in intermittent contact with the islands and coast of western Greece. So there was just enough acquaintance running west from the Aegean—little though it may seem—for Greeks there to utilize, in the same range of venture that took them east to the Levant. Out that way, through events of the previous age when the world of Mycenae was falling, Greeks had been left not in Cyprus only but even in Cilicia; eastward acquaintance thus could run to the corner where Cilicia meets the coast of the Levant stretching north. And not far below, yet well above Phoenicia, where the Orontes river opens the way from inner Western Asia, was the port best known to us for the new Greek trade, at the site called nowadays Al Mina.

I

That these first new Greeks in the East must be viewed in one with the first in the West, where they sailed in quest of products beyond what the East could or wished to afford them, recent archaeology has been showing in a manner unattainable forty years ago. David Ridgway, in his study here following, pays his modern generation's tribute to its first English forerunner, vivid still to my own and to myself, the nobly gifted venturer Alan Blakeway, who perceived, and affirmed against all the banes that beset him, that Italy must have had Greeks along its seaboard, sailing there for trade, before the time came for colonies. The fact that even of the colonies, when Greeks began to found them, the first was said to be Cumae, close beside the Bay of Naples, could point him up the coast to where he recognized his earliest vases among those that, with the eyes of his time, he could see as Greek and brought from the Aegean: namely, in the cultural domain of the Etruscans. That Etruscan culture later, after the founding of most of the colonies and when the Greek trade had passed nearly all into the hands of Corinth, became so Hellenized as to fit the subsequent story that the Tarquins, kings of Rome, were bred from Demaratus, a noble of Corinth and one of Etruria's leading Hellenizers, was viewed by Blakeway as a sequel to the early stage, when the first Greek goods in Etruria were pre-colonial. Why should the first Greeks have advanced up the coast so far, beyond the Straits of Messina and the sites of their ensuing colonies, if not to trade with Etruria, and most for its metals, notably iron? Thomas Dunbabin, a dozen years after Blakeway, gave his question the same positive reply. And while all this early trade can now be shown as a panorama, with Al Mina giving an Oriental stiffener to its dating, archaeology has found the Greek cities that commenced it to be cities of Euboea—the island along the middle-Aegean flank. Lefkandi, the site of major British excavations, lies between the two most famous, Chalcis and Eretria. It is Euboean ceramic industry, thus now well known from its vases, that prevails in the initial Greek phase at Al Mina, from around 800. And so it does in the West.

Here, on the island of Ischia, off the point between the Bay of Naples and the site of ensuing Cumae, subsequent ancient record tells that the same two cities, Chalcis and Eretria, jointly founded a first Greek settlement. Its name was Pithekoussai; now, excavation has been bringing it fame. Giorgio Buchner, after locating its acropolis, has long been arduously working in an adjacent major cemetery; the prevailing early vases in its graves are the same Euboean. Mr Ridgway, for a good while now the excavator's colleague, has written for this book an account which surveys the whole wide setting, from east to west, and from Pithekoussai out to the Campanian mainland and to southerly Etruria. There too, the position that Blakeway found has been transformed by excavation and fresh research. Such work is still proceeding, in hands Italian,

British and other, both in Ischia and at important points elsewhere. It is moving towards an historically valid pattern, of Italic and Etruscan relationship with Greeks, of Greeks with each other, and of all with the distant Orient, which at certain points has lately been made in part already explicit, notably at Veii, as will be seen from Ridgway's pages.

Meantime, whatever is still to come, we have the pre-colonial stage, when voyaging was made for trade, and settlement only to subserve it, firmly now declared—and much as the prophetic Blakeway would have wished. We have it even ascertained that Pithekoussai had iron from the Etruscan-held ironfield in Elba. And for Italy on northward, and beside and beyond in Europe, the gain from all this is both a steadier chronology, from the seventh and late eighth century back to the early eighth and ninth, and along with it a lesson: that where venture sets out, and has power to get what it wants, as in the present case trade in distant products, not only will it keep what it wants and so fulfil its purpose, but through success will create conditions for stable settlement to follow. Where archaeologists must do without the aid of any history, they may think as though the trade were a self-explanatory process, forgetting the factor of power and the potential for spreading settlement. 'Diffusion of culture', abstracted from all such things, can then appear dubious. But the trading enterprise of Greeks, and their colonies, are realities of history: never dubious in themselves, and admitting doubt only about place, occasion, date and circumstance—doubt which archaeology, once equipped and acting thoroughly, can assuage and turn to confidence. This can then bring archaeology's aid elsewhere.

The first Western Greeks: Campanian Coasts and Southern Etruria

BY DAVID RIDGWAY

Introduction

In two papers published in 1935 the late Alan Blakeway concluded that post-Mycenaean Greek commerce with the West preceded the foundation, in the eighth century B.C., of the first Western Greek colonies (Blakeway 1935a, b). Blakeway's method was no less significant than his conclusions: a number of pungent observations bears witness to contemporary need for the lesson that Greek—and Western Greek—history should not necessarily be regarded as the prerogative solely of professional Greek historians. The key point in Blakeway's argument was the apparently novel demonstration that certain 'barbarian' contexts in the West had yielded imported and imitated Greek Geometric vases earlier, typologically, than the earliest examples then known from Greek colonial contexts. As a result, the idiom of 'pre-colonial trade' entered the respective languages of Greek history and barbarian archaeology. The subsequent excavation at a Greek colony demonstrably earlier than any known to Blakeway has since resulted in the assumption of an 'early colonial' (It. 'proto-coloniale' [1]) period in Italy, commercial in tone, Euboean in origin and essentially apart from subsequent Western Greek history: 'the main wave of agricultural colonization begins later, in the 730s' (Andrewes 1967, p. 49). Nor is this all that has happened in the last thirty-five years.

This paper will re-examine—with particular reference to Campania and Etruria and from a Western, occasionally barbarian, point of view—Blakeway's concept of the chronological priority of 'trade' over 'the flag' in the light of the primary evidence

[1] This word was extensively used in a round-table conference (Naples—Ischia, March 1968) on pre- and early colonial activity in the West, of which the proceedings were published after the completion of the present paper. See Postscript, pp. 37–8. 'Proto-coloniale' is better than 'para-coloniale', used by Ridgway 1967, p. 319.

II

that has become available since he wrote.[1] In the order of their treatment here, the new facts can be classified under the following headings:

(i) the emergence of the Euboeans into the archaeological record of the ninth and eighth centuries, not only in Euboea itself but also in the Near East (see the map, Fig. 1);

(ii) the current (1952–) excavation of the Euboean colony at Pithekoussai on the island of Ischia in the Bay of Naples;

(iii) 'new light on the Villanovans', shed not only in south Etruria (where their name means 'people of the culture prior to the Orientalizing Etruscan'), but also in Campania (the region centred on Naples). Each area now has yielded pottery, in particular, which to Blakeway would have seemed Cycladic (meaning Aegean-island Greek), from new—and better understood—Villanovan contexts.

It will be clear by now that (in anyhow two of its three parts) this paper will try to assess, in English, the salient features of a discussion that for obvious territorial reasons has so far been conducted in Italian—by the present writer among many others. As production, publication and discussion of the relevant evidence are incomplete still, this is a 'preliminary report', but in the hopefully valid sense of a true 'dispatch from the front' (see Postscript, pp. 37–8 below).

I. EUBOEANS IN THE EAST: AL MINA

The emergence of the Euboeans into the historical record of both Euboea and the Near East has taken place since Blakeway's time. A new dimension to their history was provided by Sir Leonard Woolley's excavations at Al Mina,[2] the major Iron Age port and entrepôt at the mouth of the Orontes, in North Syria, that provided Greeks with their most important gateway to the empires beyond: and 'it seems likely . . . that it was the Euboeans who led the Greeks to Al Mina, together perhaps with islanders of the Cyclades . . .' (Boardman 1964, p. 65). That several of the wares found

---

[1] This paper will not mention Sicily. Coldstream 1968, pp. 373ff., is a convenient introduction, with further references, to what has happened since Blakeway argued for 'trade before the flag' there as well.

[2] Al Mina excavation reports: Woolley 1937, 1938. Other reports: Robertson 1940 (early Greek vases); Beazley 1939 (Attic red figure vases); Lane 1938 (medieval finds); Robinson 1937 and Allen 1937 (coins); Taylor 1959 (Cypriot and Syrian pottery). Further discussions: Smith 1942; Robertson 1946; Woolley 1948; Boardman 1957 (esp. pp. 5ff., 24ff.), 1959; Birmingham 1961; Coldstream 1968, pp. 313ff. Säflund 1957, pp. 16ff., bases a low Greek chronology on the misprinted caption to Woolley 1937, pl. xiv: Boardman 1957, p. 8 n. 45, 1958 and cf. 1965. Recent general accounts of Euboean enterprise in the East: Dunbabin 1957; Boardman 1964; Coldstream 1968, pp. 302–21.

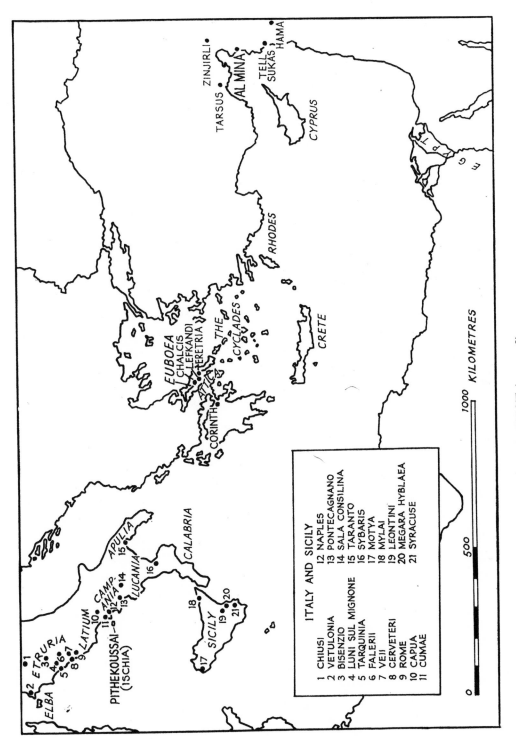

ITALY AND SICILY

1 CHIUSI	12 NAPLES
2 VETULONIA	13 PONTECAGNANO
3 BISENZIO	14 SALA CONSILINA
4 LUNI SUL MIGNONE	15 TARANTO
5 TARQUINIA	16 SYBARIS
6 FALERII	17 MOTYA
7 VEII	18 MYLAI
8 CERVETERI	19 LEONTINI
9 ROME	20 MEGARA HYBLAEA
10 CAPUA	21 SYRACUSE
11 CUMAE	

0   500   1000   KILOMETRES

FIG. 1   MAP, TO SHOW EUBOEANS EAST AND WEST (pp. 1–38).

at Al Mina are distinctively Euboean is confirmed by recent work and discoveries not only in the Western Euboean colony of Pithekoussai but also in Euboea itself: the work of John Boardman on both pottery and history (Boardman 1952, 1957, etc., and 1970); the British excavations at Lefkandi, midway between Chalcis and Eretria (Popham and Sackett 1968), and associated topographical activities (Sackett *et al.* 1966); the Greek-Swiss excavations at Eretria (Schefold 1966; Schefold *et al.* 1967; Karagiorghis and Kahil 1967; Kahil 1968)—all these factors have contributed to a picture that is considerably richer in detail than that available in the mid thirties. The following conclusions have been drawn from current discussions of the evidence for Euboean enterprise in the East in general and at Al Mina in particular: they are stated briefly here as a prelude to the Western story, and with no pretence at originality.

The pebble foundations of the walls in the lowest levels at Al Mina rest on virgin soil (Woolley 1938, pp. 16, 155), and there seems no reason to doubt that the emporium was in itself a new foundation, which either numbered Euboean merchants among its founders (Coldstream 1968, p. 345) or anyway 'only assumed real importance as an emporium when the Greeks began to visit the port and established a small community there' (Boardman 1964, p. 67). An upper limit of 825 B.C. has been suggested for the Syrian and Palestinian material found in the earliest levels (Taylor 1959, p. 91). This agrees as well as can be expected with the date for the earliest Greek pottery from the same levels: Middle Geometric *skyphoi*, or two-handled cups, painted with pendent concentric semicircles, for which Euboea is now seen to be a major source, and Atticizing Middle Geometric pieces from the Cyclades (Coldstream 1968, pp. 310 n. 3, 312, 345). In any case 'the destruction of Tell Sukas . . . in *c.* 850 B.C. ought to provide an upper limit for the establishment of Greek traders on the North Syrian coast' (Coldstream 1968, p. 312): after this episode, associated with the Assyrian punitive campaigns of Shalmaneser III in 853–844, Syria was comparatively untroubled until the conquest of the Levant by Tiglath-Pileser III in 746–727 B.C. There was thus a lull of a century or so in which Euboean and Cycladic merchants were able to establish themselves on the North Syrian coast: and peaceful conditions were no doubt good for trade.

Unfortunately, not all the pottery from Al Mina can now be assigned to its original position in the levels, of which Woolley distinguished ten. The lower six (levels x–v) are relevant to our present purpose: for ease of reference these have been treated by Boardman (Boardman 1964, p. 62) as constituting a *first period* (levels x–vii), covering the earliest history of the town to *c.* 700, and a *second period* (levels vi–v) to *c.* 600. It should always be borne in mind that, although the finds of both periods consist largely of pots and sherds, 'the excavation was in the town and warehouses, and we unfortunately know nothing of the cemeteries and sanctuaries, Greek or native' (Boardman 1964, p. 62): the nature of the evidence at this end of the story is fundamentally different from that at Pithekoussai and in the West generally.

The oldest Greek pottery at Al Mina is Atticizing Euboean and Cycladic, with some Attic and an interesting class of locally made products (Boardman 1959). It may be assigned to levels VIII and earlier (Coldstream 1968, pp. 313ff.)—the remains of levels IX and X are very fragmentary, and it is of course probable that the town covered a smaller area in its early stages (Woolley 1938, pp. 16, 155). 'No other Greek styles are represented until the arrival of Corinthian and Rhodian pottery during the last quarter of the eighth century' (Coldstream 1968, p. 345). The only apparent exception to the rule that 'from Corinth the earliest stratified sherds occur in levels VII–VI' (Coldstream 1968, p. 316) is a Euboean imitation of an 'intermediate' (Late Geometric/Early Protocorinthian) Corinthian type of two-handled bowl (*kotyle*), found in level VIII.[1] A suitable date for this piece would be *c.* 720 B.C.: which is not only good for the division between Corinthian Late Geometric and Early Protocorinthian in general, but also coincides with the lower limit for levels X–VIII proposed on the basis of the Syrian and Palestinian evidence (Taylor 1959, p. 91). It is therefore reasonable to sub-divide the first period at Al Mina into a phase (levels VIII and earlier: up to *c.* 720 B.C.) in which Greek trade was wholly in Euboeo-Cycladic hands, followed by a phase (level VII: *c.* 720 B.C. onwards) in which Euboeo-Cycladic merchants and material were supplemented by new arrivals from Rhodes and Corinth 'among their residents, or at least among their visitors' (Coldstream 1968, p. 385).

In fact the Greek element in level VII 'seems to expand at the expense of the Levantine'. It is clear stratigraphically that level VII is a rebuilding of level VIII (Woolley 1938, pp. 18, 154): such repairs 'imply considerable havoc among the warehouses' (Coldstream 1968, p. 385), which in turn may be associated with the crushing of the rebel Levantine cities by Assyrian forces and the sack of the neo-Hittite city of Hama by Sargon II in 720 B.C.—which meant the end of the export of Greek pottery inland. These warlike events in the Near East, and the consequent decrease in the Levantine element at Al Mina, have been linked with the foundation of Phoenician Motya (*c.* 720–710 B.C.) in Western Sicily: 'the fall of Hama, perhaps, may have inclined some Phoenician merchants to leave the North Syrian coast, in search of more tranquil markets in the western Mediterranean' (Coldstream 1968, p. 388).

The break between the first and second periods at Al Mina is represented architecturally in level VI by 'a complete replanning of the warehouses, which must have

[1] Boardman 1957, pl. iib (a); Coldstream 1968, pp. 315 no. 30, 316 and cf. pl. xlih—from Ischia.

been caused by some major disturbance soon after 700' (Coldstream 1968, p. 385). It is more than possible that this disturbance was an indirect result of the revolt in 696 of the Assyrian governor in Cilicia, supported by the Greeks at Tarsus—an episode which culminated in the destruction of Tarsus by Sennacherib and could well have made Greeks in general unpopular with Assyrians (Boardman 1964, p. 70; 1965, p. 14). In the present context, however, it is more important to note a feature of the second period that is apparently unconnected with any local cause or effect. '. . . most of the Greek pottery arriving at Al Mina in the seventh century is coming from parts of Greece other than those which served the Greeks living there in the eighth century. The Euboean interest has virtually disappeared' (Boardman 1964, p. 73). The disappearance of the Euboean presence at Al Mina in the seventh century has been linked with the so-called Lelantine War between Eretria and Chalcis at home around 700,[1] after which both cities 'retire from the arena for many years' (Boardman 1964, p. 73): and the archaeological record at Al Mina is dominated by Corinthian and East Greek vases.

The story of Euboean activity at Al Mina can thus be summarized as follows:

Euboeans In: 1a—*c.* 825—*c.* 720
    —levels VIII and earlier
    —trade wholly in Euboeo-Cycladic hands: some Attic and Atticizing, including Cycladic, Euboean and local versions.
   1b—*c.* 720—*c.* 696
    —level VII
    —predominantly as before, but now with some Corinthian and Rhodian pottery and 'visitors'.

Euboeans Out: 2—*c.* 696 onwards
    —levels VI upwards
    —virtually no Euboeo-Cycladic; mainly Corinthian and East Greek.

II. EUBOEANS IN THE WEST: PITHEKOUSSAI

Blakeway identified the Greek affinities of many of the vases he observed in Etruria as 'Cycladic', and this—given the dependence of the Cyclades on Euboea [2]—was already symptomatic of Euboeans in the West: a concept which we can now examine against the background of their slightly earlier enterprise in the Near East. In the

---

[1] Boardman 1957, pp. 27ff.; Forrest 1957; D'Agostino 1967; Coldstream 1968, pp. 368ff.
[2] For the geographical and political dependence of the Cyclades on Euboea see Boardman 1957, pp. 9, 24f., 25 n. 153.

West, Blakeway saw Cumae as the 'one Greek colony . . . whose foundation falls within the pre-colonization period' (Blakeway 1935a, p. 200), and his brief reference to Pithekoussai, on Ischia near by—known, of course, to him only from the literary sources—show him ready to think of it as 'the centre from which much of the early Greek Geometric in Etruria was distributed' (Blakeway 1935a, p. 180). The fact that this was not immediately seen to be so, to any great extent (Cook 1962, p. 114; but see now Postscript, pp. 37–8), in no way lessens the importance of Giorgio Buchner's excavations, begun in 1952, in the cemetery, on the acropolis and elsewhere at Pithekoussai. Cumae was already 'a most ancient foundation—the oldest of all those in Sicily and Italy' (Strabo V, c 243 = V, 4, 4): Pithekoussai, whence Cumae was traditionally founded (Livy VIII, 22, 5–6), has amply justified its claim to be even older. Pithekoussai and Cumae must now be seen as the essential components of the 'early colonial' or '*proto-coloniale*' period referred to above, preceded in time only by those Greek elements whose arrival in the West is still demonstrably earlier than that of the earliest imports known at Pithekoussai. The contents and possible significance of this 'pre-colonial' horizon will be examined in the next section: meanwhile we must turn to Pithekoussai itself, and use the evidence of topography and excavation to determine the nature and date of the settlement there.

Topography (Pls. I, II)

> . . . orbataque praeside pinus
> Inarimen Prochytenque legit sterilique locatas
> colle Pithecusas, habitantum nomine dictas.
> > Ovid, *Metamorphoses*, XIV, 88–90

Telling how Aeneas touched the islands at the north end of the Bay of Naples on his way, Ovid remarks their names: '. . . the fleet, though with loss of its helmsman, reaches Inarime and Prochyte [both implying volcanoes, one now Procida]; also Pithecusae, on its barren hill, named from the folk there.' (trans. C. F. C. Hawkes.)

The location of Pithekoussai satisfies all the requirements of pioneers in a strange land (Boardman 1964, p. 177): the acropolis of Monte di Vico is a short, rocky, steep-sided peninsula at the north-west corner of the island, about 18 km. as the crow flies from Cumae on the mainland. The town site itself is convenient of access only by an easily defensible route up the east slope, and has ideal harbours in the form of a narrow inlet immediately to the west—the modern Baia (or Spiaggia) San Montano, backing on to the colonists' cemetery in the Valle San Montano—and the broader curve to the east that is now the sea-front of Lacco Ameno. Evidence for Greek activity elsewhere on what is, after all, a fair-sized island (46·3 sq. km.: cf. Capri—10 sq. km.; Procida—3 sq. km.) is very thin on the ground.

In her account of the geography of Ischia, Dora Buchner Niola clearly shows that the '*risorsa fondamentale*' of the island in historical times has always been agriculture (Niola 1965, ch. VI *passim*)—but only in the specialized sense of viticulture (Niola 1965, p. 103, fig. 12). This is a direct result of the island's hilly terrain, of the climate and of the soil—mainly a very porous volcanic tufa, rich in minerals but poor in clay content and in humus. A non-geographer may perhaps be forgiven for concluding that only the vine is capable of retaining moisture, and that its roots serve to bind the soil so that it is not washed off the necessarily narrow terraces by the normally heavy winter rains. However this may be, the fact remains that areas of arable land suitable for other types of agriculture are few and far between, and very small. A great deal of the island is known to have been covered with *boscaglia* (low wooded scrub) until the sixteenth century A.D., and this is not likely to have been less thick or extensive in the eighth century B.C. Ischia's heavily eroding hillsides could hardly be less like the rolling plains of, say, Leontini in Sicily or (on the southerly mainland) Sybaris; and the poverty of the modern inhabitants has been alleviated only by the regular seasonal influx of tourists characteristic of the last two decades of the present century.

The excavations

'. . . the island of Ischia, formerly Aenaria, off the coast of Campania. I have been informed by Professor Ernest Gardner that little excavation has ever been done on the island, but there is no reason why Greek burials should not exist there.'

Purser 1927, p. 36

Giorgio Buchner's first series of campaigns (1952–61) in the Valle San Montano at the foot of Monte di Vico (Pl. II) produced almost 730 tombs.[1] Much of the pottery is Protocorinthian (Buchner 1964, p. 267), and of this a good deal belongs to the Early Protocorinthian or 'globular *aryballos*' phase, datable now to *c.* 720–690.[2] The earlier

---

[1] Preliminary information about the Pithekoussai excavations: Buchner 1954a, b, 1961, 1962, 1964, 1966a, b, 1970 and forthcoming; Stoop 1955; Trendall 1956, 1967. The definitive report on the 1952–61 excavations, edited by Dr Buchner and the present writer, is scheduled to go to press in early 1973: it will be published by the Accademia dei Lincei as an early volume in its projected new series of *Monumenti Antichi* monographs.

[2] Phase when the *aryballos* (flask for perfumed oil, buried with the dead) was of the early globular-bodied form. For dating see Buchner and Boardman 1968, p. 59 n. 78; but see also Coldstream 1968, p. 330, with the Bocchoris scarab in a grave dated *c.* 710–705 B.C. (*ibid.*, p. 327).

part of the eighth century is represented by a certain number of tombs earlier than the 'globular aryballos period'; some of them contained locally made imitations of the earliest, 'Aetos 666', type of Corinthian Late Geometric round kotyle, of which imported examples were also found sporadically in the cemetery.[1] In the second series of excavations (1965–   ), about 90 m. south-east of the first, the proportions are rather different (Buchner 1970 and forthcoming); although the material is not yet available for detailed study, it is already clear that far more eighth-century tombs can be assigned to the 'Aetos 666' period, which precedes anything known from colonial Cumae. At the time of writing, the total number of tombs excavated stands at 1,033, ranging in date from the eighth century B.C. to Roman times; the excavated areas together represent probably less than 5 per cent of the total surface area of the cemetery. The aim of the current series of excavations is to make a transversal cut across the valley; roughly half of this has now been done; the second instalment of the project entails the first excavation near the foot of the acropolis itself, and it remains to be seen whether this will produce any Greek imports earlier than those found so far. Since 1965 Dr Buchner has also carried out three rescue excavations in the area: an ancient dump (the 'Scarico Gosetti') filling a rain-water channel on the east slope of the acropolis; a votive deposit in the Mezzavia area, about 350 m. south-west from San Montano, which produced figurines of horses, mules, carts and boats together with Transitional and Early Corinthian pottery dated *c.* 635–620 (Trendall 1967, pp. 30f.); a building complex, also in the Mezzavia area ('Mazzola'), which—like the 'Scarico Gosetti'—has produced to date a good deal of imported material as early as (but not earlier than) any at present known from the cemetery (see Postscript, pp. 37–8).

The 1952–61 excavations in the Valle San Montano cemetery produced a number of pieces that are already well known: the Nestor Cup,[2] the Shipwreck Krater[3] and the Bocchoris scarab[4] are redolent of a certain degree of sophisticated contact with the outside world in the eighth century. In the absence of full excavation reports, however, it may not be generally apparent that evidence for sophistication of this order is more usual than exceptional in the eighth-century material from the Pithekoussai tombs

[1] Buchner 1964, pp. 264ff., fig. 1a = Coldstream 1968, pl. xixj (and v. *ibid.*, p. 101); Ridgway 1967, p. 315 n. 27.
[2] Buchner and Russo 1955; Jeffery 1961, pp. 235f.; Guarducci 1967, pp. 226f.; Metzger 1965 is an effective reply to Carpenter 1963, pp. 83ff., and see now Guarducci 1970, pp. 51–7. Associations: Trendall 1956, p. 61, fig. 14. Assigned to the first phase of the Rhodian Late Geometric 'Bird-kotyle Workshop' by Coldstream 1968, p. 277.
[3] Brunnsåker 1962. The drawing Buchner 1966b, p. 8 supersedes Buchner 1954b, p. 42, fig. 1 (widely reproduced) and Brunnsåker 1962, p. 171, fig. 7.
[4] Bosticco 1957, p. 218 no. 102, pp. 225, 227 no. 2; Momigliano 1963, p. 105; Buchner 1966a, p. 10; Coldstream 1968, pp. 316f., 327. Associations: Stoop 1955, fig. 17.

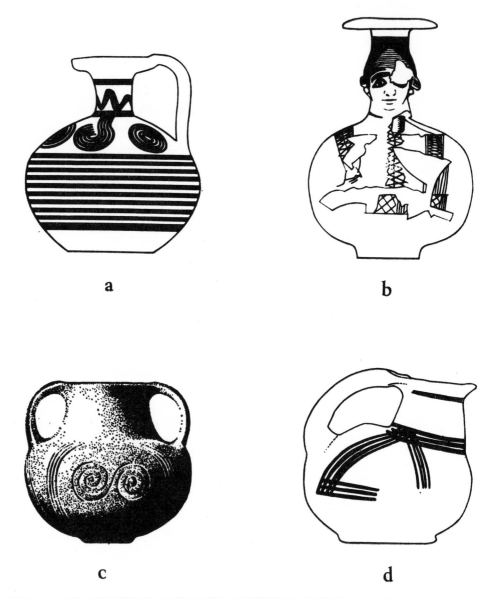

FIG. 2   PITHEKOUSSAI: IMPORTED POTTERY, EIGHTH CENTURY B.C., FROM THE VALLE SAN MONTANO CEMETERY (pp. 15–16). a, Rhodian aryballos (tomb 233 ht. 8,5 cm.); b, North Syrian face-aryballos (tomb 517: ht. 11,7 cm.); c, spiral amphora of impasto, brought from Etruria (tomb 233: ht. 7,6 cm.); d, askos, brought from Calabria (tomb 102: ht. 8,1 cm.).

and other sites. Both the Scarico Gosetti and the Mazzola excavations have yielded many fragments of figured kraters, or *krateres* (wine-mixing bowls), imported and local (Trendall 1967, p. 31, fig. 2; and see Postscript, pp. 37–8), as well as further graffiti on eighth-century sherds; and meanwhile the side-long *alpha* (Guarducci 1967, p. 225) inscribed on a sherd from the cemetery has been taken as suggesting a degree of local evolution of the Greek alphabet prior to the date indicated by comparanda and associations for the Nestor Cup itself. The latter is by no means the only vase that had come from Rhodes: the cemetery has produced dozens of Rhodian globular aryballoi (Fig. 2, a)[1] of a type widely exported from *c.* 725 and occasionally found in Etruria. The Bocchoris scarab is one of more than a hundred scarabs found to date in eighth-century contexts in the cemetery;[2] some (not many) occur in seventh-century contexts—and again there are a few in Etruria. There are eighty-seven seals of the North Syrian or

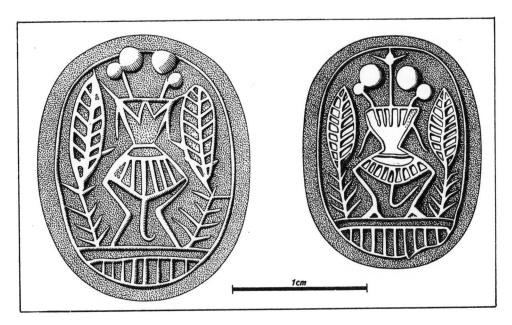

FIG. 3   SEALS, OF THE 'LYRE-PLAYER GROUP' (pp. 15–16). Left, from Pithekoussai: right, from Etruria (Falerii).

[1] On the type see Coldstream 1968, p. 276, pl. lxiib and Friis Johansen 1957, p. 17, fig. 19, p. 33, figs. 55–6, p. 47, fig. 96, p. 71, figs. 142–3 (Exochi). To Friis Johansen's list (*ibid.*, p. 155) add: Bernabò Brea and Cavalier 1959, pl. xli nos. 2, 4, 6 (Mylai); Ricci 1955, col. 219, fig. 10. nos. 1, 3 (Cerveteri); Hencken 1968a, p. 346, fig. 344b (Tarquinia); see also Coldstream 1969, pp. 4, 7 n. 33. The decoration on the examples from Mylai and in Etruria seems to have disappeared, and this is also true of many at Pithekoussai.
[2] Bosticco 1957 accounts for 31 of the Pithekoussai scarabs. Etruria: *ibid.*, p. 216 n. 2; *Q.F.*(1), p. 221, fig. 94k; *Q.F.*(2), p. 130, fig. 52; *Q.F.*(3), p. 139, fig. 30 no. 16 (Veii, Quattro Fontanili: glass paste, amber, faience).

Cilician class known as the Lyre-Player Group; thirty-four were found in the first series of excavations in the cemetery (Buchner and Boardman 1968), and fifty-two have been found so far in the second series. It is now thought that the greater number of the tombs with such seals may date from the third quarter of the eighth century (Buchner and Boardman 1968, p. 59, n. 79). Pithekoussai has yielded to date more than one-third of the total number of the Lyre-Player Group known from the entire ancient world; of the five seals of this class recorded from Etruria, one can be paralleled exactly at Pithekoussai (Buchner and Boardman 1968, no. 43 from Falerii—cf. no. 5). Aryballoi and other vases from the Near East also occur; they include a North Syrian face-aryballos (Fig. 2, b) with parallels at Tarsus and Zinjirli (Buchner 1964, p. 271 n. 11; 1966b, p. 7; Coldstream 1969, pl. iif). Imported Euboean vases of the eighth century have naturally been found (Buchner 1964, pp. 267ff.; Coldstream 1968, pp. 189ff.; Boardman 1970, pp. 110ff.): they include a class previously thought to be Cretan.[1] There are Euboean imitations of Protocorinthian that include bird-kotylai previously known only from Euboea itself—and Al Mina.[2] The presence of similar fibula-types in Etruria and at Pithekoussai will be noticed in the next section; an impasto spiral amphora from Etruria (Fig. 2,c), associated at Pithekoussai with Early Protocorinthian, has been much discussed (Ridgway 1968a, pp. 239f.; Buchner 1970, pp. 89ff., figs. 22–23); and a 'barrel-vase' from a tomb in the second series of excavations finds its closest parallel, both for form and decorative motifs, in Etruria from the Olmo Bello cemetery at Bisenzio.[3] From elsewhere in the Italian peninsula, Apulia (Buchner 1964, fig. 6b, as Mayer 1914, pl. xvii, nos. 3, 5–8; De la Genière 1968, pp. 45f.) and Calabria (Fig. 2,d, askos. De la Genière 1968, p. 240), are represented by vases painted in the respective indigenous Geometric styles. Other fabrics present in eighth-century contexts at Pithekoussai include Argive Monochrome, Attic ('SOS' amphoras) and Phoenician Red Slip. In the latter connection it is worth pointing out that parallels exist at Pithekoussai for many of the objects illustrated in a recent account of the excavation, at Riotinto in southern Spain, of the remains of a community of eighth-seventh-century silver miners (Blanco and Luzón 1969). In the opinion of the excavators these were either Phoenicians themselves or natives in close contact with Phoenicians. It is particularly interesting that a small three-legged bowl (Blanco and Luzón 1969, pl. xxivd) from

[1] The class has long been known from Cumae, where it was defined as Cretan by Payne 1931, p. 5 n. 1, followed by Blakeway 1935a, p. 202, and Dunbabin 1948, p. 8. A Euboean identity was proposed by Buchner 1964, pp. 267ff. and accepted by Coldstream 1968, pp. 194f.
[2] Coldstream 1968, p. 194 and cf. note 1, p. 9 *supra*.
[3] Buchner 1970, p. 94; cf. Åkerström 1943, pl. xii no. 4 (Bisenzio); see also *Sotheby Sale Catalogue* 13th June 1966, no. 46 (no provenance); a vase of similar form, with little or no decoration remaining, is displayed in the Museo Etrusco at Chiusi.

Riotinto has parallels not only at Pithekoussai, where one is associated with a Phoenician Red Slip *oinochoe* (wine jug or flagon) (Buchner 1964, fig. 6a = Jully 1968, pl. i, no. 2, as Cintas 1950, pl. lxxiv, top), but also at Tarquinia (Hencken 1968a, p. 348, fig. 346e, g, i), where three are associated with a Rhodian aryballos of the type noted above and with a 'lion fibula' identical with that found at Pithekoussai in the same tomb as the Bocchoris scarab (Buchner 1966a, p. 11 n. 24).

The contents of the Scarico Gosetti, excavated in 1965, were unstratified and ranged in date from the Apennine Bronze Age to the second century B.C. (Campanian black-glaze), with the exception both of anything Greek earlier than the earliest vase-types known from the cemetery and (virtually) of native Iron Age material corresponding with that from Castiglione d'Ischia (Buchner 1937; Buchner and Rittmann 1948, pp. 35ff.) and pre-Hellenic Cumae. In addition to pottery, the channel produced 'a fair quantity of iron-slag, two bottoms of rough pots the insides of which are encrusted with iron-slag—in other words they had been used as crucibles—and several fragments of bellows-mouthpieces of terracotta' (Buchner 1966b, p. 12). Parallels for these mouthpieces (*tuyères*, Fig. 4) from Greek Marseilles, and Ampurias by the eastern Pyrenees, are admittedly dated as late as the second half of the sixth

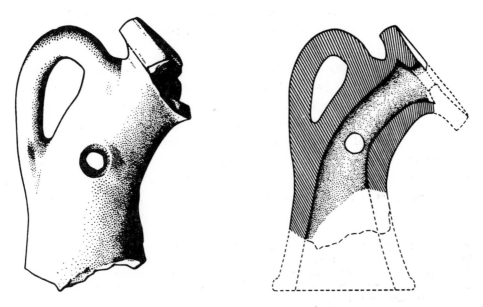

FIG. 4 PITHEKOUSSAI: CLAY MOUTHPIECE (*TUYÈRE*) FOR BELLOWS, FROM THE SCARICO GOSETTI, ht. *c.* 20 cm. (pp. 17–18).

century,[1] but the cemetery had already yielded a piece of iron-slag, in an unequivocally eighth-century context (Buchner 1966b, p. 12). And the analysis of a piece of iron mineral from the Scarico Gosetti has shown conclusively that it was mined on Elba (Marinelli *apud* Buchner 1970, p. 97f.).

The nature of the settlement

'Even more than by the beauty of land and sky, and the excellence of the waters, the Chalcidians and Eretrians were probably attracted by the commercial opportunities which Ischia offered.'

Pais 1908, p. 183

R. M. Cook once suggested that Pithekoussai was settled by Greek colonists intent on agriculture, who chose it for its fertility and for its impregnability as an island, and that Cumae—which has no harbour (but see now Paget 1968)—represents the logical extension of agriculture, rather than trade, to the mainland (Cook 1962). This view seemed at one time to have crystallized into dogma in some quarters (Woodhead 1962, p. 33; Graham 1964, pp. 218f.), though not in others:[2] it recalls A. Gwynn's classic paper on the causes of Greek colonization (Gwynn 1918), and contrasts sharply with T. J. Dunbabin's conviction, thirty years later, that Cumae—then still the earliest known Greek foundation in the West—owed its existence to interest in the metals of Etruria.[3]

The facts of topography and excavation, summarized above, yield two pieces of evidence which lend strong support to the commercial rather than to the agricultural hypothesis: they are in turn borne out by the simplest interpretation of the recently acquired archaeological evidence as a whole. Firstly, Ischia itself: a modern account of the island's natural resources suggests very strongly that it would not have been chosen by knowledgeable colonists whose sole or principal motive was the traditional pressing need for good cornland. Secondly, the smelting of iron ore from Elba at Pithekoussai, as early as the eighth century, is now proved (as we have seen) beyond reasonable doubt.

[1] Benoît 1948; 1965, pl. xv, nos. 1–3 (Marseilles); Almágro 1945, p. 67 and fig. 13, no. 3 (Ampurias); see also Jully 1968, pl. viii.
[2] Boardman 1964, pp. 176f.; Buchner 1964, pp. 273f.; 1966a, p. 8; 1966b, p. 12; D'Agostino 1967, pp. 23f.; Humphreys 1965, p. 425; Bérard 1960, p. 71; Andrewes 1967, pp. 49, 102f., 123f.; Coldstream 1968, pp. 370f.
[3] Dunbabin 1948, pp. 7f.; Vallet 1958, p. 57; Heurgon 1961, pp. 20, 151; Gabrici 1913, cols. 168, 364.

These two factors confirm S. C. Humphreys's view that the initial organization of Pithekoussai was different from that of subsequent colonies. Mrs Humphreys pointed out that the identification of the earliest post-Mycenaean Greek establishments abroad—Al Mina and Tell Sukas, on the coast of Syria—as *emporia* rather than food-producing townships (*poleis*) makes for a better appreciation of the relevance of commerce. (She wrote, Humphreys 1965, p. 424, '*vediamo infatti che la fondazione di un insediamento all'estero per ragioni commerciali nell'ottavo secolo non era impossibile*'.) Furthermore, it may be pointed out that Pithekoussai is one of a number of early Greek foundations in the West which, like Al Mina and Tell Sukas in the East, are near the sites of former Mycenaean trading stations (Immerwahr 1959, p. 298): *Pithekoussai*: Castiglione d'Ischia, and Vivara;[1] *Syracuse*: Plemmyrion; *Megara Hyblaea* (again Sicily): Thapsos; *Taranto* (Apulia): Scoglio del Tonno; *Al Mina*: Sabouni (Woolley 1948; Boardman 1957, p. 7 n. 32; Hankey 1967, p. 112); *Tell Sukas* (same location: Hankey 1967, pp. 113f.). And '. . . it would be odd if in the early Iron Age sailors from the Ionian islands did not sometimes cross the straits' (Cook 1960, pp. 34f.): Professor Cook has himself implied the survival of knowledge of the West from Mycenaean times, and it may have extended not only to Magna Grecia but also to Etruria. The allegedly Mycenaean sherds (LH III A-C)[2] that have been found in a native (Apennine Culture) context at Luni, in the province of Viterbo, could conceivably be connected with Late Mycenaean interest in the natural resources of Elba and north-west Etruria (Pugliese Carratelli 1962, pp. 7ff; 1966, pp. 157f.). To be passed in Mycenaean times the opposite way, to Greece, we have an axe-mould of stone, very likely North Italian (not the whole mould, but a half-piece, slightly damaged) at Mycenae (well known, from the 'House of the Oil Merchant', LH III B),[3] and an Italian vase in an LH III C context at Lefkandi (Popham and Sackett 1968, p. 18, fig. 34); it is not fanciful to see a Villanovan belt from Euboea (Close-Brooks 1967a) as a later counterpart of these earlier shippers' oddments. Main cargoes of consumer goods, thus implied, suit both the periods.

Throughout the half-century before *c.* 700/690, the Euboeans at Pithekoussai

---

[1] Taylour 1958, pp. 7f., pl. viii. One of the 'Geometric' sherds from Castiglione d'Ischia (Buchner and Rittmann 1948, pp. 41f.; Johannowski 1967, pp. 159, 167) has now been recognized as Mycenaean: Buchner 1970, p. 96f. and fig. 25c.

[2] Östenberg 1967, pp. 128–51, 245–54; also illus. Ridgway 1968b, p. 41 fig. 15. Hencken 1968a, p. 448; 1968b, pp. 191f.; and Peroni 1969, p. 171f. discuss the Mycenaean-Apennine synchronization. See also Johannowski 1967, p. 159.

[3] Wace 1953, p. 15, pl. ixb; Childe 1960; Müller-Karpe 1959, text vol., p. 93, fig. 9. On this type of bronze axe, see now MacNamara 1970, pp. 245–6, fig. 1 no. 2.

steadily acquired a wide range of goods, many of them luxuries, originating from a wide variety of centres in the Near East, Greece and Italy itself. The nature of the goods that have survived in the graves excavated cannot really be explained by reference to piracy or to the imposition of tolls on passing merchant-ships. In the nature of things, such ships would be on their way either to or from Etruria. Their masters would have needed not merely 'a useful place to stop and revictual' (Cook 1962, p. 114), which they could have done almost anywhere, but '*una base amica in cui poter svernare, riparare le navi, o ricevere carichi già raccolti per loro da mediatori*'—a friendly base for wintering, mending ship, or loading cargoes assembled in advance for them by agents—preferably with a '*modicum* [my italics] of good land from which to support themselves' (Humphreys 1965, p. 425; Hammond 1967, p. 122): in other words a 'home base', not too far off, with residents. And the natural advantages of the acropolis and harbours at Pithekoussai make it an obvious choice for an early headquarters at the western end of any sea-borne trade between Etruria and the Aegean.

Such an interpretation inevitably recalls Blakeway's conclusions of thirty-five years ago: literary evidence has been complemented by archaeology at the western end of the story. We are left in no doubt that the arrival of Protocorinthian in the West and the first steps in the 'Hellenization of Etruria' were bound up with Euboean enterprise.

Blakeway held that the 'strong causal connection between commerce and colonization' that resulted in the presence of a diversity of Greek fabrics in the West was succeeded in the seventh century by an 'overwhelming preponderance of the pottery of Corinth' (Blakeway 1935a, pp. 203–4). The evidence from Pithekoussai now shows clearly that Western trade was in the hands of the Euboeans until the beginning of the seventh century. Then, with the transition from the Protocorinthian globular aryballos to the ovoid variety, the pottery is almost exclusively Corinthian; and the overall image of seventh-century Pithekoussai comes to differ but little from that of the normal run of Western colonies. We have observed a similar and contemporary succession in the previous section: the first and second periods at Al Mina.

There is thus a very strong case for accepting that 'with the possession of the base of Al Mina in the East and that of Pithekoussai in the West, the Euboeans were, from about 775 to 700 B.C., the masters of the trade between the Eastern Mediterranean and Central Italy' (Buchner 1966b, p. 12). The importance that Blakeway attached to trade as a factor in early colonization is wholly confirmed: the necessary adjustment of his dates and attributions requires little more effort than the substitution of the epithets 'early colonial' (*proto-coloniale*) or 'Euboeo-Cycladic' for the greater part of his 'pre-colonial'. The agricultural possibilities of Ischia—or the lack of them—

are unlikely to have been a factor in the development of a commercial operation of this type and on this scale.

It should be noted, however, that the parallel between Pithekoussai and Al Mina is incomplete in one important respect [1]—quite apart from the fundamental difference in the nature of the evidence available for interpretation. Whereas Pithekoussai was a new and wholly Greek settlement in apparently virgin territory overseas, Al Mina was a settlement of Greeks in a foreign city where supplies could presumably be acquired without difficulty. Although the evidence from the hinterland of Campania suggests that, in the West, the Euboeans may well have been moving into a wide-ranging Villanovan community with a comparatively stable organization, it is intrinsically likely that the Euboeans resident on Ischia would have felt the need to provide for themselves if the need arose (Humphreys 1965, p. 425); and the evidence of Ischia in historical and modern times suggests that a subsistence economy of precisely this nature is the most that the island could have supported.

Objections : gold-mines, fertility and pottery exports

Two inconvenient facts remain to be discounted: (i) a Greek author specified Ischia's 'gold-mines', and fertility, as natural advantages enjoyed by the early settlers there; and (ii) Professor Cook has pointed out 'there is little or nothing of Ischian make among the early Greek pots found in Etruria' (Cook 1962, p. 114; Coldstream 1968, p. 371).

(i) The author is Strabo (of the time of Augustus).[2]

> 'Pithekoussai was once settled by Eretrians and also Chalcidians, who, although they had prospered there on account of the fruitfulness of the soil (εὐκαρπία) and on account of the gold-mines (τὰ χρυσεῖα), forsook the island as the result of a quarrel . . .'
>
> Strabo, Geography V, c 247 = V 4, 9
(trans. H. L. Jones)

Not unlike χρυσεῖα is the Greek word χυτρεῖα, meaning 'potteries', conceivably too 'deposits of potters' clay'; it is a rare word, so does not seem particularly convincing as a replacement for χρυσεῖα here by emendation, as E. Pais and J. Bérard

---

[1] I am grateful to Professor Cook for pointing this out to me.
[2] I am grateful to M. W. Frederiksen and M. L. West for helpful discussion and correspondence about this passage.

have proposed.[1] Ischia does, however, possess a good source—the only one in the general area of the Bay of Naples—of potters' clay. It was used from an early stage at both Pithekoussai and Cumae. By the sixth century Pithekoussai was supplying architectural terracottas to mainland Campania; and in Hellenistic and Roman times there was a notable production of wine-jars and black-glaze pottery (Buchner and Rittman 1948, pp. 45, 54–60). Pliny, in fact (*Nat. Hist.* III, VI 82), derives the Greek name 'Pithekoussai' not from *pithekoi* (πιθήκοι), meaning 'monkeys', but from potters who made *pithoi* (πίθοι, 'jars'): *non a simiarum* ['monkeys'] *multitudine, sed a figlinis doliorum* (makers of 'jars', so perhaps of pots in general). It has been objected [2] that Pliny's *figlinis doliorum* is simply an explanation, thought by him possible, of the derivation of 'Pithekoussai' from 'pithoi', rather than reliable evidence for the existence of flourishing potteries; and that in any case potteries and their products would not have had the same significance in the eyes of an ancient writer that they have for a modern archaeologist. If these objections are valid, we are left in all probability with χρυσεῖα again—for which indeed Dr Buchner, in conversation with the writer, has suggested the translation, possible at least theoretically, 'goldsmiths' workshops'. This is attractive, but difficult to prove. Anything which Strabo says need not be taken as applying literally to the early eighth century B.C. (see below): even if it cannot (yet) be demonstrated, it is surely not beyond the bounds of possibility that some Orientalizing or Etruscan goldwork could have been made on Ischia. However this may be, gold-*mines* are geologically out of the question: they would surely have been mentioned by other writers (especially by Pliny, *Nat. Hist.*)—and no gold has been found in the excavations. It follows therefore that, if by χρυσεῖα Strabo and his readers understood 'gold-mines', then he and they were—and are (Hammond 1967, p. 118; Scullard 1967, p. 179)—wrong.

Fertility (εὐκαρπία) sounds like a superficial (not necessarily eye-witness) impression —rather like the ubiquitous '*Isola Verde*' of modern tourist literature—of the island's vineyards and remedial waters.[3] The impression need not have been Strabo's own, for much of his information about Campania was no longer true in the Augustan period; many points of his more obscure erudition are found in Hellenistic writings, especially the *Alexandra* of Lycophron, and in many cases they can be shown to derive ultimately from Timaeus (writing around and after 300), Lycophron's principal source of Western knowledge. In the case of Ischia, the connection of 'Pithekoussai' with

---

[1] Pais 1908, pp. 183ff. Pais had previously proposed χαλκεῖα ('bronze-foundries'), on the analogy of Aenaria (the Roman name of Ischia): Bérard 1957, p. 43 n. 1.
[2] By M. L. West in a letter to the present writer.
[3] Pliny, *Nat. Hist.*, XXXI, v, 9; Statius, *Silvae*, III, v, 104.

pithekoi had been alluded to in the *Alexandra*; [1] Strabo then repeated it, and his account of an eruption here, of Monte Epomeo, is from Timaeus, whom he quotes as saying it was shortly before his own (Timaeus') time.[2] By that time, it is more than probable that vine-growing on Ischia (then under the control of Naples) had been organized on a large scale. But neither remedial waters nor Hellenistic vineyards imply the type or degree of fertility that would have attracted a mainly agricultural community in the eighth century B.C. We can only conclude that either Strabo's text or his (source's) knowledge of the place was at fault, if by εὐκαρπία we are meant to understand any exceptional degree of fertility, over and above mere possibilities of cultivation that could make the island independent of the mainland if necessary.

(ii) Professor Cook on the pots. There is no insurmountable reason why there should be vases 'of Ischian make among the early Greek pots found in Etruria'. The trade was in metals and ores, not pottery, and we should not look for more than the inevitable side-effect—and invaluable trace element—constituted in fact by the presence of scarabs and seals, *en masse* at Pithekoussai and sporadically in Etruria (Ridgway 1970, pp. 28f.), together with the occasional exotic pot travelling in either direction (see now Postscript, pp. 37–8). Trade could well have been carried by a land-route rather than by sea: the current work of Drs W. Johannowski and B. D'Agostino indicates close and continuous contact between Etruria and the hinterland of Campania from the ninth century B.C. onwards.

The date of the settlement

Giorgio Buchner places the foundation of Pithekoussai in the first half of the eighth century, 'say about 775 B.C.' (Buchner 1966b, p. 12); J. N. Coldstream places it 'not later than *c.* 760' (Coldstream 1968, p. 354); and the extent of the habitation at Mazzola, taken with the quantity of 'Aetos 666' kotylai from the Scarico Gosetti and the second series of excavations in the cemetery, certainly implies the presence of a substantial population by *c.* 750. We should remember, of course, that our knowledge depends upon work that essentially is still in progress. So far the 'Aetos 666' kotyle is the earliest Greek type *found* at Pithekoussai and in the West generally, but excavations now (October 1971) in progress, especially in that part of the Valle San Montano which is nearest the foot of the acropolis, may yet produce earlier material. On

[1] Monkeys: Lycophron, *Alexandra*, 688–93; Strabo XIII, c 626 = XIII, 4, 6.
[2] Strabo, V, c 248 = V, 4, 9; Jacoby, F 58. Monte Epomeo is not a volcano, but a result of Ischia's status as a 'volcano-tectonic horst': for references to the vulcanological literature and further discussion see Buchner 1970, p. 99, n. 1.

the other hand, they may not: the 'Aetos 666' type currently stands at the beginning of the Pithekoussai sequence not only in the cemetery, but also at the Mazzola site and in the unstratified material from the Scarico Gosetti—which looks like a reliable cross-section of the material in use at Pithekoussai between the Bronze Age and Roman times.

In the present state of knowledge, then, it is still true that the earliest Euboean type at Al Mina, namely the Middle Geometric skyphos with pendent concentric semicircles, does not occur in the West: 'Euboean workshops may have stopped making them by the time Pithekoussai was founded' (Boardman 1965, p. 13 n. 27; cf. 1964, p. 65). However, imported Euboeo-Cycladic Middle Geometric skyphoi with chevrons, earlier than anything known so far from Ischia (but not earlier than the earliest material from Al Mina), have been found in native Iron Age contexts in Campania and in southern Etruria. These will be mentioned in the next section.

It remains to note that three unimpressive sherds from the native site at Castiglione d'Ischia have recently been invoked, as 'Geometric', to provide some earlier Greek pottery from somewhere on the island,[1] and so a brief period of pre-colonial 'trade before the flag' with the native Iron Age inhabitants attested at the site (*contra* Coldstream 1968, p. 355, Buchner 1970, pp. 95ff. and fig. 25). This is certainly wrong: one of the sherds is in fact Mycenaean, and the other two (one certainly, one almost certainly) do not belong to 'chevron skyphoi'.

III. MAINLAND CAMPANIA AND SOUTHERN ETRURIA IN THE EIGHTH CENTURY B.C.

Blakeway's pioneer picture of relations between Greek and native in mainland Italy has been changed radically with the demonstration that, from the third quarter of the eighth century, Euboean Greeks had taken up residence for commercial reasons on the island of Ischia in the Bay of Naples. This final section will briefly turn to mainland Campania, and up to southern Etruria, and define the remains, somewhat exiguous, of the 'pre-colonial' Greek phenomenon there. It then can comment on the same area in the light of the subsequent presence and activity of Greeks in their earliest 'colonial' setting.

Pre-colonial trade with the Villanovans

Knowledge of southern Etruria's own Iron Age culture, and Campania's, is on a

---

[1] For references see note 1, p. 19 *supra*. Johannowski 1967, p. 167 ('*frammenti di tazze di tal tipo . . .*') is factually wrong, and p. 181 n. 82 ('*Non dissimili da queste sono alcuni skyphoi euboici dell'area della città . . .*') is very misleading: Gierow 1969, p. 140 n. 4, has already been misled.

much sounder footing now than it was in the nineteen-thirties. More cemeteries have been excavated, and—equally important—blocks of old and new material are being published in an accessible and usable form. This is particularly true of Latium and southern Etruria,[1] where the recent Tarquinia and Veii publications have released a flood of Villanovan evidence for study and interpretation. And interpretation has not been lacking in this 'new wave' of interest: Dr Hencken's views on the affinities and antecedents of the Villanovans and early Etruscans, arising out of his catalogue of their cemeteries at Tarquinia, have been discussed by Professor Pallottino (Pallottino 1968 on Hencken 1968a)—who himself originated much that is still fundamental to current Villanovan thinking (Pallottino 1939, 1947). The present writer has commented elsewhere on the methods and conclusions of the 'Swedish school of chronology' as applied to their invaluable *corpora* of raw material (Ridgway 1968a).

In mainland Campania the old and in some ways unreliable evidence from pre-Hellenic and early colonial Cumae has been supplemented by the work of Drs D'Agostino and Johannowski, respectively and in particular at Pontecagnano and Capua and by Mme de la Genière at Sala Consilina.[2] Campania now has a sequence of its own, with a wide distribution of affinities in Etruria, that is said to continue unbroken from early graves which are Villanovan, with typical biconical ossuaries for cremations, down to the Orientalizing and subsequent Etruscan periods—from the ninth to the fifth century B.C. Though there are inevitable influences from the local 'Fossa Culture' (so called from its tradition of inhumation-graves), the similarities with Etruria suggest a degree of close and continuous contact that could have been maintained by traffic up and down the Liri and Sacco valleys. Early affinities have also been noted with Iron Age material from adjacent Latium and the Alban Hills.

In the present context the most appropriate starting-point is Veii, in Etruria close to Latium and the Tiber. Blakeway, there, was forced to admit defeat: 'There is, I understand, a large quantity of Geometric material from [Veii] in the Villa Giulia [museum] which is as yet unpublished, inaccessible and invisible' (Blakeway 1935a, pp. 174, 195 n. 4). This material in Rome, much of it important, has been augmented since his day, from the current (now partly published) excavations at Veii in the Villanovan cemetery of Quattro Fontanili. Dr Close-Brooks has recently completed an interim discussion of this cemetery (Close-Brooks 1965; 1967b); she proposes the

[1] Gjerstad 1953–66 (Rome); Gierow 1964–6 (Latium generally); Hencken 1968a (Tarquinia); Veii: *Q.F.* (1,2,3) and the forthcoming publication of the Grotta Gramiccia material by Dr A. P. Vianello de Cordoba. A re-publication by Miss I. Pohl of the material from the Sorbo cemetery at Cerveteri is in the press.
[2] Salerno 1962; Johannowski 1963, 1965, 1967; D'Agostino 1964, 1965, 1968; De la Genière 1968.

following absolute chronology for the divisions based on association-tables of the grave-groups, in their horizontal stratigraphy on the site (Close-Brooks 1967b, p. 329):

I . . . finishes *c.* 800
IIA . . . *c.* 800–*c.* 760
IIB . . . *c.* 760–*c.* 720
IIIA . . . *c.* 720 onwards

In Period I iron is rare and the use of bronze is mainly functional. Period IIA, on the other hand, displays a notable increase in the use of iron and of metal in general. This sudden awareness of metallurgy coincides with the arrival of Euboeo-Cycladic Middle Geometric skyphoi, painted with a narrow panel of vertical chevrons in the handle-zone: 'chevron-skyphoi', or alternatively 'Cycladic cups'. This looks like a clear case of cause and effect. And it is difficult to think of the cause being anything other than Euboean interest in the metals of Etruria—often proposed, sometimes contested, and now demonstrated by mineralogical analysis. At what need not be a very much later period (pp. 17–18), iron was mined on the metal-rich island of Elba (off northern Etruria), and worked on Ischia—where the occurrence of iron ore in nature is as geologically impossible as that of gold. If the 'Aetos 666' Corinthian Late Geometric kotyle is really the earliest imported Greek type taken by the Euboeans to their settlement on Ischia, then these Middle Geometric skyphoi from native contexts on the mainland are the symbol of what little now remains to us of Blakeway's period of 'trade before the flag'.

The present writer has published a study of the Veii chevron-skyphoi elsewhere (Ridgway 1967), and there is little point in retailing the same information with adjustments and additions here. After that paper appeared, Dr Johannowski published a picture of a similar skyphos from Capua (Johannowski 1967, pl. viiib), and mentioned the existence of more there; others have been noted from Pontecagnano (D'Agostino 1967, p. 31 n. 12). These new finds must be considered in connection with the two examples of the same type that have long been known from the pre-Hellenic Osta cemetery at Cumae (Ridgway 1967, p. 311 n. 4, pl. lviia, b); and it will be possible to do that when the Capua and Pontecagnano material is published definitively (see Postscript, pp. 37–8). In the present state of the evidence from the hinterland of Campania, only a few points can be made.

Dr Johannowski at one point seems to minimize the possibility of a close connection between these first Greek contacts with Campania and southern Etruria, and 'true' colonization: the presence of Middle Geometric skyphoi on the mainland but not at Pithekoussai 'justifies the hypothesis that the link between these first contacts and true colonization may be nothing more than a preconceived idea' (Johannowski 1967, p. 174). The hypothesis rests on the identification of some chevron-skyphoi in Campania, and apparently from Veii as well, as not merely Attic*izing* Greek but as real imported Attic—and, as such, an isolated phenomenon. Chevron-skyphoi belong to the early eighth century, and the next Attic products do not arrive in the area until much later in the same century (Coldstream 1968, p. 84—Pithekoussai grave 129). This is ingenious, and even attractive: Johannowski points to evidence for a similar and contemporary phenomenon in Cyprus and the Near East. On the other hand, in the West at any rate, the concept stands or falls on the identification of some Western chevron-skyphoi as Attic: for what it is worth, the present writer does not think that any of them are.

Dr Johannowski's announcement of the discovery in 1966-7 of imported Corinthian Late Geometric 'Aetos 666' kotylai at Capua (Johannowski 1967, p. 184) tends if anything to underline the validity of the pre-colonial concept. If this is the earliest type found at the early colony of Pithekoussai, it could also be the very latest type in the pre-colonial phase on the mainland—and could in fact represent the division between 'trade' and 'flag', to be dated in absolute terms to *c.* 760.

On this reckoning, the end of the pre-colonial period coincides with the transition at Veii from IIA to IIB. What was it for? The chevron-skyphoi both in Campania and at Veii are accompanied by other *exotica*: an Egyptianizing statuette of faience from Cumae is well known (Gabrici 1913, col. 110, fig. 51), and can be matched at Veii (*Q.F.*(3), pp. 130f., fig. 26 no. 18). J. N. Coldstream has written in terms of such trinkets being 'hawked to the natives by Euboean or Cycladic merchants . . . traders with Levantine contacts' (Coldstream 1968, p. 355). This is no doubt true as far as it goes; the present writer is still tempted to take it a step further with the introduction of the lately unfashionable concept of the prospector—or the advance party spying out the land, and making the first contacts with the natives of a strange country. The remains of the pre-colonial period in Etruria, exemplified by the new finds at Veii, show an increased local awareness of metallurgy, associated with Euboeo-Cycladic Middle Geometric imports; the Euboean Late Geometric colonists at Pithekoussai can now be linked with iron from Elba. The establishment of a permanent Euboean 'home base' abroad—with all that such an operation inevitably required in the way of investment of men and resources—would surely not have been contemplated without a preliminary period of elementary market research; and it surely would never have been undertaken at all unless the cause had been seen to take effect, with the mechanics of supply and demand arranged. After all, it cannot be a coincidence that the first Euboean colony in the West is placed in the northernmost corner of this whole 'Magna Grecia', and that a Euboean factor in the previous development of Villanovan metallurgy can be postulated on the basis of evidence from Veii, the southernmost of the great Villanovan-Etruscan centres.

Early colonial contact with the Villanovans

R. M. Cook's dictum that 'there is little or nothing of Ischian make among the early Greek pots found in Etruria' has been discussed in the previous section. The extraordinary variety and sophistication seen in the later eighth-century material at Pithekoussai is certainly not reflected in contemporary Villanovan contexts: and given that the *raison d'être* of Pithekoussai was an interest in the natural resources of Etruria, ceramic evidence is not to be expected there. Imports into Campania, Johannowski points out, actually cease with the foundation of Pithekoussai (Johannowski 1967, p.168).

Apart from comparatively stray finds such as seals and scarabs, solid evidence for contact between the early colonists and the Villanovans is to be sought in another class of artefact: namely fibulas of bronze. The adoption of the long foot for fibulas of various types has been much discussed (Müller-Karpe 1959, pp. 28, 38; Hencken 1968a, Appendix B). This is a characteristic of the early colonial material at Pithekoussai, from the earliest known graves onwards (associated in more than one case with a local version of the 'Aetos 666' kotyle), but not of the pre-Hellenic graves at Cumae. Before the evaluation of the Quattro Fontanili evidence from Veii, it followed that there were two possibilities (Buchner 1962, p. 258): either (i) the Euboeans had adopted a native type of fibula by the time they took up residence on Ischia, which means that the native fashion did not have time to develop from 'short pre-colonial feet' to 'long early-colonial feet'; or (ii) the Euboeans brought the idea of the long foot with them—perhaps with some fashion of dress which required its essential properties. A significant contribution to this discussion has now been made by Dr J. Close-Brooks. She has shown that some types of fibula with long feet at Veii in Period IIIA can be paralleled at contemporary Pithekoussai, in Early Protocorinthian contexts dated *c.* 720–690. Since it is clear at Veii that the long foot is not so much a sudden fully formed introduction as the result of a previous and gradual process of local growth, Dr Close-Brooks concludes that the relevant fibulas of late eighth-century Pithekoussai were either imported directly out of Etruria, or else copied and adapted from such imports (Close-Brooks 1967b, pp. 327ff.). Such fibulas as were imported would no doubt have followed the same path as the well-known small impasto spiral amphora at Pithekoussai (Fig. 2, c): this would be at home in a IIIA context at Veii. And the fact that, in quantity, the fibulas involved by far exceed the pottery underlines the metallurgical purpose in the link between southern Etruria and the earliest and most northerly Greek colony in the West.

Acknowledgements

My two biggest debts are to Professor C. F. C. Hawkes, who first encouraged me in my choice of *precolonizzazione* as a subject of research and has continued to do so, and to Giorgio Buchner, who honoured me in 1966 with the invitation to collaborate with him in the definitive publication of his 1952–61 excavations at Pithekoussai. I gratefully acknowledge the financial assistance I have received in the successive forms of a State Studentship, a Sir James Knott Fellowship in the University of Newcastle upon Tyne, a Leverhulme European Fellowship, and grants from the British Academy and from the Craven, Meyerstein (Oxford) and Munro (Edinburgh) Committees. J. Boardman, R. M. Cook, M. W. Frederiksen and A. J. Graham read an earlier version of this paper; I am most grateful to them for their comments, and to J. Close-Brooks, J. N. Coldstream, B. D'Agostino, A. P. Vianello de Cordoba and W. Johannowski for many conversations from which I have learnt more than they have. No one except myself, however, should be blamed for any errors of fact or interpretation—whether original or not—that still remain.

Bibliography

ÅKERSTRÖM, Å., 1943. *Der Geometrische Stil in Italien.* Skrifter utgivna av Svenska Institutet i Rom, 4°, no. 9. Lund.

ALLEN, D. F., 1937. 'Coins of Antioch etc. from Al Mina.' *Numismatic Chronicle,* ser. 5, 17, pp. 200–10.

ALMÁGRO, M., 1945. 'Excavaciones de Ampurias: últimos hallazgos y resultados.' *Archivo Español de Arqueología,* 18, pp. 59–75.

ANDREWES, A., 1967. *The Greeks.* London.

BEAZLEY, J. D., 1939. 'Excavations at Al Mina, Sueidia III: the red-figured vases.' *Journal of Hellenic Studies,* 59, pp. 1–44.

BENOÎT, F., 1948. 'Soufflets de forge antiques.' *Revue des Études Anciennes,* 50, pp. 305–8.

—, 1965. *Recherches sur l'Hellénisation du Midi de la Gaule.* Annales de la Faculté des Lettres, Université d'Aix-en-Provence, n.s., 43.

BÉRARD, J., 1957. *La colonisation grecque de l'Italie et de la Sicile dans l'antiquité: l'histoire et la légende.* Université, Faculté des Lettres, Paris.

—, 1960. *L'Expansion et la colonisation grecques.* Paris.

BERNABÒ BREA, L., and CAVALIER, M., 1959. *Mylai.* Istituto Geografico De Agostini, Novara.

BIRMINGHAM, J., 1961. 'The overland route across Anatolia in the eighth and seventh centuries B.C.' *Anatolian Studies,* 11, pp. 185–95.

BLAKEWAY, A., 1935a. 'Prolegomena to the study of Greek commerce with Italy, Sicily and France in the eighth and seventh centuries B.C.' *Annual of the British School at Athens,* 33 (1932–3)[1935], pp. 170–208.

—, 1935b. '"Demaratus": a study in some aspects of the earliest Hellenisation of Latium and Etruria.' *Journal of Roman Studies,* 25, pp. 129–49.

BLANCO, A., and LUZÓN, J. M., 1969. 'Pre-Roman silver miners at Riotinto.' *Antiquity*, 43, pp. 124–31.

BOARDMAN, J., 1952. 'Pottery from Eretria.' *Annual of the British School at Athens*, 47, pp. 1–48.

—, 1957. 'Early Euboean pottery and history.' *Annual of the British School at Athens*, 52, pp. 1–29.

—, 1958. 'Al Mina and Greek chronology.' *Historia*, 7, p. 250.

—, 1959. 'Greek potters at Al Mina?' *Anatolian Studies*, 9, pp. 163–9.

—, 1964. *The Greeks Overseas*. Harmondsworth.

—, 1965. 'Tarsus, Al Mina and Greek chronology.' *Journal of Hellenic Studies*, 85, pp. 5–15.

—, 1970. 'Euboean pottery in West and East.' *Dialoghi di Archeologia*, 3(1969) [1970], pp. 102–14.

BOSTICCO, S., 1957. 'Scarabei egiziani della necropoli di Pithecusa nell'isola di Ischia.' *Parola del Passato*, 12, pp. 215–29.

BRUNNSÅKER, S., 1962. 'The Pithecusan Shipwreck.' *Opuscula Romana*, 4, pp. 165–242.

BUCHNER, G., 1937. 'Nota preliminare sulle ricerche preistoriche nell'isola d'Ischia.' *Bullettino di Paletnologia Italiana*, (1936–7), pp. 65ff.

—, 1954a. 'Scavi nella necropoli di Pithecusa 1952-3.' *Atti e Memorie della Società 'Magna Grecia'*, pp. 3–11.

—, 1954b. 'Figürlich bemalte spätgeometrische Vasen aus Pithekussai und Kyme.' *Mitteilungen des Deutschen Archäologischen Instituts : Römische Abteilung*, 60-1, pp. 37–55.

—, 1961. s.v. 'Ischia.' *Enciclopedia dell'Arte Antica*, 4, pp. 224–9. Rome.

—, 1962. (Contribution to discussion), *Atti del 1° Convegno di studi sulla Magna Grecia, Taranto 1961 = Greci e Italici in Magna Grecia*, pp. 256–9. Naples.

—, 1964. (Contribution to discussion), *Atti del III° Convegno di studi sulla Magna Grecia, Taranto 1963 = Metropoli e Colonie di Magna Grecia*, pp. 263–74. Naples.

—, 1966a. 'Relazioni tra la necropoli greca di Pitecusa (isola d'Ischia) e la civiltà italica ed etrusca dell' VIII sec.' *Atti del VI° Congresso Internazionale delle Scienze Preistoriche e Protostoriche, Roma 1962*, 3, pp. 7–11. Florence.

—, 1966b. 'Pithekoussai: oldest Greek colony in the West.' *Expedition* (Summer 1966), pp. 4–12.

—, 1970. 'Mostra degli scavi di Pithecusa.' *Dialoghi di Archeologia*, 3 (1969)[1970], pp. 85–101.

—, forthcoming. s.v. 'Ischia: aggiornamento.' *Enciclopedia dell'Arte Antica*, supplementary vol. forthcoming.

BUCHNER, G., and BOARDMAN, J., 1968. 'Seals from Ischia and the Lyre-Player Group.' *Jahrbuch des Deutschen Archäologischen Instituts*, 81 (1966) [1968], pp. 1–62.

BUCHNER, G., and RITTMANN, A., 1948. *Origine e passato dell'isola d'Ischia*. Naples.

BUCHNER, G., and RUSSO, C. F., 1955. 'La coppa di Nestore e un'iscrizione metrica da Pitecusa dell'VIII secolo av. Cr.' *Accademia Nazionale dei Lincei: Rendiconti*, 10, pp. 215–34.

CARPENTER, R., 1963. Review of JEFFERY 1961. *American Journal of Philology*, 84, pp. 76–85.

CHILDE, V. G., 1960. 'The Italian axe-mould from Mycenae.' *Civiltà del Ferro*. Documenti e Studi: Deputazione di Storia Patria per le provincie di Romagna, 6, pp. 575–8. Bologna.

CINTAS, P., 1950. *La céramique punique*. Institut des Hautes Études de Tunis. Paris.

CLOSE-BROOKS, J., 1965. 'Proposta per una suddivisione in fasi.' *Notizie degli Scavi di Antichità*, pp. 53–64.

—, 1967a. 'A Villanovan belt from Euboea.' *Bulletin of the Institute of Classical Studies*, 14, pp. 22–4.

—, 1967b. 'Considerazioni sulla cronologia delle facies arcaiche dell'Etruria.' *Studi Etruschi*, 35, pp. 323–9.

COLDSTREAM, J. N., 1968. *Greek Geometric Pottery*. London.

—, 1969. 'The Phoenicians of Ialysos.' *Bulletin of the Institute of Classical Studies*, 16, pp. 1–8.

COOK, R. M., 1960. *Greek Painted Pottery*. London.

—, 1962. 'Reasons for the foundation of Ischia and Cumae.' *Historia*, 11, pp. 113–14.

D'AGOSTINO, B., 1964. 'Necropoli arcaica in località Turni.' *Notizie degli Scavi di Antichità*, pp. 40–99.

—, 1965. 'Nuovi apporti della documentazione archeologica nell'Agro Picentino.' *Studi Etruschi*, 33, pp. 671–83.

—, 1967. 'Osservazioni a proposito della guerra lelantina.' *Dialoghi di Archeologia*, 1, pp. 20–37.

—, 1968. 'Tombe orientalizzanti in contrada S. Antonio (Pontecagnano).' *Notizie degli Scavi di Antichità*, pp. 75–196.

DE LA GENIÈRE, J., 1968. *Recherches sur l'Âge du Fer en Italie Méridionale: Sala Consilina*. Publications du Centre Jean Bérard, I. Institut Français, Naples.

DUNBABIN, T. J., 1948. *The Western Greeks*. Oxford.

—, 1957. *The Greeks and their Eastern Neighbours*. Society for the Promotion of Hellenic Studies: Supplementary Paper no. 8. London.

FORREST, W. G., 1957. 'Colonisation and the rise of Delphi.' *Historia*, 6, pp. 160–75.

FRIIS JOHANSEN, K., 1957. 'Exochi, ein frührhodisches Gräberfeld.' *Acta Archaeologica*, 28, pp. 1–192.

GABRICI, E., 1913. *Cuma = Monumenti Antichi*, 22.

GIEROW, P. G., 1964–6. *The Iron Age Culture of Latium*, I, II: i. Skrifter utgivna av Svenska Institutet i Rom, 4°, no. 24, 1–2. Lund.

—, 1969. 'Da Alba Longa a Lavinio.' *Opuscula Romana*, 7, pp. 139–48.

GJERSTAD, E., 1953–66. *Early Rome*, I–IV. Skrifter utgivna av Svenska Institutet i Rom, 4°, no. 17, 1–4. Lund.

GRAHAM, A. J., 1964. *Colony and Mother City in Ancient Greece*. Manchester.

GUARDUCCI, M., 1967. *Epigrafia Greca*, I. Rome.

—, 1970. 'Epigrafi greche arcaiche.' *Accademia Nazionale dei Lincei: Rendiconti*, 35, pp. 51–65.

GWYNN, A., 1918. 'The character of Greek colonisation.' *Journal of Hellenic Studies*, 38, pp. 88–123.

HAMMOND, N. G. L., 1967. *A History of Greece to 322 B.C.* Oxford.

HANKEY, V., 1967. 'Mycenaean pottery in the Middle East: notes on finds since 1951.' *Annual of the British School at Athens*, 62, pp. 107–47.

HENCKEN, H., 1968a. *Tarquinia, Villanovans and Early Etruscans*. American School of Prehistoric Research, Bulletin no. 23. Peabody Museum, Cambridge, Mass.

—, 1968b. Review of ÖSTENBERG 1967. *American Journal of Archaeology*, 72, pp. 191–192.

HEURGON, J., 1961. *La vie quotidienne chez les Étrusques*. Paris.

HUMPHREYS, S. C., 1965. 'Il commercio in quanto motivo della colonizzazione greca dell'Italia e della Sicilia.' *Rivista Storica Italiana*, 77, pp. 421–33.

IMMERWAHR, S., 1959. Review of TAYLOUR 1958. *American Journal of Archaeology*, 63, pp. 295–9.

JACOBY, F., 1923 sqq. *Fragmente der griechischen Historiker*. Berlin-Leiden.

JEFFERY, L. H., 1961. *The Local Scripts of Archaic Greece*. Oxford.

JOHANNOWSKI, W., 1963. 'Gli Etruschi in Campania.' *Klearchos*, 5, pp. 62–75.

—, 1965. 'Problemi di classificazione e cronologia di alcune scoperte protostoriche a Capua e Cales.' *Studi Etruschi*, 33, pp. 685–98.

—, 1967. 'Problemi relativi alla "precolonizzazione" in Campania.' *Dialoghi di Archeologia*, 1, pp. 159–85.

JULLY, J., 1968. 'Le marché du métal en Méditerranée occidentale au premier âge du fer: Sémites et Étrusques.' *Opuscula Romana*, 6, pp. 27–61.

KAHIL, L. G., 1968. 'Céramique géométrique et subgéométrique d'Érétrie.' *Antike Kunst*, 11, pp. 99–101.

KARAGIORGHIS, V., and KAHIL, L. G., 1967. 'Témoignages eubéens à Chypre et chypriotes à Érétrie.' *Antike Kunst*, 10, pp. 133–5.

LANE, E. A., 1938. 'Medieval finds at Al Mina in North Syria.' *Archaeologia*, 87, pp. 19–78.

MacNAMARA, E., 1970. 'A group of bronzes from Surbo, Italy: new evidence for Aegean contacts with Apulia during Mycenaean IIIB and C.' *Proceedings of the Prehistoric Society*, 36, pp. 241–60.

MAYER, M., 1914. *Apulien vor und während der Hellenisierung*. Leipzig-Berlin.

METZGER, H., 1965. 'Sur la date du graffite de la "coupe de Nestor".' *Revue des Études Anciennes*, 67, pp. 301–5.

MOMIGLIANO, A., 1963. 'An interim report on the origins of Rome.' *Journal of Roman Studies*, 53, pp. 95–121.

MÜLLER-KARPE, H., 1959. *Beiträge zur Chronologie der Urnenfelderzeit nördlich und südlich der Alpen*. Römisch-Germanische Forschungen, 22. Berlin.

NIOLA, D. BUCHNER, 1965. *L'isola d'Ischia: studio geografico*. Memorie di geografia economica e antropica, n.s. 3. Naples.

ÖSTENBERG, C. E., 1967. *Luni sul Mignone e problemi della preistoria d'Italia*. Skrifter utgivna av Svenska Institutet i Rom, 4°, no. 25. Lund.

PAGET, R. F., 1968. 'The ancient ports of Cumae.' *Journal of Roman Studies*, 58, pp. 152–69.

PAIS, E., 1908. *Ancient Italy: historical and geographical investigations in central Italy, Magna Grecia, Sicily and Sardinia*. Chicago.

PALLOTTINO, M., 1939. 'Sulle facies culturali arcaiche dell'Etruria.' *Studi Etruschi*, 13, pp. 85–128.

—, 1947. 'Nuovi orientamenti sulla cronologia dell'Etruria protostorica.' *Atti della Pontificia Accademia Romana di Archeologia: Rendiconti*, 22, 1946–7, pp. 31–41.

—, 1968. Review of HENCKEN 1968. *Studi Etruschi*, 36, pp. 493–501.

PAYNE, H., 1931. *Necrocorinthia*. Oxford.

PERONI, R., 1969. 'Per una revisione critica della stratigrafia di Luni sul Mignone e della sua interpretazione.' *Atti del I° Simposio di Protostoria d'Italia, Orvieto 1967*, pp. 167–73.

POPHAM, M. R., and SACKETT, L. H. (eds.), 1968. *Excavations at Lefkandi, Euboea 1964–6: a preliminary report*. London.

PUGLIESE CARRATELLI, G., 1962. 'Achei nell'Etruria e nel Lazio?' *Parola del Passato*, 17, pp. 5–25.

—, 1966. 'Greci d'Asia in Occidente tra il secolo VII e il VI.' *Parola del Passato*, 21, pp. 155–65.

PURSER, O., 1927. 'Ancient pottery at Shanganagh Castle.' *Proceedings of the Royal Irish Academy, Section C*, 37 (1924–7), pp. 36–52.

QF(*1*), (*2*), (*3*). Various authors. 'Veio: scavi in una necropoli villanoviana in località "Quattro Fontanili".' *Notizie degli Scavi di Antichità*, (1) 1963, pp. 77–279; (2) 1965, pp. 49–236; (3) 1967, pp. 87–286.

RICCI, G., 1955. 'Caere III: Necropoli della Banditaccia: zona A "del recinto".' *Monumenti Antichi*, 42, cols. 201–1048.

RIDGWAY, D., 1967. '"Coppe cicladiche" da Veio.' *Studi Etruschi*, 35, pp. 311–21.

—, 1968a. Review-discussion of GJERSTAD 1966 and GIEROW 1964–6. *Journal of Roman Studies*, 58, pp. 235–40.

—, 1968b. 'Archaeology in Central Italy and Etruria 1962–67.' *Archaeological Reports 1967–68*, pp. 29–48.

—, 1970. 'Il contesto indigeno in Etruria prima e dopo l'arrivo dei Greci.' *Dialoghi di Archeologia*, 3 (1969)[1970], pp. 23–30.

ROBERTSON, C. M., 1940. 'Excavations at Al Mina, Sueidia IV: the early Greek vases.' *Journal of Hellenic Studies*, 60, pp. 2–21.

—, 1946. Postscript to ROBERTSON 1940. *Journal of Hellenic Studies*, 66, p. 125.

ROBINSON, E. S. G., 1937. 'Coins from the excavations at Al Mina (1936).' *Numismatic Chronicle*, series 5, 17, pp. 182–96.

SACKETT, L. H., et al., 1966. 'Prehistoric Euboea: contributions toward a survey.' *Annual of the British School at Athens*, 61, pp. 33–112.

SÄFLUND, G., 1957. 'Über dem Ursprung der Etrusker.' *Historia*, 6, pp. 10–22.

SALERNO, 1962. Catalogue: *Mostra della Preistoria e della Protostoria nel Salernitano*. Salerno.

SCHEFOLD, K., 1966. 'Die Grabungen in Eretria im Herbst 1964 und 1965.' *Antike Kunst*, 9, pp. 106–24.

SCHEFOLD, K., et al., 1967. 'Die Ausgrabungen in Eretria 1964.' *Archaiologikon Deltion*, 20 (1965) [1967], pp. 262–88.

SCULLARD, H. H., 1967. *The Etruscan Cities and Rome*. London.

SMITH, S., 1942. 'The Greek trade at Al Mina: a footnote to Oriental history.' *Antiquaries Journal*, 22, pp. 87–112.

STOOP, M. W., 1955. 'Some observations on the recent excavations on Ischia.' *Antiquity and Survival*, 4, pp. 255–64.

TAYLOR, J. DU PLAT, 1959. 'The Cypriot and Syrian pottery from Al Mina, Syria.' *Iraq*, 21, pp. 62–92.

TAYLOUR, LORD WILLIAM, 1958. *Mycenaean pottery in Italy and adjacent areas*. Cambridge.

TRENDALL, A. D., 1956. 'Archaeology in Sicily and Magna Graecia.' *Archaeological Reports 1955* (Supplement to *Journal of Hellenic Studies*, 76), pp. 47–62.

—, 1967. 'Archaeology in Southern Italy and Sicily, 1964–66.' *Archaeological Reports 1966–67*, pp. 29–46.

VALLET, G., 1958. *Rhégion et Zancle: histoire, commerce et civilisation des cités chalcidiennes du détroit de Messine.* = Bibliothèque des Écoles Françaises d'Athènes et de Rome, fasc. 189. Paris.

WACE, A. J. B., 1953. 'Mycenae: preliminary report on the excavations of 1952.' *Annual of the British School at Athens*, 48, pp. 3–18.

WOODHEAD, A. G., 1962. *The Greeks in the West.* London.

WOOLLEY, C. L., 1937. 'Excavations near Antioch in 1936.' *Antiquaries Journal*, 17, pp. 1–15.

—, 1938. 'Excavations at Al Mina, Sueidia I, II.' *Journal of Hellenic Studies*, 58, pp. 1–30, 133–70.

—, 1948. 'The date of Al Mina.' *Journal of Hellenic Studies*, 68, p. 148.

Postscript (October 1971)

Since this paper was completed in December 1969, publication has modified the picture presented above with a rapidity that defies any hasty synthesis. A new basic source of information is now available: the published account of the 'Incontro di studi sugli inizi della colonizzazione greca in Occidente' (Naples-Ischia 1968) = *Dialoghi di Archeologia*, 3 (1969), fascicule 1–2 [1970], pp. 1–234, with 32 figs. My own limited references above to items in this volume do not begin to do justice to the wealth of systematic and incidental information presented verbally in 1968 and now published with a verbatim record of all discussion of the papers read. In particular, much material from Capua is illustrated and discussed in this volume: figs. i–xiii and the Appendix, pp. 213–19, to Dr Johannowski's paper, pp. 31–43, are especially valuable. Relevant Capua material has also been published recently by N. Valenza in *Klearchos*, 41–4 (1969), pp. 91–118.

Other excavation reports have also appeared, concerning both the Eastern and Western ends of the story. The following are fundamental:

(1) P. J. Riis, *Sukas I : the north-east sanctuary and the first settling of Greeks in Syria and Palestine* (Publications of the Carlsberg Expedition to Phoenicia, I: Copenhagen, 1970)—with an authoritative review of skyphoi with pendent concentric semicircles in Chapter 7, pp. 126–75 *passim*.

(2) G. Buchner, 'Recent work at Pithekoussai (Ischia), 1965–1971.' *Archaeological Reports 1970–71* (1971), pp. 63–7. It now appears that at the Mazzola site only one building was intended for living in. The others, all dating from the middle of the eighth to the beginning of the seventh century, were concerned in one way or another with the working of bronze and iron. This provides further confirmation for the connection of the search for metals with early Greek expansion in the West. On the (much) wider implications of this see now A. M. Snodgrass, 'The first

European body armour' in *The European Community in Later Prehistory : Studies in honour of C. F. C. Hawkes* (ed. John Boardman, M.A. Brown and T. G. E. Powell; London, 1971), especially pp. 43 ff. Furthermore it is revealed that the Mazzola site has yielded so much figured Geometric that the excavator is now disposed to think in terms of a school of figured drawing that is nothing more or less than a locally produced branch of Euboean Late Geometric. This has important implications not only for the class of small closed vases previously thought to be Cretan (note 1, p. 16 *supra*), but also for the 'Cycladic' (Blakeway) affinities of the Geometric in Etruria. In a word, as a result of the new (*and non-cemetery*) evidence from Pithekoussai, we are beginning to discern which decorative ideas in Etruria may find parallels at Pithekoussai and in Euboea generally. An interesting foretaste of this situation was given by J. N. Coldstream in his discussion of 'A figured Geometric oinochoe from Italy'—presumably Etruria: now in the British Museum—in *Bulletin of the Institute of Classical Studies*, 15 (1968), pp. 86–96.

(3) B. d'Agostino, 'Tombe della prima età del ferro a S. Marzano sul Sarno', *Mélanges École Française de Rome*, 82 (1970), pp. 571–619. This is a full publication, with detailed analysis, of Iron Age tombs (some with painted pottery) from the mainland of Campania.

(4) *QF(4)*: the fourth instalment of the catalogue of material from the Quattro Fontanili cemetery at Veii: *Notizie degli Scavi di Antichità*, 1970, pp. 178–329.

Commentary 2

Houses in Prehistory, and the Celts

The archaeology of Greeks on the seaboard of Italy, with a little light from texts and an Oriental dated background, brings a scheme of stages and aims—pre-colonial and then colonial: trade and wider influence—into a case of what prehistory calls 'diffusion of culture'. 'Culture', furthermore, from being something perceived through history, as in 'Hellenic culture' or 'Egyptian culture', or else through ethnology, has given prehistory the word that makes its concept of '*a* culture': such a culture as the Villanovan, or the Hallstatt, or the Bell Beaker, named from a site with 'typical' finds, or a 'typical' kind of object. These prehistoric cultures, defined from material remains which discovery shows to recur in association within a region, resemble those of ethnology or history in some ways. Archaeology has resources for investigating them all. But in those that have to be treated as prehistoric, or are totally so, prehistory starts from material remains yet may always think beyond them. Just as in an early Greek assemblage, from a grave perhaps in Italy or Sicily, the Hellenist knows that the aryballos vase contained a typical Hellenic toiletry, perfumed oil for rubbing on the skin, and is thus Hellenic not only in form but also in social purpose, so the pre-historian knows, when meeting a find that is classed as typical, that it served a social purpose in its 'culture'. What the purpose was, may be obvious or obscure. Were the mugs called bell beakers for drinking ale, or milk? Was the axe with hole for the shaft, called a battle-axe, really for battle? At least it is clear that a grave for the dead, if covered by a barrow, was meant to endure in social memory; and that great collective tombs of stone had a purpose in community religion. But what matters the most to this conception of a 'culture', is the prehistorian's choice, amongst its traits, of what shall be typical. Frequency of occurrence, in observed association, of course will often determine this. But it need not do so always.

Consider the house. One would think that the structure of this, whether standing

III

or inferred from the plan of its emplacement in the ground, its situation alone or in numbers and its size, with any internal features, would be typical indeed; and that difference in houses ought to distinguish different cultures. In early historic or proto-historic times, quite true, archaeology has not greatly been concerned with house-plans, to distinguish (for example) Greek from Etruscan; it is rather when temples rise on the scene, and settings for athletics, drama or market, that Greek architectural forms stand out, as again in the Hellenistic Orient. But turn to Europe earlier, and you find within the Iron Age, especially from the central regions northward and west-ward, a range of emplacement groundplans for what mostly were certainly houses, which requires explanation with aid from ages earlier still. European archaeologists have their golden age for groundplans, house plans above all, in the Neolithic—or in this along with its metal-conscious Chalcolithic sequels. The most ancient venturers then, advancing their agricultural livelihood, building in south-east Europe small rectangular houses of mud-brick, ignored the Asiatic tendency to compound them together like cells, with roofs all flat; they kept them free-standing, the roofing pitched from a median ridge, and made increasing use of wattlework and stake or post up-rights. How there spread beyond those regions, north-west through the Continent's centre, agricultural communities building houses far longer, supported on posts of stout timber set in rows, and how house-forms also elongated became the rule farther east, and eventually northward too, are among prehistory's proudest showings. North-ern Europe—meaning the lands around the westerly Baltic—built long wooden post-supported houses also later. But how these might be related to the earlier, is not so plain. For further stages ensued, Neolithic and Chalcolithic variously, when houses were still rectangular or oblong but of normal one-family size: sometimes apsidal—curved outwards at the back—sometimes (whether thus or fully rectangular) with a porch, in front of the oblong hall that could hold the hearth. While this porched or 'megaron' form is earliest known in Anatolia, whence its use embraced the Aegean and attained a special development in Greece, such houses however simplified came to be normal far across Europe, from eastern to west-central, before (at the least) 2000 B.C. What, then, of Mediterranean lands, and of the West?

Beyond the lands where easterly connections were strongest, in those of Mediter-ranean Italy and west from that again, one is met by a different notion, that of a house built circular, or oval or anyhow rounded, without any side laid straight. Habitation having often been not in houses at all, but caves, Neolithic cases are sparsely known, but are manifest in Apulia, and in southern Spain have lately been discovered in a context where the pottery is bell beaker. That means around or again before 2000 B.C.; and one would expect that already earlier, if it was really from the Mediterranean that the West had attained its first agricultural economy, similar round-house plans would have been found right through it, round the Alps and over France to the British Isles. They would help to attest a venture, by slowly spreading early cultivators, pastoral in habits too, corresponding to those made east of them. Yet the evidence is far less clear. Beside the Alps, Swiss Neolithic houses from the start appear rectangular; and though there and in France and the British Isles too, Neolithic 'cultures' generally seem inter-related, an Irish site (Lough Gur) has house plans round and rectangular both, straight sides distinguish all the few yet cited for Britain, and the 'culture' whose forms of house are best known to include the round one is no earlier than the Beaker (as at Gwythian in Cornwall). Thus if it be true, as has been stated, that, in whatever materials built, the circular form is standard here by a date soon after 2000, the Beaker folk might well appear the people most responsible.

Then what about 'cultures' afterwards? and what about the Celts? As the Beaker folk's beakers are in the British Isles so plentiful, owing largely to its social custom of burying a whole one with the dead, and as they include so many kinds, and in general are so plainly derived from beakers found on the Continent, this folk's archaeological remains altogether have made it our favourite prehistoric body of 'invaders'. Never mind that after a while the beaker pottery ceased to be made; that the same is true later, in the Early or Middle Bronze Age, of more insular pottery sometimes showing influence from its styles. Yesterday's prevalent doctrine was that when the Beaker folk had ventured, group by group, into Britain and Ireland, they acted as a 'catalyst', on Neolithic residues, strong enough to excuse us any but minor incursions later. So no wonder that houses of Britons in the Iron Age, indeed from the Middle Bronze Age on, are often shown to have been round. And these, speaking broadly, were the Britons who were our Celts. Of course they were branches of those who were at home in mainland Europe; but the branching, even though it went on later, must have started as early as Bell Beaker times. 'Celt', in this broad sense, quite true, refers to language; and prehistoric dialects that issued in later Celtic ones must themselves have been owed to branching, out of Indo-European, the ancient dialect-cluster or tree from which languages in much of Europe and Asia grew likewise. As for the house, speakers of dialects ancestral to Celtic, in Central Europe at least, will have been dwellers in those houses of family size, seen above to have been built not round but rectangular, or sometimes with apse or distinctively with porch, and attested there already before 2000 B.C. But through their mixing here and there with the Bell Beaker folk, and intruding such mixtures into its spreading to the British Isles, dialects that they spoke could have moved (so to say) from the rectangular into the round house, which thus became our typical house for speakers of later Celtic. Yesterday's theorists supposed, however, that this act of moving house was essentially insular. If north-western Spain and Portugal had it, at least it was there peninsular. On the Continent proper, Celtic houses remained rectangular, as did houses in the north, or around the Danube or the Alps. Thus the contrast in house plan (minor incursions apart) showed the Beaker folk's invasion to be the last in our prehistory. Later 'cultures' (minor incursions again apart) owed their other changes of character to influence, not to immigrants.

Venture, in a doctrine such as that, had got to be early. Thoughts of it in later prehistory will pass, if at all, only for movements either minor, or (presumably) superficial: as those of Celts into Spain, or into Italy or down the Danube, may be guessed to seem in the eyes of those who find such doctrines logical. Yet archaeology, on whose findings they are taken to be built up, can only claim to be logical where the findings give it a base. How would Pithekoussai look, or Cumae or any Greek colony, to a prehistorian bringing to it only such logic as was brought to the Celtic round houses? Even if accepting neither venturers nor colonists, but reducing all to 'influence' not definable as through settlement, he might still compare the pottery here with its like found in Greece, and see that its tradition there was older, so that here the source must be Greek. He might even end by conjecturing, besides trade, a minor incursion. He could hardly explain everything as home-grown in Italy—unless through failing to compare it with Greece at all. But in the case of the Celtic houses, this is just what has been happening. The non-invasion hypothesis, for Britain after the beakers, was floated on non-comparison with related parts of the Continent. Rectangular houses, farther away, were assumed to be universal. There was also something of blindness towards the British evidence itself; and anyhow a preference, common to all who held the hypothesis, for expounding later prehistory in terms not of venture, but of resistance, following venture which itself could be only earlier.

Dr Harding, first concerned with wholly British Iron Age findings, but with eyes for the Continent too, here returns to some basal logic. Archaeology works by inference which has got to be based on fact. For comparing any two regions, it ought to search for fact in both of them: from the best excavations possible, and the best other sources too. The question what is a 'culture' could then be posed in more adequate terms. West European house-forms, pre- and protohistoric equally, make a problem for sorting out which will probably strain archaeology's patience. It is one of illuminating culture through investigating structure. Social questions, even linguistic ones, are involved with it potentially. But fact, mostly from the earth, must come first.

PLATE I   THE ACROPOLIS OF PITHEKOUSSAI: MONTE DI VICO (pp. 11 ff.)
Island of Ischia (province of Naples).
Ridgway, 'First Western Greeks'.
Ph.: Leonard von Matt

PLATE II PITHEKOUSSAI FROM MONTE EPOMEO: MONTE DI VICO, VALLE SAN MONTANO, BAIA SAN MONTANO (pp. 11 ff.).

Ridgway, 'First Western Greeks'.

Ph.: J. Klein

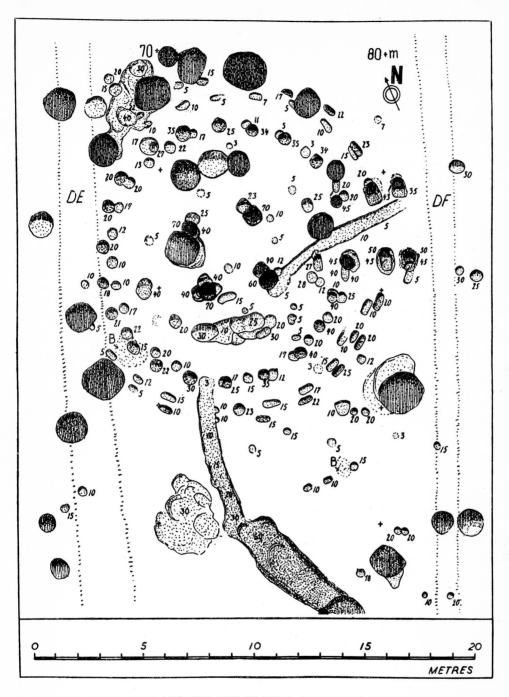

PLATE III   LITTLE WOODBURY, WILTSHIRE, G. BERSU'S EXCAVATION PLAN
OF HOUSE I, 1939 (p. 45), showing pits interfering, and central square of four large re-cut
post-holes. After *Proceedings of the Prehistoric Society* VI (1940), fig. 20.
Harding, 'Round and Rectangular Houses'.   *Ph.: R. L. Wilkins*

PLATE IV   NATIVE HOUSES IN CENTRAL EUROPE, ASSAILED IN THE ROMAN
WARS OF 167–80 (p. 47).   After Bellorius, 1704: engravings by Bartolo (9, 17) of reliefs on
the Column of Marcus Aurelius, Rome.
Harding, 'Round and Rectangular Houses'.

Ph.: R. L. Wilkins

Round and Rectangular: Iron Age Houses, British and Foreign

BY DENNIS HARDING

IV

British archaeology in the 1960s made it almost an axiom that British houses, in the Iron Age, were built to a circular plan, while rectangularity, long established on the Continent, remained there nearly universal. Thus concentric settings of post-holes, which retained the upright timbers of round houses, first recognized by Bersu for Britain at the now classic site of Little Woodbury in Wiltshire (see below, with Fig. 5,B and Pl. III), and exemplified more recently elsewhere, as at Pimperne, Dorset (Harding and Blake 1963), and in Wiltshire at Longbridge Deverill (Chadwick 1961) had come to be regarded as entirely typical, in southern Britain anyhow, of Iron Age settlements. Even in the Highland Zone, where the relative paucity of find-material has so often made it hard to identify pre-Roman Iron Age habitation, the recurrence of circular groundplans, whether for timber or stone construction, has nonetheless been taken as evidence of culture allied to native Iron Age tradition (e.g. by Jobey 1962). Except for a religious building—as at Heathrow, London [1]—for small 'granaries', and for further cases, to be mentioned here below, rectangular plans have not (unless for burials: Stead 1965, figs. 3, 10) been expected from Bronze or from pre-Roman Iron Age Britain. Declaring the apparently invariable use of circular domestic buildings to be one of his principal characters for the period in this country, Dr Hodson (1964, pp. 99–100) remarked that the contrasting distribution, of circular houses in Britain and rectangular houses on the Continent, was one so firmly established that it was unlikely to be seriously challenged by future discoveries. Outside the British Isles, he believed, Iron Age circular houses occurred regularly nowhere but in one extremely

[1] Grimes 1948, 1961. Distinct from this quadrilateral plan, and recalling the early Greek *megaron* form, is that traced within the hill-fort at South Cadbury in Somerset: *Current Archaeology*, 18 (Jan. 1970), pp. 185–7. To the numerous round-house plans traced in the successive excavations there, Musson 1970 may serve as an introduction.

peripheral region, that of the 'castro culture' of north-western Iberia, stone-built and seeming too late in their dating to give acceptable origins for the British ones. For those who rejected the older conventional view, that our Iron Age cultures were the product of immigration from the Continent, here was a further point where Britain stood in 'splendid isolation' from the rest of Europe. And for round houses here, viewed for the Iron Age as insular, insular antecedents were not hard to find.

British houses prior to the Iron Age, at all events through the Bronze Age, must normally be seen as round, in their structure and plan, already. What is more, they can mount a better claim today, than ever formerly, to give Iron Age round houses an insular 'native' pedigree. In 1969, Michael Avery and Joanna Close-Brooks, re-interpreting the Bronze Age house plans traced at Shearplace Hill in Dorset, and in 1970 C. R. Musson, on those and others, as at Itford Hill (Fig. 5,A) mainly in Sussex, each showed in only slightly different ways how reviewing of Bronze Age data can

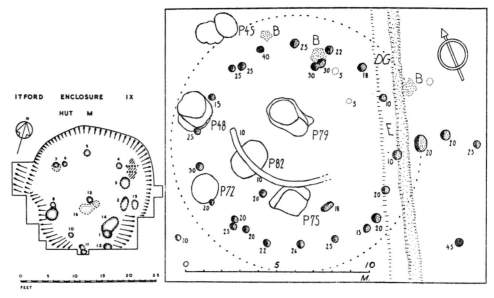

FIG. 5
A. HOUSE IN BRITISH BRONZE AGE SETTLEMENT, ITFORD HILL, E. SUSSEX (pp. 44, 46). Scale 1:200. *After Burstow and Holleyman 1957* (Hut M, Encl. IX).
B. HOUSE II IN BRITISH IRON AGE FARMSTEAD, LITTLE WOODBURY, WILTSHIRE (pp. 43, 45). Scale 1:200. *After Bersu 1940*, adjusted to his text; added dots show circle for outer wall now guessed, its post-holes presumed ploughed away. B, tree-holes (different age); DG field-edge (more recent) sunk by ploughing; E, entrance into house; P, earlier pits, filled in. Figures by post-holes are their depths in cm. from excavation surface.

bring the claim a new force.[1] On the Iron Age side, further, where at Little Woodbury in Wiltshire, from the excavations of 1938–9 by Gerhard Bersu (Bersu 1940), his House I has been taken as a 'classic' British round house (my Plate III), Musson proffers a fresh interpretation of his own, putting others' previous doubts into positive form. He explains it as built twice over, the second phase being quite distinct; and has shown 'a fair chance' that the central square of post-holes—trunk-sized, and seen hitherto as a key to its whole design—was dug for some different structure when no house was standing at all. Of the posts that the house has in each of its phases, in big concentric rings, the inner ring will have borne the main thrust of the conical roof; the outer, under its eaves, and clad with daub-covered wattlework, formed the circular exterior wall. Standing in shallower holes accordingly, some destroyed by modern ploughing, this ring allows the conjecture that Bersu's House II (Fig. 5B), outside the ring in which its holes did survive, had had an outer ring too (dotted circle here), which has vanished.

Here a further factor is relevant besides. Both houses had a porch, planned to stand across their circles, with posts flanking the entry, set in holes that were fairly deep. House I's had a pair where the entry crossed each of its circles—the main and the outer or wall ring—and a front pair, projecting. Across House II's surviving main ring (Fig. 5B) the entry was at E: that is certain, from the width between the post-holes there, and from holes for the porch outside them. One of these, on the south side, fits the guess for the house's wall ring; another, beyond to east, must mark the porch's front. Bersu, who regarded the structure as never finished, doubted holes on the north: one (at B) showed action by tree-roots. Musson however, by guessing that the north side holes had been there, but were ploughed away with the wall ring, gives us a porch to match House I's (Plate III). So we may welcome both of the excavated Little Woodbury house-sites as examples of the same large round-house plan. The projecting porch, and the circular build that required no central element, show exactly the kind of structure which more recent excavation has been proving among British Iron Age house plans elsewhere: at Pimperne and Longbridge Deverill, mentioned already, and amongst the many findings at South Cadbury (p. 43, n. 1) in Somerset. This then is the kind of house for which the argument, so far followed, claims a 'native' pedigree through the Bronze Age.

It is clear, to be sure, that Britain had had a long-established practice, which can be traced well back in the Bronze Age, if not further, of building circular dwellings—

[1] Avery and Close-Brooks 1969, re-interpreting Rahtz in Rahtz and ApSimon 1962; Musson 1970, re-interpreting Burstow and Holleyman 1957 (Itford), with e.g. Curwen 1934, Holleyman and Curwen 1935, and especially Ratcliffe-Densham 1966.

with use, where wanted, of timber posts. Yet the Bronze Age groundplans of these recovered hitherto are seldom at all as large, or as regular, as those of the Iron Age. The comparison in Fig. 5 (from the excavators' originals) is not of extreme examples. It brings out the contrast, but the likeness too. The Iron Age layout, in symmetry and size, suggests innovation; yet at Shearplace Hill, the Avery/Close-Brooks demonstration lets us see, back in the Middle Bronze Age, houses with a porch, fit to be seen as prototypes of the Iron Age elaborate ones, and with diameter approaching 12 metres already. At the smaller size presented in Fig. 5A from Itford, Musson's case for an outer ring of wall, close to the terrace-scarp (shown on the plan by its steep-slope hatching), adds a metre to the diameter on either side of the house's post-ring, making the interior 6 metres across instead of 4. And at this size also, the porch is unmistakable. Simple though it is, moreover, it yet would need the roofing, carried across the post-ring into the cone of the main rafters, that is shown by the Shearplace model to anticipate that of the Iron Age. Dimensions altogether, of course, in either period, are a factor especially critical as applying to the roof. The conical form of that, with its rafters meeting in a peak, and the bracing-strength required against their weight, and against the wind, calls for greater skill the greater the dimensions to be covered. Iron Age men, with iron tools to cut and shape their timbers, could stretch constructional skill to a high degree of sophistication, giving a symmetry and regularity to the full-sized layout, which the Pimperne house displays in pre-eminence. And though we may not yet have discovered the best that Bronze Age men could do, this Iron Age mastery of the technique need not surprise us. That it was reached in a tradition practised in both periods, is nowadays not in doubt; nor need this have been confined to the type that we have here been considering, the round house with porch. What must, on the other hand, be brought into question is the 'axiom' that would make the type peculiarly insular. The like applies to the belief that on the Continent, houses of these periods were almost everywhere rectangular. For even north-west Iberia, with its 'castro' circular houses, may prompt some search for others of their kind; and if that be successful, should not Britain prompt one too? Was circular building a British or insular tradition that was isolated totally, or anyhow as much— against rectangular building on the mainland—as some modern thinkers have supposed? From either of the viewpoints, the question calls for evidence. After the British, we must turn to the Continental.

First, it must be emphasized that statements such as Dr Hodson's concerning the 'Continental' tradition of rectangular building really refer to the Central European (and possibly the Northern) convention, rather than any yet at all fully demonstrated in areas bordering on the Atlantic or the Channel. Much more excavation here, with extensive stripping of Iron Age settlements, requires to be undertaken, particularly in France. Meantime, however, domestic houses in this region need not be expected to conform exclusively to the rectangular pattern long familiar, far inland, at the Mont Beuvray (Côte d'Or, and not far short of Burgundy).

Besides the small and not always exactly rectangular groundplans there (fig. 124 in Piggott 1965), we might expect larger ones of the same late pre-Roman age, not yet replaced from Italian models but of a rectangularity made distinctively long, as in the contemporary Late La Tène culture east of the Rhine, represented in classic form at the oppidum of Manching, in Bavaria beside the upper Danube (Krämer 1960, 1961, 1962). Yet farther from the reach of the rectangular convention, which was oldest in Central Europe, the case might be different. The Greek geographer Strabo, probably using Posidonius, a personal observer of the Gauls before Caesar's conquest, states of them unequivocally (IV, iv, 3): 'Their houses are large and circular, built of planks and wickerwork, the roof being a dome of heavy thatch.' That description, even to the use of planks as well as wattling, might equally well have been written of houses over in southern Britain, like that at Pimperne, if any observer had come and seen them. In Gaul, even in the north, such houses need not have been the only ones, but we ought to allow for enough to bear out this factual description's terms. So its record, our plainest for Gaul, stands at variance with the belief—whether drawn from Manching or the Mont Beuvray—that mainland houses were all rectangular.

One further source of information—long available to prehistorians, though used by them too seldom, perhaps on account of its being Roman—relates not to Gaul but actually to Central Europe itself. More than two hundred years from Caesar, in Rome on the Column of Marcus Aurelius, the sculptured reliefs that commemorate his wars show the dwellings of hapless natives, which his soldiers are setting on fire, most frequently as circular; rectangular buildings are rarer, and this argues quite convincingly that north of the Middle Danube (where his wars were fought) such circular huts were then not only present, but common (Pl. IV).[1] The dilemma is evident. We need a solution which will not only reconcile the facts we have, but also bring the houses' apparent distributions, insular and mainland, rectangular and round, into a more coherent archaeological frame for all these regions of Europe.

The next stage in our enquiry must be to return to the testimony of excavation: to consider first of all whether, like Strabo and the sculptures, it can show (besides the

---

[1] Rather than standard publications (even Caprino 1955; e.g. Tav. xxvii) showing the Column's reliefs from photographs (or photographs of casts), I have here preferred older engravings, and chosen pls. ix and xvii from Bellori 1704: splendid in its kind, his work was also done when the condition of the sculptures could have been sharper than they were more recently.

Iberian case) round buildings on the Continent. Half a century ago, Bersu and Goessler (1924) excavated an oval house on the Lochenstein, a hill near Balingen in Württemberg—a site too long forgotten in our preoccupation with the more common rectangular house-type of Central Europe. A more convincing plan from the first century B.C. (Late La Tène, according to M. Hatt's latest view, by letter 14th February 1972, and not 'precocious Gallo-Roman' as originally thought) was published some twenty years ago from a site in Alsace, Achenheim (Hatt and Heintz 1951; I owe Miss N. K. Sandars, and the editor (C.F.C.H.) thanks for information, and J. J. Hatt for permission to re-draw). Here a circular house (Fig. 6A), some 6 metres in diameter, was defined by the double ring of holes for the stakes that held the clay-covered wattling of its wall. Central within the interior was a circular pit; and this was evidently just similar to that which lately, in northern Champagne, has been determined as a sunken fireplace, again placed centrally, in a house of 'Marnian' Early La Tène (Ia), at Chassemy (Aisne), the wall of which had been built likewise with stakes, but in plan was rectangular (Rowlett and Boureux 1969). Of the posts for its long ridged roof, in twin rows, the middle four had holes placed close around the fire-pit; posts for the Achenheim roof, of course a cone, could have stood there also, though no holes could be used by Hatt for his elevation. Lastly, and again rectangular (or at least with the long sides parallel), houses with a similar central pit have been explored at Aulnat (Puy-de-Dôme), in the centre of France near Clermont-Ferrand. Here the twin rows of post-holes pass beside four extra middle ones, standing around the pit; the age is La Tène II–III, roughly around 100 B.C., and the current excavations, directed by R. Périchon, have resumed those started in the 1940s by J. J. Hatt himself.[1] The Chassemy house being earlier than these by a good 300 years, it is striking that beyond this series, and past the time of Caesar's conquest, the Achenheim house with the central pit should yet have been of circular build. One is bound to agree with Hatt in taking this to have been traditional. Recognition seems at hand, in fact, that through most of the Iron Age anyhow, north-west and west and north of the Alps, round and rectangular traditions existed together.

The round tradition, too, could take more forms than the one we have seen at Achenheim. Returning to the 'Marnian' area, we find at Berry-au-Bac (Aisne) a house of diameter about 5 metres but of slightly irregular circular plan, with floor

---

[1] I have to thank Professor Hawkes and M. Périchon for use of correspondence between them (1970–1), with information then unpublished, on the Aulnat excavations; for progress reports by the director and colleagues, see *Revue archéologique du Centre*, 1964 onwards. For the previous work by J. J. Hatt, see *Bulletin historique et scientifique de L'Auvergne*, 62 (1942), with plan pl. i.

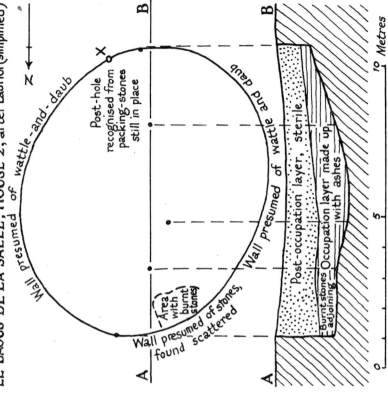

LE BAOUS DE LA SALLE, HOUSE 2, after Lauriol (simplified)

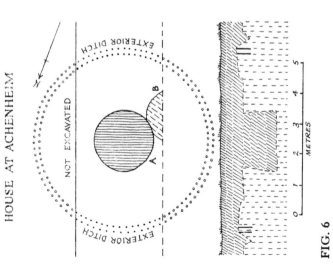

HOUSE AT ACHENHEIM

FIG. 6

A. ROUND HOUSE, FIRST CENTURY B.C., AT ACHENHEIM IN ALSACE (p. 48), as planned on exposure in clay-workings, 1945. Scale 1 : 125. *After Hatt and Heintz 1951;* A, sunken fireplace; B, more ancient (Hallstatt) floor-remains. Entrance to house not found. Exterior wall of wattle is marked by the double ring of holes for its supporting stakes; section (across diameter) shows these and the ditch outside them. Roof (elevation omitted) must have been conical, slanting over. *Drawn by Marion Cox.*

B. ROUND-OVAL HOUSE, FINAL BRONZE AGE (no. 2), AT LE BAOUS DE LA SALLE, BIZE-AUDE, S. FRANCE (p. 50) Scale 1 : 125. *After Lauriol 1958* (adapted; black dots mark measuring-points for section). *Drawn by Marion Cox.*

recessed into natural subsoil (Chevallier and Ertlé 1965). Finds included fragments of carinated vases, Early La Tène and thus pointing to a date, within or still close to the fifth century B.C., broadly contemporary with the rectangular house at Chassemy, also in the Aisne though farther north. And since the filling above the sunken floor shows up such a house's outline, even in the absence of recorded post-holes, there can be more for us to learn of the range of groundplans. Thus in the Languedoc (southern France), where rectangular ones should be likely, in the Iron and indeed the Late Bronze Age—brought down the Rhône from some inland quarter—excavations at the place named Le Baous de la Salle, near Bize in the Aude, more than a dozen years ago disclosed such a sunken-floored house, with groundplan very definitely oval (Fig. 6B: Lauriol 1958).[1] Measuring 9·70 metres by 8 and sunk into bedrock, its floor was made up progressively with ash from its hearth (marked by cobblestones crazed from burning), behind which its wall had been set with larger stones (found scattered), while elsewhere the wall was of wattlework daubed with clay, as many fragments showed. Of holes for its stakes or posts, one was located, being packed with stones; as internal posts on the floor of rock could have been steadied without them, we cannot judge the roof, but the type of house is definite. The site had a number of houses (this was no. 9); and when motorway construction disclosed another, at the 'Boussecos', not far off (Lauriol 1963), the houses were similar again: round or sub-circular and at least once oval, 6 metres by 4·50, (the hearth here was a fire-pit), and with clay fragments proving wattled walls. The period of both, from their pottery, was the same: Late Bronze Age ('Final'), reaching Iron Age in date, or roughly ninth to seventh century B.C. And beside the Rhône in Isère, at Sérézin-du-Rhône, excavation in 1961 attested a house 6 metres by 5·50 approaching the oval, and with pottery likewise assigned to the Late Bronze Age (Combier 1961).

If therefore, with rectangular house plans in Gaul, we have circular, sub-circular and oval ones too—the oval bidding for status as a standard sub-group, in age going back to Late Bronze—this tradition of building round, and ignoring rectangularity, might surely take, as a further form, the one known best from Britain: that of a circular house with projecting porch. And thus we are led to the important work in the east French region of the Franche-Comté, by P. Pétrequin and colleagues at Dampierre-sur-le-Doubs, published by them a few years back (Pétrequin, Urlacher, and Vuaillat 1969). This was a substantial Late Bronze Age settlement, of two successive periods, respectively of Final Bronze I and II (in the system of J. J. Hatt): not so late as III, within the eighth–seventh centuries, but reaching to it from a start not later than the

[1] I am much obliged to M. Lauriol, and the editor for whom he wrote, for permission to have his drawing adapted here.

tenth, and perhaps before 1000 B.C. In the period I so starting, the site was divided into a cemetery zone to south, for cremations in pits with sherds (not urns), and a habitation zone to north, with a few non-cemetery pits, and dotted more or less densely with post-holes. Between the zones ran a trench for a palisade, ending to east at the marshes of the river Doubs; Fig. 7B (from the excavators' fig. 22, by their courtesy) shows nearly all its length, and all the habitation-zone that had been spared by the eastward marsh. The post-hole spread bears sorting into patterns, with north–south

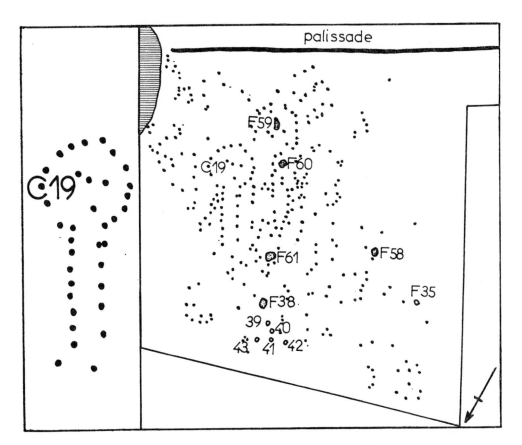

FIG. 7 SETTLEMENT OF FINAL BRONZE I, DAMPIERRE-SUR-LE-DOUBS, NEAR MONTBÉLIARD, E. FRANCE (pp. 50–2, 53)
A. House c 19, plan of post-holes with the double row approaching its porch. Scale 1:200.
B. Plan of this whole period's habitation-zone, with post-holes of c 19 and all others, pits (F+number), and trench for palisade dividing it from the cemetery-zone (cremations). Scale 1:400. *After Pétrequin, Urlacher and Vuaillat 1969.*

lanes between the denser groupings; guesses at structure from these (as in such cases elsewhere: e.g. Musson 1970, pair of plans p. 267) may vary in plausibility, and the group near the middle of the palisade, appearing rectangular, may be accepted or doubted. But the excavators' caution has permitted one group (therefore numbered, C19) to stand as a round house with porch: 16 post-holes for its roof-supporting ring, and two for the porch's front (to north). The main ring is 5 to 6 metres in diameter; with the porch and a vanished wall-ring, the area roofed might nearly be 30 square metres. Fig. 7A here shows the post-hole plan enlarged, to the scale of our British examples (Fig. 5), with the long double row of post-holes approaching the porch, like a fenced-off lane or a corridor, which the excavators prudently refrained from annexing to their plan (fig. 25) of the house as such. With or without this feature, then, not far from 1000 B.C., Bronze Age people in eastern France could have a round house, porched, like the British. Somewhat larger than that illustrated in our Fig. 5A, it is nearer to the dimensions now inferred at Shearplace Hill (p. 46 above); and in the Iron Age, its closest British counterpart published is the plan of the principal house at Standlake, on the Upper Thames in Oxfordshire (Riley 1946–7, fig. 9). Finally, passing to Dampierre's second period, Final Bronze II around the ninth century B.C., we find nearly all the site given over, including the former cemetery zone, to substantial post-built houses of oblong plan, two of them apsed at one end (with partial wooden plank flooring), and otherwise all consistently rectangular. The tradition of Central Europe, then, with the culture called 'Urnfield' (from its cemeteries of cremation-urns; though at Dampierre none was found), had now superseded the round house here— although not, as we have seen, in France everywhere.

If the porched round house was here in use as early as 1000, how much was it used on the Continent before? And for how long? The next period previous is the Middle Bronze Age, when it was used in Britain as at Shearplace Hill. For its Iron Age distributions to be explained, now or in future, we should search at least as far back as this, in the second millennium B.C. There may be more than one counterpart, within mainland Western Europe, to the 'Deverel-Rimbury culture' in which we first encounter it in Britain. But the one that has shown it over there, and no later, is as near as it well could be, namely the so-called Hilversum culture, spread from Boulogne to the southern Netherlands. And there, in the province of North Brabant, well known for resemblances to Britain in this period's mode of burial, houses of this form have now been disclosed in habitations. The principal excavation to be published, so far, is that of a farmstead settlement near Nijnsel (Beex and Hulst 1968); the chief part of the plan is here presented in Fig. 8, by permission of the Rijksdienst voor het Oudheidkundig Bodemonderzoek. Of the post-hole groups for quadrangular buildings,

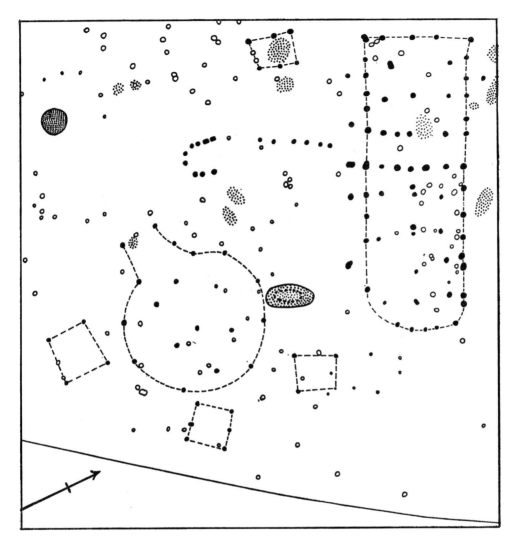

FIG. 8 (pp. 52–4, 55) BRONZE AGE FARMSTEAD NEAR NIJNSEL, NETHERLANDS (PROV. NOORD-BRABANT): centre-west portion of plan. Scale 1 : 200. *After Beex and Hulst 1968.*

there were several of the small size interpreted as 'granaries'; but the most important revealed the groundplan of the farmstead's principal dwelling. It was large and long, with an apse at one end (inviting comparison with those of Dampierre period II); and in the aisles formed by its three lines of roof-supporting post-holes, and the transverse passage between the rows that divide its length into two, it plainly foreshadows the plan of the later 'long houses' of northern Europe. Yet this was not all, for directly to south of it was the very clear plan of a substantial round house. Measuring approximately 8·50 metres in diameter, it is once again distinguished by entry through a porch, which projects outwards from the main circle of post-holes. Internal support for the roof was provided by a number of other posts, arranged rather irregularly in a ring. North of Nijnsel, comparable huts of circular or sub-circular plan have been discovered in recent years at Zijderveld (Hulst 1965, 1966) and Dodewaard (Hulst 1967), which, despite their irregular disposition of post-holes, nonetheless retain the projecting porch as a prominent feature.

In view of the links, in burial forms at least, seen for Britain and the Netherlands in the early Middle Bronze Age (Smith 1961), it perhaps might be argued that the notion of such a building was implanted there as a result of emigration from Britain. Yet it scarcely seems convincing to derive the much wider later round-house distribution from origins at all so strictly localized; a preferable solution would be to view these Middle Bronze Age groups, Hilversum and Deverel-Rimbury both, as regional manifestations of a broader European tradition. Its origins and development, of course, will require much further research. But we can no longer doubt that, by the time of the Final Bronze and Iron Age, circular building was much more widespread in France and elsewhere than many British prehistorians have believed. This should include the Iberian peninsula, not reviewed in the present article. In consequence, the contrast in building practice between Britain and Western Europe will be seen to be more apparent than real. Its importance in the long-drawn controversy on British 'insularity', as against an 'invasion hypothesis', has been much exaggerated. What really distinguishes the major British round houses, of the Iron Age, from the Continental examples cited here is their greater size. Not only does this presuppose more perfect structural symmetry, and superior engineering skills, but it may also reflect a difference in their occupants' social status, in contrast to a community living in smaller, individual, dwellings.

On the Continent, amongst sites known to the author, only one included sub-circular houses of dimensions comparable to the large round houses of Britain. This is the Iron Age site in Belgium, on the Hoever Heide near Lommel (prov. Limburg: De Laet 1961). Its two emplacements lack both the symmetry of layout of the Wessex round houses, and the circular settings of post-holes which in the British examples provided the principal roof-support. Rather do they resemble the oval houses known in the south (Fig. 6B). But they anyhow leave the idea of total contrast, between circular British and rectangular Continental building fashions, as still more an erroneous simplification. Once the wider view is taken, rectangularity becomes an aspect of the movement and influence out from Central Europe, associated mainly, though not indeed exclusively, with the 'Urnfield culture' before and after 1000 B.C. Presumably the North European plain had its own traditions, and here the discovery at Nijnsel that, alongside the round house, a form of long house was in use already in the early Middle Bronze Age, should invite more excavation of sites of that period. Round building appears mainly Atlantic, or at all events Western. How and when it became so is a further question, but the issue for us here is now no longer one of black or white. Instead, we may reasonably expect to find that, from the Low Countries out over France and beyond, there was a shifting admixture of influences in which both traditions met. For just as rectangularity, in Central Europe, was of course much older than 'Urnfield' times, which only mark a swell in its diffusion westwards, so in the West itself we may see an ancient tradition, of circular house construction, extending back through the Bronze Age. From that, in the British Isles on the north-west, the Peninsula on the south-west, and the broad lands between, the tradition can have been developed towards the features it shows in the Iron Age. Thus Britain and the mainland opposite would be parts of one whole.

Finally now, turning back to rectangularity once again, we must ask how and when any influence or movement, effecting its diffusion, might in fact reach Britain. Did this really never happen till the Romans came, to bring it? Behind our exhortations to Continental colleagues, to expose more habitation-sites, have we sites of our own already, which we have failed to understand? And which include, already of the Iron Age, some rectangular plans of houses? At Park Brow in Sussex, indeed (Wolseley, Smith and Hawley, 1927, pp. 32–6 with fig. P), and the Dorset Maiden Castle (Wheeler 1943, p. 124, fig. 22), minor claims of the kind will not compare with Krämer's houses at Manching. Both the post-hole groupings involved would currently be better explained as for granaries, or even for pairs of drying-racks or emplacements for weavers' looms. And somewhat irregular groups of post-holes elsewhere, in excavations whether in Scotland (Steer 1956: West Plean) or England in Buckinghamshire (Cotton and Frere 1968: Ivinghoe Beacon) and Wiltshire (Wainwright 1970: Budbury), if for rectangular structures really, could never be used for claiming these as a standard type of house.

Perhaps the biggest single hindrance to the recognition of rectangular houses in Britain has been our preoccupation with post-holes, which happen to be an essential of our southern porched round houses. A rectangular house, in fact, does not require many posts, if any. One may build it virtually free-standing at ground level by giving it a frame of sill-beams, of which no trace need survive archaeologically—unless the beams, or any footing-stones under them, were purposely sunk in a bedding-trench, or became embedded subsequently, in wind-blown dust or vegetable undergrowth. Traces of beam or bedding-trench, then, may survive to furnish a structural outline, like that on site IV on Micklemoor Hill, West Harling, Norfolk (Clark 1953, pp. 12–14, fig. 9). Alternatively, the house could be built on the log-cabin principle, requiring posts at the four corners only, or six posts if longer. Amid the wealth of miscellaneous pits, post-holes and intrusions which prolonged occupation of an Iron Age settlement invariably produces, it is improbable that the archaeologist will be able to identify, and justify, those few post-holes which are such a house's residual elements. It could be, then, that the odds favour the recognition of circular buildings, rather than rectangular, particularly on the south and east English chalk, where the topsoil is often so shallow that any structural foundations, unless dug well into bedrock, may by now have been ploughed away.

Once we accept the principle that a pattern of post-holes is not a *sine qua non* for tracing Iron Age houses, several excavated and published sites emerge, where rectangular buildings may be recognized. I have attempted elsewhere (Harding 1971) to demonstrate this for the Upper Thames valley, where rectangular house sites may be inferred at Wigbald's Farm, Long Wittenham (Savory 1937) and adjacent to the hill-fort on the Sinodun Hills (Rhodes 1948). In both cases substantial post-holes are lacking, and the crucial evidence comprises a compacted floor-level, indicating the rectangular outline of a building. At the former site the entire occupation area is recessed into the ground, as at the oval house shown in Fig. 6B, and those similar in France and Belgium that I have cited (pp. 48–50); the Sinodun site gives the possibility also of a low enclosing wall of chalk rubble. And ironically enough, the one site where the whole known settlement gave no sign of circular houses, but only oblong floors like these, is one whose find-material has always made it stand as a type-site for the earliest standard Iron Age in Britain—the famous Wiltshire habitation-site at All Cannings Cross (Cunnington 1923, fig. 2), whence here Fig. 9. The floors, of which this plan shows almost all, were all rectangular, or nearly so, formed of compacted chalk rubble with some flint and sarsen blocks. The excavators thought them paved areas serving as forecourts to houses of which no further trace survived, but they seem far more likely to have been the floors of the buildings themselves. Although not elongated in plan like Central European long houses, but averaging 8 metres in length and 5 in width, these houses at All Cannings Cross would have been very comparable, in dimensions and design, to those at the Mont Beuvray (p. 47). Once again, indeed, they appear to have lacked accompanying post-holes, though it is conceivable that some were present, but still remain to be found. Not all the floors need be contemporary with one another: in view of the over-sailing and re-alignment of several, it is evident anyhow that more than one building phase is represented. But the nature of the settlement, as one where the houses were rectangular, and thus to be presumed of

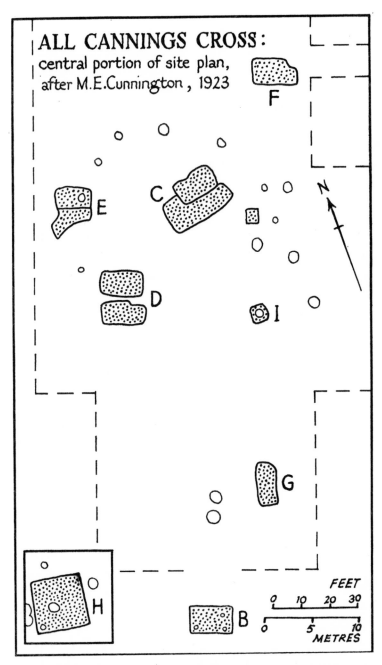

ALL CANNINGS CROSS:
central portion of site plan,
after M.E.Cunnington , 1923

FEET

METRES

FIG. 9 (p. 56) BRITISH IRON AGE SETTLEMENT, ALL CANNINGS CROSS,
WILTSHIRE: centre portion of plan. Scale 1 : 400. H (inset) was some 55 m. south of G. *After
Cunnington 1923. Drawn by Marion Cox.*

foreign type, can scarcely be doubted. It is fully as significant, for British Iron Age studies, as the foreign nature of the site's fine decorated pottery. Its neglect for so long is in itself a measure of our insular obsession with the concept of circular architecture. And in Herefordshire, on hillforts through the years to 1970, successively at Croft Ambrey, Credenhill, and Midsummer Camp, Mr Stanley Stanford (1967; 1970) has been finding that in the western British province small rectangular dwellings were the rule. This is the further case that I promised above (p. 43) that I would notice. Simple in plan as these are, and small in area by comparison with contemporary houses in Central Europe, there can be no denying the dominance in western Britain of rect-angular over circular. Whether other examples listed by Stanford in southern Britain can all be treated as dwellings is questionable; only for those exceeding 7 sq. m. in area is he prepared to press the case strongly. And since he wrote, discoveries in Hamp-shire (Balksbury, Danebury) and Cotswold (Crickley) have given fresh examples.

At the outset of this study we noted that some prehistorians have regarded the apparently contrasting pattern of house-types in Britain and on the Continent as a measure of the insularity of the British Iron Age, devoid of intrusive elements from abroad. That contrast now being qualified, both by the discovery of circular build-ings in Continental Europe and by a reappraisal of the evidence for rectangular construction in Britain, we must now question the validity of the inference that Iron Age settlements in Britain reflect only insular origins. That Iron Age round houses have antecedents in the British Bronze Age is not in question. But we can no longer argue conversely against the 'invasion hypothesis' on the grounds that all immi-grants would have brought with them their mode of rectangular buildings, since any might have come over from parts of the Continent where both rectangular and circular houses were in use. And in such circumstances, they might well have deferred to the native preference, particularly if they were dependent upon indigenous builders and craftsmen with the engineering skill for their construction.

I shall not, in this essay, pass on to the 'Belgic' period, in which southern Britain received a full Late La Tène culture. Debate has begun, in fact, on its whole invasive character; and for that, the reader must turn to volume II of this series and read the study there by Michael Avery. Yet the culture's remains of houses here, insofar as known from excavation, would not suggest an improvement, to say the least, upon its predecessors' (e.g. Hawkes and Hull 1947, pp. 46ff.; Ward Perkins 1938, pl. lxx). Here, literary sources afford no consolation. Caesar (*de Bello Gallico* V, 12) tells us only that the native buildings in the maritime states of south-eastern Britain were numerous, and were very like those of the Gauls. Whether we believe them to have been rectangular or circular in plan, therefore, depends upon which view we take of

Gallic buildings. But the implications of our failure to locate in numbers rectangular Belgic dwellings in the south-east are clear. Either any invaders were content for the most part to adopt British practice in domestic building, or they already had a similar one themselves, or excavation has still to find a superior one that they brought, or the debate on their invasion has to erode much old belief. Whichever we prefer, the same reasoning should be applicable equally to the position in our earlier centuries. What is sauce for the Belgic goose should be sauce for the earlier ganders. And though we may retain the round-house plan as a type of the British Iron Age, it would be imprudent, in view of the findings on the Continent, now to regard it any longer as an exclusive sign of British insularity.

Bibliography

Avery, M., and Close-Brooks, J., 1969. 'Shearplace Hill, . . . a suggested re-inter-
pretation.' *Proceedings of the Prehistoric Society*, 35, pp. 345–51.

Beex, G., and Hulst, R. S., 1968. 'A Hilversum-Culture settlement near Nijnsel . . ,
North Brabant.' *Berichten van de Rijksdienst voor het Oudheidkundig Bodemonderzoek*
18, pp. 117–30.

Bellori, G. P. (= J. P. Bellorius), 1704. *Columna Cochlis M. Aurelio Antonino
Augusto dicata . . . a P.S. Bartolo aere incisa.* Rome.

Bersu, G., 1940. 'Excavations at Little Woodbury, Wiltshire: Part I.' *Proceedings of
the Prehistoric Society*, 6, pp. 30–111.

Bersu, G., and Goessler, P., 1924. 'Der Lochenstein bei Balingen.' *Fundberichte aus
Schwaben*, n.s., 11 (1922–4), pp. 73–103 and pl. iv. *See also* Wolseley, Smith, and
Hawley 1927, pp. 26–9.

Burstow, G. P., and Holleyman, G. A., 1957. 'Late Bronze Age settlement on
Itford Hill, Sussex.' *Proceedings of the Prehistoric Society*, 23, pp. 167–212.

Caprino C., *et al.*, 1955. *La Colonna di Marco Aurelio.* Rome.

Chadwick (Hawkes), S., 1961. 'Early Iron Age enclosures on Longbridge Deverill
Cow Down, Wiltshire.' In *Problems of the Iron Age in Southern Britain* (ed. S. S.
Frere). University of London Institute of Archaeology, Occasional Paper no. 11,
pp. 18–20.

Chevallier, R., and Ertlé, R., 1965. 'Un fond de cabane gauloise à Berry-au-Bac
(Aisne).' *Revue Archéologique de l'Est et du Centre-Est*, 16, pp. 206–14.

Clark, J. G. D., and Fell, C. I., 1953. 'An Early Iron Age site at Micklemoor Hill,
West Harling, Norfolk . . .' *Proceedings of the Prehistoric Society*, 19, pp. 1–40.

Combier, J., 1961. 'Information archéologiques . . . Grenoble: Sérézin-du-Rhône
(Isère).' *Gallia Préhistoire*, 4, pp. 316–18.

COTTON, M. A., and FRERE, S. S., 1968. 'Ivinghoe Beacon excavations.' *Records of Buckinghamshire*, 18, 3, pp. 187–260.

CUNNINGTON, M. E., 1923. *All Cannings Cross*. Devizes.

CURWEN, E. C., 1934. 'A Late Bronze Age farm on New Barn Down, Clapham, nr. Worthing.' *Sussex Archaeological Collections*, 75 (1934), pp. 137–70.

DE LAET, S. J., 1961. 'Opgravingen en vondsten in de Limburgse Kempen.' As reprinted in *Archaeologica Belgica*, 55.

GRIMES, W. F., 1948. 'A prehistoric temple at London airport.' *Archaeology*, 1, pp. 74–9, esp. figs. 3 and 4.

—, 1961. 'Heath Row ("Caesar's Camp") Harmondsworth.' In *Problems of the Iron Age in Southern Britain* (ed. S. S. Frere). University of London Institute of Archaeology, Occasional Paper no. 11, p. 25, fig. 7.

HARDING, D. W., 1971. *The Iron Age in the Upper Thames Basin*. Oxford.

HARDING, D. W., and BLAKE, I., 1963. 'An Early Iron Age settlement in Dorset.' *Antiquity*, 37, pp. 63–4 and pl. viii.

HATT, J. J., and HEINTZ, G., 1951. 'Découverte d'une cabane gallo-romaine précoce à Achenheim.' *Cahiers d'archéologie et d'histoire d'Alsace*, 9, pp. 47–52.

HAWKES, C. F. C., and HULL, M. R., 1947. *Camulodunum*. Society of Antiquaries of London, Research Report, no. 11. Oxford.

HODSON, F. R., 1964. 'Cultural grouping within the British pre-Roman Iron Age.' *Proceedings of the Prehistoric Society*, 30, pp. 99–110.

HOLLEYMAN, G. A., and CURWEN, E. C., 1935. 'Late Bronze Age Lynchet-settlements on Plumpton Plain, Sussex.' *Proceedings of the Prehistoric Society*, 1, pp. 16–38.

HULST, R. S., 1965, 1966. 'Zijderveld, gem. Everdingen.' *Nieuwsbulletin van de Koninklijke Nederlandse Oudheidkundige Bond* (1965), pp. 107, 138; (1966), p. 93. (Cited with house-plan in BEEX and HULST 1968).

—, 1967. 'Hien, gem. Dodewaard.' *Nieuwsbulletin van de Koninklijke Nederlandse Oudheidkundige Bond*, p. 64.

JOBEY, G., 1962. 'An Iron Age homestead at West Brandon, Co. Durham.' *Archaeologia Aeliana*, 40, pp. 1–34. Newcastle.

KRÄMER, W., 1960. 'The *Oppidum* of Manching.' *Antiquity*, 34, pp. 191–200.

—, 1961. 'Neue Funde aus dem Oppidum von Manching.' *Germania*, 39, pp. 299–383.

—, 1962. 'Manching II: Zu den Ausgrabungen in den Jahren 1957 bis 1961.' *Germania*, 40, pp. 293–317.

LAURIOL, J., 1958. 'Un gisement . . . Bronze Final-1er Age du Fer: les fonds de cabanes du Baous de la Salle.' *Cahiers Ligures de Préhistoire et d'Archéologie*, 7, pp. 16–51. Montpellier. Summary in *Gallia* 1959, pp. 457–9.

—, 1963. 'Trois nouveaux gisements du Bronze Final à Bize (Aude), les habitats de Boussecos.' *Cahiers Ligures de Préhistoire et d'Archéologie*, 12, pp. 131–41. Montpellier.

MUSSON, C., 1970. 'House-plans and prehistory.' *Current Archaeology*, 2, 10 (= no. 21, July 1970), pp. 267–75; and for Wales, pp. 276–7.

PÉTREQUIN, P., URLACHER, J.-P., and VUAILLAT, D., 1969. 'Habitat et sépultures de l'Age du Bronze Final à Dampierre-sur-le-Doubs (Doubs).' *Gallia Préhistoire*, 12, pp. 1–35.

PIGGOTT, S., 1965. *Ancient Europe*. Edinburgh.

RAHTZ P., and APSIMON, A., 1962. 'Excavations at Shearplace Hill, Sydling St Nicholas, Dorset.' *Proceedings of the Prehistoric Society*, 27, pp. 345–51.

RATCLIFFE-DENSHAM, H. B. A. and M. M., 1966. 'Amberley Mount: its agricultural story from the Late Bronze Age.' *Sussex Archaeological Collections*, 104, pp. 6–25.

RHODES, P. P., 1948. 'A prehistoric and Roman site at Wittenham Clumps, Berkshire.' *Oxoniensia*, 13, pp. 18–31.

RILEY, D. N., 1946–7. 'Late Bronze and Iron Age site on Standlake Downs.' *Oxoniensia*, 11–12, pp. 27–43.

ROWLETT, R. M. and S.-J., and BOUREUX, M., 1969. 'A rectangular Early La Tène Marnian house at Chassemy (Aisne).' *World Archaeology*, 1, no. 1, pp. 106–35 (house 9).

SAVORY, H. N., 1937. 'An Early Iron Age site at Long Wittenham, Berkshire.' *Oxoniensia*, 2, pp. 1–11.

SMITH, I. F., 1961. 'An essay towards the reformation of the British Bronze Age.' *Helinium*, 1, pp. 97–118.

STANFORD, S. C., 1967. 'Croft Ambrey hill-fort—some interim conclusions.' *Transactions of the Woolhope Field Club, Herefordshire*, 39, 1, pp. 31–9.

—, 1970. 'Credenhill Camp, Herefordshire: An Iron Age Hill-Fort Capital.' *Archaeological Journal*, 127 (for 1970; pub. 1971), pp. 82–129.

STEAD, I. M., 1965. *The La Tène Cultures of Eastern Yorkshire*. Yorkshire Philosophical Society. York.

STEER, K., 1956. 'The Early Iron Age homestead at West Plean, Stirlingshire.' *Proceedings of the Society of Antiquaries of Scotland*, 89 (1955–6), pp. 227–51.

WAINWRIGHT, G. J., 1970. 'An Iron Age promontory fort at Budbury, Bradford-on-Avon, Wiltshire.' *Wiltshire Archaeological Magazine*, 65, pp. 108–66.

WARD PERKINS, J. B., 1938. 'The Roman Villa at Lockleys, Welwyn, Hertfordshire.' *Antiquaries Journal*, 18, pp. 339–76.

WHEELER, R. E. M., 1943. *Maiden Castle, Dorset* (Society of Antiquaries of London, Research Report, no. 12. Oxford).

WOLSELEY, G. R., SMITH, R. A. and HAWLEY, W., 1927. 'Prehistoric and Roman settlements on Park Brow.' *Archaeologia*, 76, pp. 1–40.

Commentary 3
From Venture to Resistance:
Rome in the British North

Protohistoric Europe had its first great age in the half-dozen centuries from the landing of Greeks on Ischia. Its chieftain-led societies and Bronze Age economy, gaining from the collapse in Greece of the old Mycenaeans, and drawing fresh strength out of interludes of turmoil, began to pass to its Iron Age in the first of those centuries; by the end of the next, Europe had started to find its links with the south transformed, as the Mediterranean venturing advanced and multiplied. Its strengthening through turmoil arising within itself, meantime, had been coming about by land, and from the east: peoples strong in their horses, and bringing their own knowledge of iron, had transformed its means both for aggression and for prosperity, so that in the seventh and sixth centuries B.C., north of the Alps, its Hallstatt civilization stood at the middle of a chain of cultures, similarly led and flourishing, from the Oxus to the Tagus. But all along that, wherever there were points of entry, through Caucasus, Balkans or Alps, but most from the sea, the mounting southerly enterprise was continually in action, Oriental, Greek and Etruscan, with Phoenician farthest to west. And when Greeks, beyond the colonies in Sicily and southern Italy, before a declining Phoenicia had yet been overstepped by Carthage, made for Spain, and past the Etruscans for Mediterranean Gaul, they touched both the western and middle-western parts of the chain, and in each came to acquaint themselves with Celts. The sequel, in the later sixth century B.C., with Carthage now rising and an advancing Persia threatening, was the venture of Greek trading deep into middle-western Europe, freshly affecting the Hallstatt Celts, and thus, indirectly, the British. So the builders and inhabiters of archaeology's Celtic houses, rectangular or round, belong to its moving into history.

So does the trading into their territory by Greeks. Amongst the aims of this, we can scarcely doubt, was a share of the precious tin which, with its sources in Spain and

Portugal now available only to Carthage, had to be sought either from far inland, in Bohemia or beyond, or from its northern Atlantic sources, Brittany and Cornwall. Just as for Greeks three centuries earlier, venturing up by Pithekoussai, an aim had been precious iron from Etruscan-held Elba, now there was an aim in trade for tin, amongst whatever other goods the Celtic lands might offer. This aim, in spite of fresh barbarian interludes of turmoil, and the swing of Celtic culture from the Hallstatt to the La Tène, was kept alive in Mediterranean Gaul's Greek metropolis, at Marseilles, henceforward to the time of Caesar. The half-dozen centuries which we started from had ended, in the thirty to fifty years following 225 B.C., when Celtic North Italy, with lands adjoining, was won by Rome, when Rome defeated Hannibal and took what Carthage had held in Spain, and when Rome's advances eastward as well as westward had brought her the power, wherever it might be used, for initiatives in Europe. Conflicts to east, and to west in inland Spain, spared the Celts of inland Gaul till after 125 B.C.; but Rome's then annexing the southern part of this, which had started from a plea by Marseilles, led almost straight to the situation grasped in 58 by Caesar, for the initiative which took him in two years to the British Channel.

Trading by Greeks of Marseilles, through Gaulish agents, will of course have been what made the Channel real to the southern mind. The Marseilles explorer Pytheas, long before, had been to explore it; trade across it in British tin is on record for times close to Caesar's; and the metal-bearing coasts of its Atlantic end were already amongst his aims before the winter of 57. Thus the revolt there, early in 56, which prevented him from crossing, moved him naturally both to anger and to resolve to make amends, as soon as he could, by crossing at the other end. There too there was Gaulish trade; and had already been migration, to south-eastern maritime Britain: starting in hostile raids 'ex Belgio', and leading into settlement which stressed the two lands' close resemblance. Caesar's resolve, fulfilled first briefly in 55, and in 54 through his major British venture, had sprung thus from his awareness that a trade in distant products, notably such as the British tin but of course of wider value, could only make Roman profit if secured from recurrences of turmoil by extending annexation. After the prior start in the south of Gaul, he was doing this now throughout it; but the problem set by the Channel was that he could not just stop there. The British Isles, attainable from Gaul and also Spain, were islands that looked to both; and unlike Germany, vast but coercible by a continuous land frontier, they opened on to water, which would never be long controlled from stations on the mainland alone. Thus the form to which Mediterranean enterprise now had been brought, in modern terms Roman imperialism, once Caesar had forced it outside Mediterranean latitudes, had to be forced beyond the water if its western wing was to be safe.

This is not the place to consider either what Caesar effected in maritime Britain and behind it, or the peoples and powers he found there. Of what he noted at the time, one of the resemblances to Gaul—that in houses—has been cited here above (p. 58); archaeology may confirm it, but these matters have further aspects, amongst them being the coins in gold which he also briefly remarked. That is a subject handled in the second of our volumes; the reader will find it there giving particular expression regarding Caesar and his opponent, the British king Cassivellaunus, to what is advanced more generally here. Not maritime Britain only, but all the lowland zone of the country up to the Mersey and Peak and Humber, looks to the mainland and resembles it. Just a hundred years from Caesar's taking command in Gaul, the case for a major conquest here was offered to the Emperor Claudius. Another twenty years, and his troops were on the Humber, facing the Peak, and as near the Mersey as Chester. The problem set to Caesar by the Channel had been answered. But where should the major conquest stop? What confronted Rome now was the British North.

Between the Yorkshire Ouse upstream from the Humber, the Derbyshire Peak and the Mersey marshes downstream from Manchester, ran the southerly border of the peoples called collectively the Brigantes. From the Durham and north Yorkshire coast they stretched to the Irish Sea. They are called by modern writers a confederacy; at the time of the Roman advance they had a queen and a kingly consort. We know few details; but a royal and chieftain class, with 'barons' and probably minor kings, can readily be supposed and appears confirmed by the archaeology, which gives us weapons and horse-gear in developed Celtic La Tène style, but contemporary pottery hand-made and coarse, when indeed there is any pottery at all. Beyond them, though the same extremes of culture are apparent, tribes with names of their own fill the ancient British Scotland, north from the Solway and Tyne: here was the Brigantes' northern boundary. On both sides of it, and on theirs in Cumbria, Cleveland and the Pennines, the moors and fells show single sites or clusters of habitation; with pottery barely any but Roman and subsequent to conquest, the remains of dwellings still declare their prevailing form as circular. A round-house emplacement proving to be like the southern in structure, when discovered and studied thoroughly as at West Brandon, Co. Durham (see Jobey 1962, p. 61 above), leaves the many upland 'hut-circles', of varying simplicity, suggesting traditions often still more deeply prehistoric. The Romans found the Brigantes tough resisters: early loss of their class of chieftains, to be supposed from the archaeology, left the people obstinately hostile. Of this, the obviously strongest demonstration comes from the Romans. With the patches of text borne history, archaeology has the roads, and the sites, some yielding inscriptions, of the very great number of forts. Through the forces deployed in these, once the venture of conquest started, the country had to be secured, policed and held to a steady subjection.

How it was done, and how combined with the fortunes of the strategy and similar occupation advanced to Scotland, is a tale closely woven into the Roman story in Britain. Evidence, here as everywhere, is archaeologically manifold: inscriptions, coins, Samian pottery, coarse pottery, weapons, tools, structures and all the precisions of excavation. Repeated from fort to fort, and in special modes for special objectives—legionary fortresses, the two great frontier lines, and other particular sites, religious, civil, industrial, rural—the work goes on, affording ever more exact comparison between its findings, at this and that site, for sounder assessment of the whole. Thus the Northern undertaking, in its broadest main lines, falls into phases of initiative and phases more defensive, filling 150 years from the time of Nero on, to the aftermath of the last long-distance northward thrust by Septimius Severus, who died at York in 211. In this ensuing phase, leading into the middle third century, when the Tyne–Solway frontier had been renewed with its arrangements altered, soldiers both serving and retired could be granted land to farm in allotments, and the civil settlements around their forts grew more prosperous and larger, with more marriages and children. Of the Brigantes then at last, our best authority—Sheppard Frere, at p. 187 of his *Britannia* (1967)—can conclude that 'the long-lasting hostility of the inhabitants of the Pennines seems finally to disappear'.

So the old disciplined venture of martial enterprise had reached stability; garrisons and local tribesmen grew, as Frere puts it, in 'community of sentiment'. But into that, at the end of the century, there intruded the start of a change: the harsh change of invasion out of the farther north of Britain, hard for even a Constantius Chlorus to retrieve, and leaving fourth-century Roman power on the defensive now entirely. The community of sentiment had to be turned to a spirit of resistance. From forts rebuilt in stone, and from new-built coastal and town defences, archaeology through this century has once more to assemble the details of military situations and events. There was a crisis in 343; worsened peril from about 360. A great storm of invasion came in 367–9. Retrieving the damage, over all the country, was arduously accomplished by the Count Theodosius. He too rebuilt in stone when he could. But with the depletion of garrisons by Maximus (383), repeating what had let in the late third-century invasion, the tale passes quickly to the last age of Rome in Britain. Thus the archaeology of forts, the essential local seats of its strength, concerns on the one hand the conquest and consolidation after, and on the other the Later Empire's defences against assault from the enemies, here Celtic and Pictish and North-European German, to whom by land and sea the initiative now had passed. From what followed, in the migrations that soon were so vastly more widespread, protohistoric Europe was to gain its second great age.

The excavator of a fort will expect the difference to be revealed in his strata. But discernment of stratification has been an art learnt only gradually. Its practice today, on virgin sites, can assure them interpretation commanding confidence; and on sites that have been explored in the past only partly, can give a reassessment almost an equal guarantee. If further virgin sites for its exercise are found, all the better; but with modern air-photographic and geophysical prospecting, the number of forts unrecognized cannot be large. The only remaining means for making the most out of the evidence will be fresh assessment of forts explored in the past, but now beyond reach: through re-examination of what their excavators recorded, in their notes and photographs, drawings and all they published, and of any of their actual finds that are still accessible. This is what Grace Simpson, in her contribution to this book, has done for the forts at Manchester, on the Irwell that feeds the Mersey, and at Temple-brough, on the Pennines' eastern side, by the Don at Rotherham. She explains the whole process, has rediscovered missing pottery, and is able to answer questions that most had given up as insoluble. Templebrough is where the Don was crossed by the Roman road from the Midlands, which together with the crossing by the road from London, at Doncaster lower down, gave the only metalled access north into Yorkshire clear of the Humber. As for the Manchester fort (*Mamucium*), located in the modern city's centre, it stood where the road between the two legionary fortresses, Chester and York, was crossed by that from the Midlands to Carlisle, and where others led off to the Lancashire coast and to forts in the Peak and Pennines, all using the gap of good ground between the flank of the hills and the Mersey marshes—a road fording the Mersey being the only other western route from lowland Britain to the North. Both are therefore critical sites for Roman military history, and for the serial tale of relations between the Roman command and the Brigantes. Dr Simpson's qualifications being well and widely known, I welcome her contribution, in all its detail, as a vital one.

Roman Manchester and Templebrough: The Forts and Dates Reviewed

BY GRACE SIMPSON

Introduction

This paper had its origin in my two chapters on Roman forts in the southern Pennines, in the thesis for which Professor Hawkes was my supervisor. Roman Manchester has continued to interest me and I have rewritten that chapter, after re-reading all the evidence and noticing details which I had missed before. They seem to me now to have importance for dating the Roman occupation of the fort. Nowhere can I find comment on these details by other writers; and believing that their evidence may be valuable as a starting point for any further excavations within the fort, I shall describe the discovery of the datable remains, especially in the area of the 1907 excavations. Those early excavators at Manchester had very high standards of recording by plan, section and photography. One day it may be possible to check their results, in the same way that excavators since 1950 have re-examined the north fort wall and confirmed discoveries made and conclusions drawn in 1898 and 1912. My own conclusion now may bring the reader some surprise: in 1950 the fort wall was being dated 'early second century', and a few years later it was 'possibly Severan'. But neither conclusion was made from evidence, only by analogy with forts elsewhere. The evidence is in the 1907 Report and it implies a later period.

A reassessment of the decorated Samian pottery will not lead to any big changes in dating the sherds from Manchester, because they have never been dated closely before. Some of the sherds were published by Roeder and Phelps (Roeder 1899), and a few others by Bruton and Phelps (Bruton 1909). They referred to publications by Dragendorff, H. Syer Cuming and James Curle; but Déchelette (1904) is not mentioned and, in consequence, some of the figures were wrongly restored. Nevertheless, Phelps drew extremely well, considering how little help there was at that early time in sigillata studies. There is no recorded evidence to date the second-century military occupation inside the fort, and the sherds illustrated below (Figs. 12–14) indicate occupation throughout that century. But not all these sherds are certainly from within the fort. Some may come from the defensive ditches. Others may come from the *vicus*. The greater importance of these sherds lies in their stylistic interest. Every sherd has some intrinsic value to students of sigillata.

At Templebrough Fort, by Rotherham (S. Yorkshire), destroyed in 1916–17, the operations on the spot by Thomas May let him rescue pottery in some amount. My discovery of the bulk of the coarse pottery he rescued was the result of a deduction I drew from his Report. I trust that this pottery also provides useful evidence, not hitherto recognized; and also that, together, these two forts, one entirely built over, one entirely destroyed, justify the method of reassessment or recension, and show it to be a necessary part of archaeological studies.

Professor Hawkes's reassessment of the excavations on rural sites made by General Pitt-Rivers from 1881 to 1897 (Pitt-Rivers 1887–98) was the first demonstration of this method which I read. The general's achievement in archaeology, wrote Hawkes, was

'. . . its transformation from an amateur study to a scientific discipline . . .

'. . . any quest for more facts about Britons and Romans [in Cranborne Chase] should begin not with fresh excavation, but with re-examination of Pitt-Rivers's work. And he recorded it so well, and preserved his finds so carefully, that this process can really amount to re-excavation of his sites.'

Hawkes 1947, p. 35

For the reader of that re-examination, those sites, and the finds associated with them, are restored by words almost into inhabited houses and settlements, set in the tranquil countryside of southern Roman Britain. The excavator had received the interpreter he needed in order to relate his discoveries to early Britain's wider agricultural and social scene.

The early excavators of Manchester asked every noted archaeologist of the time to interpret their discoveries, and they hoped that one day their many questions would be satisfactorily answered. They could have given the answers themselves, but doubt always spoiled the sensible interpretations they made from the evidence they had excavated. This hesitancy contrasts strongly with their confidence while actually working in the fort.

I. MANCHESTER 1907 EXCAVATIONS REASSESSED

Seventy to eighty years ago there was an indefatigable band of enthusiasts in Manchester who watched for the discovery of Roman coins and pottery, excavated in redevelopment areas in and around the fort, and plotted find-spots on maps. Two of them, Charles Roeder and J. J. Phelps, published their work in *Roman Manchester* (1900) by Roeder (reprinted from Roeder 1899), who himself drew the sections, with other illustrations by Phelps. In 1912 Phelps recorded his observations of the north wall of the fort, made 'at his own risk' during commercial demolition (Phelps 1912). This Report contains a most important photograph, as we shall see later. The better-known book, *The Roman Fort at Manchester*, edited by F. A. Bruton, describes the excavations of 1906–7, inside the north-west corner, and the east and west defences insofar as they survived (Bruton 1909).

The fort was in a strong position, defended on the south-east, south and west sides by the confluence of the Medlock with the river Irwell (Fig. 10). The ground fell steeply along the south side, and hypocausted buildings near the river, south from the south gate, were found in 1771. Roeder and Phelps realized that these must have been the fort bath-building. On the west side of the fort a morass was still impassable in the eighteenth century. Only on the north was the ground without a natural defence, and there a long 'Deep Foss' was visible and was drawn by Dr Clarke on his plan in Whitaker 1771. In 1840 the Rochdale Canal was opened: it had cut across about one-third of the fort. Then, in 1848, two converging railway viaducts passed right across the long axis of the fort, and the remaining ground was soon covered by streets of small houses. During rebuilding about the end of the century, Roeder noticed that two areas of civil settlement produced quantities of pottery. One was the site of the police station in Bridgewater Street which lies beyond the ditch system in front of the north fort wall. From the north gate a road must have gone north to Ribchester Fort near Preston. The other civil area was near Knott Mill, outside the east gate. Roman Manchester was an important road junction, and it was also on the direct route between the legionary fortresses at York and Chester.

Bombing during the Second World War destroyed the houses about the centre of the north fort wall, and as a result valuable information about the wall, the ditches, and the north gate has been discovered. But previously, the only large area free for excavation was in the north-west sector. There, in 1907, Bruton and his colleagues found abundant Roman remains. They were depressed, however, by their inability to expound their discoveries, and in consequence their final summing-up is too depreciatory; it is also hesitant and contradictory (Bruton 1909):

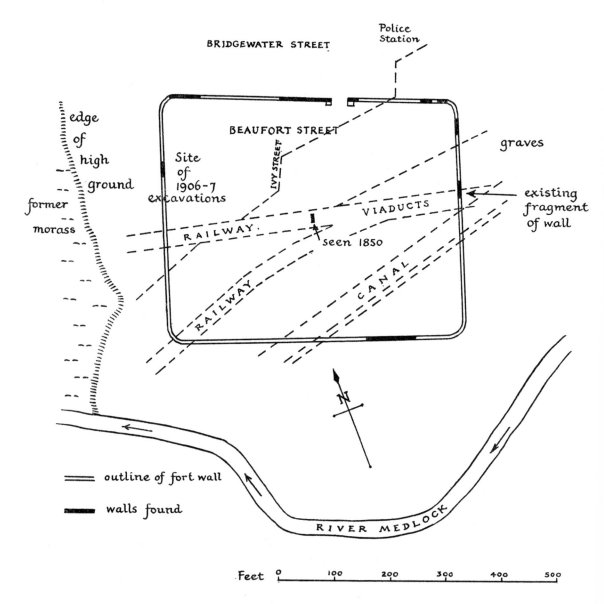

BRIDGEWATER STREET

Police
Station

edge
of
high
ground

former

morass

BEAUFORT STREET

IVY STREET

Site
of
1906-7
excavations

graves

VIADUCTS

existing
fragment
of wall

RAILWAY

seen 1850

RAILWAY

CANAL

N

═══ outline of fort wall

▬▬▬ walls found

RIVER MEDLOCK

Feet 0   100   200   300   400   500

FIG. 10 MANCHESTER ROMAN FORT: SKETCH PLAN (pp. 71–5) Simplified to
bring out the site's relation to modern features, mentioned in the text, and to natural features
also: the confluence of the rivers Medlock and Irwell is beyond the plan's limits on the west.
The fort's gates, besides that shown on the north, are not located. Scale 1 : 2000.

'. . . the area examined . . . from its position . . . could not be expected to yield results of great interest.' (p. 63)

'It is easy to suggest that [the cobble pavement] marks the line of an earlier rampart, on which the wall was subsequently built. It is not so easy to substantiate the theory . . .' (p. 65)

'After studying these complex sections for months . . . I am strongly of the opinion that any attempt to theorise upon them, *and especially to deduce from them evidence of two successive ramparts*, would be unwise and unwarranted.' (p. 69. His italics.)

'. . . it would be unwise to assume that the undulations in the neighbourhood of our section were other than natural.' (p. 70)

'The Bank of Clay east of [i.e. inside the fort] Wall.' (p. 72). On the next page Bruton makes clear that this is turf, but everywhere else they call it clay. They have to admit that it is not natural, since pottery is found beneath it.

'. . . a gap in the gravel [subsoil] full of silted earth . . . about five feet wide. Curiously, it did not occur to us at the time to consider whether this might possibly be the ditch of an earlier fort. . . . There was no evidence in favour of such a theory.' (p. 74)

'. . . evidence of reconstruction . . . is not, in itself, proof that there were two periods of occupation; and I should hesitate to draw any such conclusion . . .' (p. 135)

Although Bruton had the uneasy feeling that he had found two successive ramparts, he did not understand two essential things: that the west fort wall foundations overlay an earlier rampart, and that this rampart was over a succession of ditches and yet earlier ramparts. Fortunately these features are perfectly clear in R. H. Fletcher's very fine photographs; and John Swarbrick's plan and sections show equally clearly that the ditches (i.e. 'undulations') correspond with the succession of ramparts (Fig 11).

Starting at the lowest feature discovered in 1907, that is the 'gap in the gravel full of silted earth', quoted above, Swarbrick's Section A.A. shows at its extreme eastern end a small military-type ditch, filled with 'black earth'. There is a stone and cobble foundation at a slightly higher level, and both features are passing under Duke Street on the east. The 'undulation' in the gravel to the west of the lowest ditch might well be the ditch associated with the stone and cobble foundation, which itself would be the base for a secondary-period rampart. This secondary-period ditch is filled with 'stiff clay'. If we have here two early periods of defences, then it is possible that they are contemporary with the two late first-century periods of barrack buildings found below bombed Ivy Street (*Journal of Roman Studies*, 52 (1952), p. 91). The distance, allowing for an intra-vallum road, is feasible. The buildings were of timber in both levels, and had plenty of Flavian pottery stratified within them, but all later Roman levels had disappeared.

The third period upwards consists of a long section across two ditches (the outer one filled with 'dark coloured loamy earth', and the inner one smaller), then a turf rampart (not wholly distinguished from another above it), then an intra-vallum road called 'sand', and then the 'pieces of sandstone' founded in the 'stiff clay'; Bruton and Jones called them 'the lower stones'. They stripped a large area, and plotted every stone accurately; and, although they did not know what to make of their discovery, Swarbrick's plan, once again, removes any doubt about what these stones were. They were foundations for buildings, probably for half-timbered barrack-blocks.

The third period ended in a fire. The burnt daub from a building close to the rampart is the 'deep layer of red burnt earth' on Fletcher's photograph (Bruton 1909, pl. xxxv). This is south of Section A.A. and therefore does not appear on it. In that burnt layer were numerous nails, coins, glass and pottery, but this datable material is not identifiable in the report.

The fourth and fifth periods are represented by two turf ramparts not properly distinguished from each other or from the third one below, but portions of the three are discernible in the photographs and sections, and they are certainly associated with the succession of ditches below the fort wall foundations (Bruton 1909, pls. xxviii–xxxi, xxxiii–xxxv). In these periods four and five in the turf ramparts, datable objects can be identified for the first time since the Flavian levels. As already noted, the excavators refer to the turf-work as 'clay', and on pl. xxv it is called 'level of the clay floor'.[1] 'A considerable area of this clay floor was stripped by Mr H. L. Jones, and the plan will show that it yielded a number of finds, most of which lay directly upon it.' (Bruton 1909, p. 75.)

However, it was Bruton who found the complete, though broken, large Samian bowl in the Antonine style of CINNAMVS, and he says it was 'embedded' in this clay floor (Bruton 1909, pp. 61, 97). Near by was a complete, but broken, mortarium of second-century type, and also several mill-stones. The pottery is important mainly as marking a period of destruction, followed by a re-building (period five) which

---

[1] These turf ramparts are also called 'clay' in Section A.A., and 'sandy clay' in Section C.C.

buried both bowls. The vessels are roughly contemporary, and they may indicate that the re-build was in the late second century or early third (Severan).[1]

The most important dating evidence presented by Bruton is in Swarbrick's Section E.E., taken along the inside of the fort wall (Fig. 11). At two to three feet vertically below the edge of the fort wall lay two bronze coins: one of Trajan, died A.D. 117, and one of Julia Domna, wife of Septimius Severus, who died in A.D. 217. Her coin was too much corroded for further identification (Bruton 1909, pp. 11–14, by R. S. Conway, coins nos. 3, 11). The extent of wear on that coin, could it be determined, would not help us to date the ditch in which the coins lay, their exact position marked on the Section (Fig. 11). Elsewhere I have discussed the risks involved in dating by single coins, whether they are worn or not (Simpson 1964, p. 83). The ditch may be Severan, or later. It cannot be earlier than his reign because of this coin of Julia Domna.

The turf of the fifth rampart (called 'sandy clay') runs up to the clay and cobble foundation of the fort wall, and it seems to be cut by the foundation trench of the wall. If the ditch with the coins in it is Severan, or later, then the fort wall is later still. Is it possible to define the date of the wall construction? It is not possible at this particular place, because the wall has been robbed away above its concrete levelling-up layer. But along the north wall, and at the surviving fragment of the east wall, the remains are similar to each other and some conclusions may be drawn from their type of construction.

All the excavators, whether on the west, north or east sides, found about three feet of puddled clay containing cobbles and broken stone. Petch, digging in 1951, found these cobbles and stones in two layers with one inch of clay between (Petch 1950–1, fig. 2). On the east, Bruton described three layers set in clay to a depth of three feet. This depth corresponds to the two to three feet of clay and cobbles on the west side. Above that there is a concrete layer. On north and east sides then comes a course of horizontal stones in mortar, and then a similar course but with the stones set diagonally.

Phelps recorded the finest piece of the diagonal masonry, as disclosed by commercial contractors in 1912. His Section A shows, at the bottom, a compact mass of buff-coloured puddled clay set with cobbles of various sizes in rather irregular courses, the whole resting on undisturbed natural gravel. On the clay and cobbles '... had been

[1] There are errors in the 'Key to the "Finds" marked on the Plan' (Bruton 1909, 127–9). The CINNAMVS Dr. 37 is really no. 41, but in this key, and also *ibid.* p. 97, it is numbered 25. The real no. 25 is located in a very different part of the plan. Another mistake is brooch no. 2, *ibid.* p. 84, which is no. 34, i.e. a piece of pottery, in the Key.

poured a layer of mortar or cement in which a course of blocks of red sandstone had been set horizontally; above these a course of heavier sandstone blocks had been placed diagonally or slantwise . . .' (Phelps 1912, p. 200 and photograph of section A opposite). This diagonal course was topped by two courses of horizontally laid stone (all just as in the surviving east wall fragment), and then the modern ground level. Presumably the diagonal coursing would have been hidden from view by facing stones of regular courses.

Diagonal coursing must be distinguished from the mainly fourth- to fifth-century herring-bone walling, to be seen in several Roman villas in the Cotswolds, such as Barnsley Park and Chedworth. That was a technique which made use of the small laminated Cotswold stone. I do not know of any instance of it in military defences. Diagonal coursing appears in the core of the outer walls of several of the Saxon Shore Forts, Richborough and Portchester among them; also in the Wery Wall, the surviving fragment of the fourth-century fort at Lancaster (Richmond 1953, pp. 5-7 and pl. ii), at the lower fort at Caernarvon (Wheeler 1923, p. 95 and fig. 35; Hogg 1953, p. 182) and on the interior and exterior wall faces of Caer Gybi in Anglesey (Wheeler 1923, pp. 97-101, figs. 38-40). The town wall of Caerwent, too, has diagonal masonry in the core and in the footings (Nash-Williams 1930: the very clear photographs pl. lxxix, 1-2, opp. p. 239). With the possible exception of the lower fort at Caernarvon, those are all late third- or fourth-century walls. Diagonal coursing is not a military building technique in earlier periods in Britain. Mr B. R. Hartley kindly informs me that he has found no such masonry in recent excavations at Bainbridge, Ilkley or Bowes.[1]

Apart from this argument from building style for a late dating of the fort wall at Manchester, we have already seen from the sequence of periods of fort rebuilding, and from the evidence of the coin in the ditch below the fort wall, that the stone fort wall is a late work. Inside the fort, the latest structures are traces of gravel at a high level, which might be the fort wall backing, and some paving. At the extreme east end of Section A.A., there is a drain down the centre of a gravelled road between two barrack-blocks. If all these are contemporary, then this late fort rebuild was an impressive and extensive one. Professor Frere has noted that the date for evacuation is not clear, and this is a question involving the interpretation of lists in the *Notitia Dignitatum*

[1] I also wish to thank Dr Graham Webster, Dr Barri Jones and Mrs Janet Webster for discussing these problems with me, and for references. Mr John H. Williams also kindly sent a sectional drawing of his trench across the northern ditches in 1965: *Journal of Roman Studies*, 56 (1966), p. 200. Unfortunately the wall survived only as cobble foundations. The complex of turf or clay fill in some of the ditches is not unlike the 1907 sequence of changes and rebuilds described above.

(Frere 1967, pp. 234, 236). Plentiful coarse pottery published by Bruton and Phelps indicates occupation after A.D. 369. They cannot be blamed for not noting the find-spot of every rim-section of pottery, for even today plenty of excavators still fail to do so in their reports, although the details may be in their field note-books.

Does Manchester fort wall belong to the restoration of Britain by Constantius Chlorus, A.D. 296–306, or to the restoration by Count Theodosius from A.D. 369? Possibly to the earlier period, but only further excavation can decide.

II. THE SECOND-CENTURY DECORATED SAMIAN POTTERY FROM MANCHESTER

The drawings are by Mrs Marion Cox, from rubbings made by me by kind permission of the Director of Manchester City Art Gallery. Local soil conditions have damaged some of the glossy surfaces and often made identification difficult. The form in every case is Dragendorff's Form 37 (Dr. 37). Stanfield and Simpson 1958 is cited through-out as *S & S*; Déchelette 1904 as *D.*; Oswald 1936–7 as *O.*

FIGURES 12–14

(Fig. 12)

1–2.   The style of DRVSVS I (Potter X–3). The designs are different from *S & S* pl. xv, 193, which is also from Manchester. Trajanic.

3.   The ovolo and very fine beaded borders of the style of BIRRANTVS; *S & S* fig. 39, 1 and pl. xc, 1. The fragmentary figure is a rare type, possibly the centaur carrying a stone on its head, $D.428 = O.741$. The only other figure-types in Oswald with both arms raised are $O.121$ and $O.279$, but neither is like this example. Hadrianic.

4.   'IOENALIS style' with his ovolo 2; as *S & S* fig. 10, 2; and the man $O.570$. Trajanic.

5.   'IOENALIS style' with his ovolo 1. The warrior is $D.108 = O.179$. The horseman cannot be restored on the drawing with certainty. Trajanic.

6.   Drawn by Phelps in Roeder 1899. The ovolo has a very narrow central projection. The panel design is close to the QVINTILIANVS group; see *S & S* pl. lxxi, 31; or the early LAXTVCISSA style; as Rogers 1966, fig. III, 65. Hadrianic.

7.   Drawn by Phelps in Roeder 1899. The six-lobed detail in the festoon is copied from Phelps: the surface is now in poor condition. I wish to thank Mr Rogers for identifying the style as that of SECVNDINVS; see Rogers

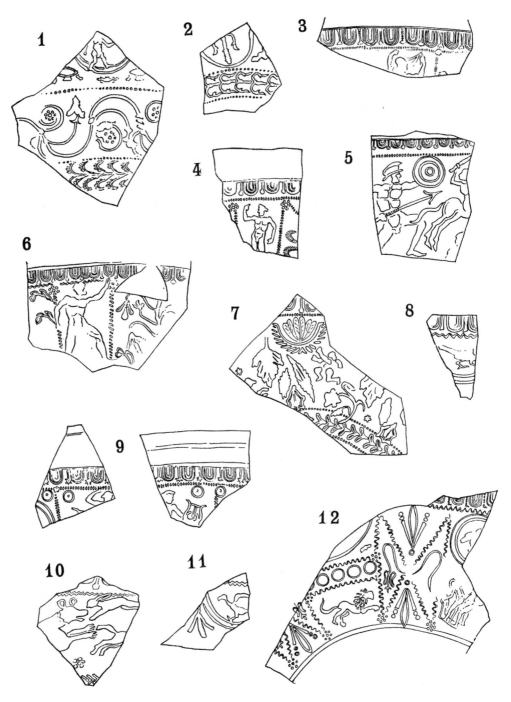

FIG. 12 SECOND-CENTURY DECORATED SAMIAN POTTERY FROM MAN-
CHESTER (pp. 77–9) Nos. 1–12. *Drawings by Marion Cox.* Scale 1 : 2.

1966, figs. III and V, 59 and 59a. Other potters used some of the details, see *S & S* pl. lxix, 10–13, and fig. 14, no. 16. The little running cupid is D.255 = O.426; Phelps had drawn it as a bird. Hadrianic.

8.   Bruton 1909, pl. lviii, 14. The distinctive ovolo, with wavy-line border below, is like one in the Rambert Collection (25646) from Vichy, in the Musée des Antiquités Nationales, Saint-Germain-en-Laye. The bird was incorrectly drawn by Phelps. Hadrianic–early Antonine.

Not illus.   Roeder 1899, opp. p. 154, in the style of the DONNAVCVS-SACER group; a large sherd showing sea-monster, the 'snake and rock' ornament, and SACER's detail 6 on *S & S* fig. 22. Hadrianic–early Antonine.

9.   Two sherds with the ovolo 1 of ATTIANVS, *S & S* fig. 23, and Apollo O.83. Hadrianic–early Antonine.

10–11.   The style of Potter X-6; cf. *S & S* pl. lxxv, 13 and 15. No. 10 is Roeder 1899, 507. Hadrianic–early Antonine.

12.   The style of CRICIRO. A similar ovolo is signed CR for CRICIRO on a Dr. 37 at Aquincum (Kuzsinsky 1932, p. 90, abra 77–8). Dr Eva Bónis kindly sent me a rubbing of the bowl. Early Antonine.

(Fig. 13)

13–14.   The style of DOCILIS; see *S & S* pls. xci, 2 and xciii, 17 and 23, also fig. 24, Nos. 3, 13, 15, 17 and 19. One figure is D.215 = O.349 and the other is smaller than D.174 = O.279. Hadrianic–early Antonine.

15.   Not attributable. Pan D.411 = O.709. Hadrianic?

16, 17, 19.   Bruton 1909, pls. lvii, 2 and lviii, 13. The style of LAXTVCISSA; his ovolo 1 and details 3, 10, 11 and 12, see *S & S* p. 184, fig. 27. The man on no. 16 can be restored as O.188, the curved object on no. 19 may be the tail of a lion, and the eagle on no. 17 is O.2183. Early Antonine.

18.   The style of ADVOCISVS; his ovolo 2 and the mask D.703 = O.1329. Now lost is a Dr. 37 with the name-stamp ADVOCISI found in 1765: see Bruton 1909, p. 179 and pl. c. Antonine.

20.   Made at La Madeleine, the ovolo is slightly damaged. See Fölzer 1913, pl. xxv, ovolo 121, and details 98 and 111. Early Antonine.

Not illus.   Bruton 1909, pl. lv, 1. A Dr. 37 made at Lavoye, now in Warrington Museum. Antonine.

21–2.   The 'small-bowl ovolo' of PATERNVS; see *S & S* p. 196, fig. 30, 4, and his leaf, *ibid.*, 8. Antonine.

23.   The rounded ovolo of PATERNVS, *ibid.*, ovolo 2, and his typical animal free-style design with detail 21. Antonine.

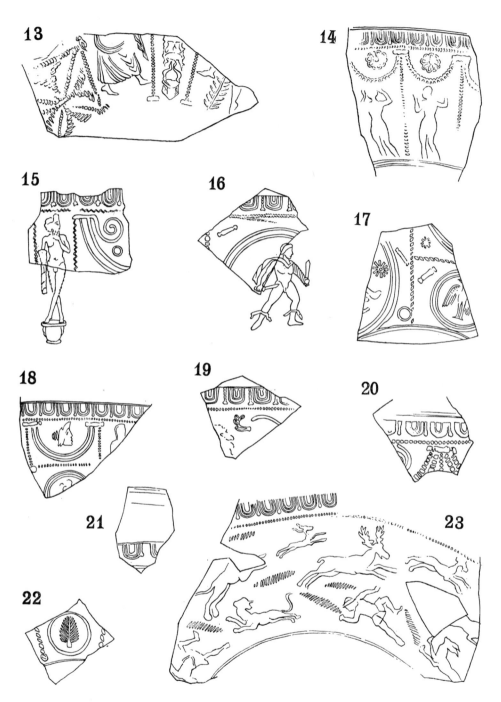

FIG. 13 SECOND-CENTURY DECORATED SAMIAN POTTERY FROM MAN-
CHESTER (p. 79) Nos. 13-23. *Drawings by Marion Cox.* Scale 1 : 2.

(Fig. 14)

24–5. Bruton 1909, pl. lviii, 4 and 4a, where Phelps drew a woman reclining, with some drapery on her knees. That drapery is really the right-hand horse's head harnessed to Luna's chariot, $O.117$. The bodies of both horses are visible on no. 25. The ovolo is damaged, and attribution is uncertain. The triton is nearest to $D.26 = O.27$. The sea-monster is $O.41$. Antonine.

26–8. The style of CASVRIVS. No. 26 has details 9 and 12. Nos. 27 and 28 have the leaf detail 6, and on no. 28 there is the asymmetrical leaf *S & S* pls. cxxxiii, 21 and cxxxvii, 56. Antonine.

29. Roeder 1899. The early style of CINNAMVS and his associates, probably with the ovolo 3B (Simpson and Rogers 1969, pp. 3–14). The sea-bull $D.29 = O.42$ in a festoon, and with the big rosette, is like no. 18 *ibid*. The little warrior is $O.177$. Early Antonine.

30. Roeder 1899, no. 508. The style of PVGNVS. The ovolo is damaged, but it is probably the CINNAMVS ovolo 3A (Simpson and Rogers, p. 4 and fig. 2, 4–6). Early Antonine.

31. Bruton 1909, pl. lviii, 9. The cupid is $O.401$ with the left hand broken off. The candelabrum is an uncommon ornament, but see *S & S* pls. cxxvi, 12 and cxxvii, 34. The sherd is not attributable. Antonine.

Not illus. Bruton 1909, pls. xxvi and lvi. The style of CINNAMVS with his ovolo 2. This is the bowl found by Bruton associated with one of the turf ramparts, see p. 74 above. Antonine.

32. Roeder 1899. CINNAMVS style with the 3B ovolo: see no. 29 above. For the same festoon, crane and pygmy, and the bear $D.817 = O.1609$, see Simpson and Rogers 1969, fig. 3, 19. For the amazon see fig. 2, 9 *ibid*., and for the lozenges in series see *S & S* pl. clvii, 11. Early Antonine.

This series of decorated potsherds implies a longer period of occupation during the second century than the time indicated by the Samian pottery at Templebrough.

III. DATABLE POTTERY AT TEMPLEBROUGH

The valley road between Sheffield and Rotherham surmounts a noticeable rise as it passes Templebrough. The fort was built upon a steep-sided plateau among the marshes of the middle Don valley. Hereabouts, the river forms the frontier between the lowland and highland zone of Britain. The river could be forded close by the fort. Probably there was early a road-link from Little Chester, in Derbyshire, and between

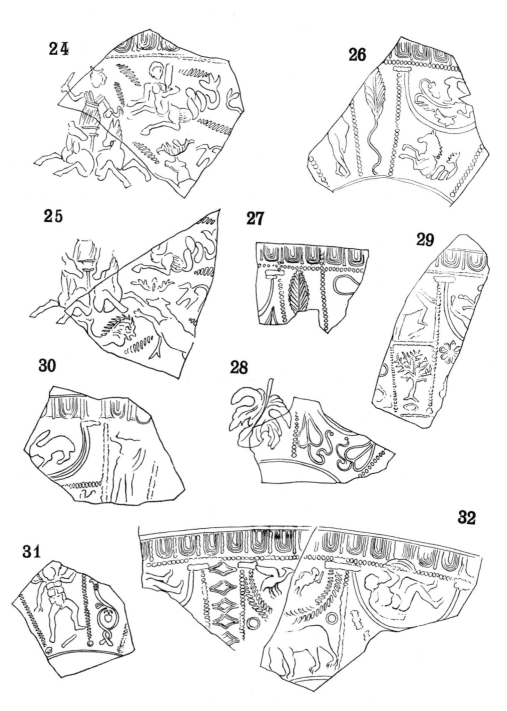

FIG. 14 SECOND-CENTURY DECORATED SAMIAN POTTERY FROM MAN-
CHESTER (p. 81) Nos. 24–32. *Drawings by Marion Cox.* Scale 1 : 2.

them these two forts controlled the eastern side of the Derbyshire uplands (Greene 1952–5, pp. 112–17). From the west gate another road ran into those uplands south-westwards, to the fort at Brough-on-Noe.

The first excavations in the fort were in 1877 (Leader 1879). It had never been built on since Roman times, and it was a cultivated field in 1913, when W. T. Freemantle saw that industrial development was near, and he tried to save it from encroachment. The opportunity was lost, and in 1916 a large extension to the steel-works of Messrs Steel, Peech and Tozer Ltd was required for war production. The whole area of the fort, to a depth of 10–15 feet, was tipped on the surrounding lower ground. The position of the south gate is behind Gate no. 4 into the Works (Fig. 15). For eight months, with labour supplied by the company, Thomas May struggled to plan the

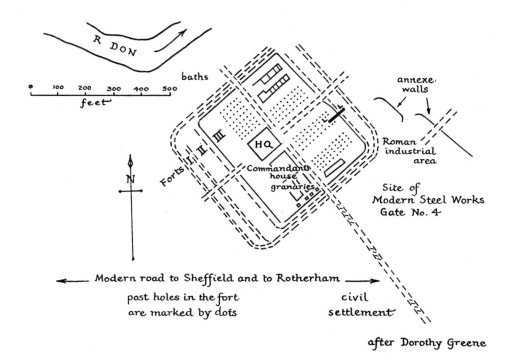

after Dorothy Greene

FIG. 15 TEMPLEBROUGH ROMAN FORTS: SKETCH PLAN (pp. 81–4, 87–9.) After the plan drawn by Dorothy Greene, from Thomas May's of 1922: shows the site's relation to the river Don, the Roman road approaching it, and to surrounding features, modern and Roman (including walls of annexed Roman enclosures). In the interior, HQ stands for Headquarters Building (*principia*); dots grouped in rectangles mark post-holes for timber buildings; LL, section by May through defences. Continuous lines mark walls, broken lines ditches (crossed by roads). Scale 1 : 4000.

remains: as each feature was exposed, it was cut away by the 'steam navvy'. He made a remarkable plan of the three successive forts, and rescued a great number of datable objects (May 1922).

Since then, various writers have associated one or another of the forts with historical events in Brigantia. No one has tried to associate the datable objects in groups, and the following notes are the first attempt to make such datable groups since May's own work was published. Whether his three forts can be truly dated by such groups will never be known. Any attempt to date Templebrough's forts will always be hypothetical. My conclusion below, however, will offer the most that I can say.

Thomas May never published the coarse pottery he had rescued from the site. It is strange that he left such a large section of material out of his book. It is especially strange since he was a master of coarse-pottery studies. He was then the equal of James Curle, of my father Gerald Simpson, and of Philip Newbold. The apparent absence of so much datable material has given several archaeologists the impression that after the Hadrianic period there was very little occupation. The material I discovered in 1957 considerably alters the size of the matter, because it consists of several hundredweights of coarse potsherds.

May (1922, p. 11; also Frere 1967, p. 85) supposed that Templebrough was founded by the governor of Britain, A. Didius Gallus (A.D. 52–7), and I agree with them. Claudius died in A.D. 54, and the decorated Samian bowls which May called Claudian (hence his attribution to Didius) are in my opinion not Claudian, but early Neronian. They have been illustrated by me elsewhere (Simpson 1964, p. 11 and fig. 1), and I think that they are very like the style of the early Neronian decorated Samian found at Trent Vale, in Stoke-on-Trent (Mountford, Gee and Simpson 1968). There are also ten cups of form Dr. 27, with grooves in their exterior footrings, a feature that is not found after about A.D. 75. Three of the ten bear potter's stamps, CAIVS, CASTVS (both Neronian potters) and FRONTINVS who worked slightly later. The most interesting evidence of early settlement at Templebrough are imitations of early Samian forms, probably, as May suggested, the products of an early local Roman kiln (May 1922, p. 109, pl. xxix, nos. 172–4): again, the parallel with the early Neronian kiln at Trent Vale is interesting.

Early Flavian occupation is attested by four South Gaulish Dr. 37, similar to those newly arrived at Pompeii before A.D. 79.[1] Domitianic South Gaulish bowls are scarcely present. There may have been a period of non-occupation in the late first century.

---

[1] A slender Dr. 18 stamped OF.MVRRA[NVS] can be matched at Corbridge, and a Ritterling type 12 can be matched at Caerhûn and Cardiff. The base from a black Gallo-Belgic platter stamped SACE is not particularly remarkable for Templebrough. Belgic platters have been

There are a great number, sixty sherds, of Dr. 37 in the style made at Banassac in South Gaul during the early second century at earliest. It may be partly contemporary with the Trajanic and Hadrianic Central Gaulish Samian also found at Temple-brough.[1] May wrote that there were only three sherds in Antonine style, but there are nineteen, including the styles of DIVIXTVS and ADVOCISVS, and of CIN-NAMVS who may have worked in the early Antonine period.[2] The apparently later potters, such as CASVRIVS and DOECCVS, are not represented. The evidence is different from Manchester (see p. 81 above), where PATERNVS and CASVRIVS styles have been found, and also different from Ilkley where all three potters' styles are well represented. Some of the plain Samian forms could be a little later, up to about A.D. 175. Antonine mortarium-makers recorded at Templebrough by rim-stamps are GRATINVS, VBRN, SARRVS, SENNIVS, SIMILIS and VOROLAS.

The following notes concern the coarse pottery which I found in February 1957, after a search through the outhouses of the Rotherham Museum. It is published here by the kindness of Mrs John Blundell (Miss Dorothy Greene) and the Curator, Mr. L. G. Lovell.

FIGURE 16

1. A deep flat-rimmed bowl, broken at the chamfer, with cross-hatching, (cf. Wheeler 1926, p. 221, C39; also no. 4 below).
2. Twenty-two rims from black flat-rimmed bowls or dishes.
3. Fourteen rims from black flat-rimmed bowls or dishes.
4. Half of a black bowl with a deep chamfer, rough acute-angled cross-hatching. Found in the well in the *principia* (p. 87), and preserved in the Museum.
5. Two rims, rounded on top, in brown ware.
   Nos. 1–5 are Hadrianic–early Antonine vessels.
6. A roll-rim in brown ware. This is a common type at Balmuildy fort (Miller

---

found in the Agricolan fort of Castlecary in Scotland (MacDonald 1934, p. 251), as Professor Hawkes pointed out to me. SACE is not recorded in *Corpus Inscriptionum Latinarum* or at Camulodunum (Hawkes and Hull 1947).

[1] Trajanic sherds: May 1922, nos. 28, 69, 70, 73, 74, 89, 94, 103B, 113, 118, 120. Hadrianic to early Antonine sherds: 99, 119, 123, 124, 133–5 by Potter X-6, 148 in SACER style. No. 123 is only one sherd illustrated by May: for the almost complete bowl which I rubbed by kindness of Miss Dorothy Greene in 1952, see Stanfield and Simpson 1958, pl. xcii, 12.

[2] May 1922, nos. 95 in DIVIXTVS style, 100, 102, 104, 105, 110, 111 and 136 by ADVOCISVS, 115B, 126, 129, 137–41 and 143 by CINNAMVS, 145, 146.

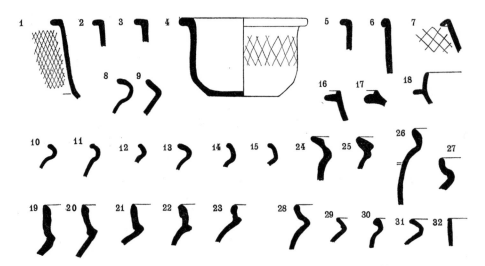

FIG. 16 COARSE POTTERY FROM TEMPLEBROUGH (pp. 85–7). Scale 1 : 4.

1922, pl. xlvii, 11–13). On Hadrian's Wall, roll-rims are more common during the third century than in the Antonine period.

7. Three drooping roll-rims in hard grey ware (cf. Balmuildy, Miller 1922, pl. xlvii, 10) with right-angled cross-hatching (cf. Ilkley fort, Hartley 1966, fig. 10, 37). Antonine.

8. Six grey-ware rims from large wide-rim jars (cf. Ilkley, Woodward 1925, pl. xxxiv, 22; Hartley 1966, fig. 9, 10). Such types had a long period of production.

9. Twelve rims in grey or black ware.

10. Ten black rims (cf. Woodward 1925, pl. xxxiv, 20).

11. Twelve black upstanding curved rims.

12. Eight grey or black beaker-rims (cf. Ilkley, Woodward 1925, xxxiv, 32; Balmuildy, Miller 1922, pl. xlv, 28). Antonine.

13. A buff-grey rim (cf. Woodward 1925, pl. xxxiv, 13).

14–15. Twenty upstanding black rims with slight beaded edges (cf. Woodward 1925, pl. xxxiv, 33–4—but they are in grey ware. Examples at Balmuildy, Miller 1922, pl. xlv, 14–16, are in black fumed ware like our Templebrough cooking-pots). Hadrianic–early Antonine.

16. Fourteen flanged bowls in black fumed ware, one illustrated by May 1922, pl. xxxiiiB, 217. Late third–early fourth century.

17. Two rims in coarse grey-brown ware, cf. no. 16.

18. *Ten imitations of Dr. Form 38* in orange or buff wares, like examples at Ilkley (Woodward 1925, p. 270, pl. xxix, 176). Woodward also noted that, at Templebrough, May had dated this form to the second century, calling six pieces imitations of the true sigillata form. However, in the third and fourth centuries,

copies in British wares are extremely common, long after sigillata manufacture had ceased.

19–23. *Derbyshire ware.*

19.   Two rims, very large and coarse.

20.   Six rims, colours including grey, yellow and red tints.

21.   Five rims.

22.   Four rims.

23.   Six rims. The type was originally described by Gillam 1939, p. 430, as late third–fourth century. Since then, evidence has accumulated to suggest that the type began in the Trajanic period in a slightly finer fabric (Brassington 1971, p. 60, excavations at Little Chester). Kilns producing it at Holbrook, Derbyshire (Kay 1962) were Antonine. The early products seem to have been used locally, and exports to the north of England were from the third century onwards.

24–6.   *Dales ware.* Calcite-gritted ware, rims with lid-seatings. No. 24 is like an example from Wetherby (Gillam 1951, fig. 1, 19); no. 25 has very large grits; no. 26 is like one from Ilkley (Gillam 1951, fig. 1, 12 = Woodward 1925, pl. xxxiv, 43).

27.   Rim of grey lid-seated jar (cf. Todd 1968, p. 202, fig. 4); smooth grey surface, with rilling, in a hard ware.

28–32.   *Hard grey gritty ware.* The pimpled surface is not so rough as Derbyshire ware: it is almost glossy, light grey in colour, often with a red-brown core. Best described by Woodward 1925, nos. 26–8. No. 28 from Templebrough is very like Woodward's no. 28 from Ilkley.

The only stratified pottery recorded by May was in the well in the *principia* (head-quarters building). This was partly timber-lined, and it had been deliberately filled up (see the sectional drawing, May 1922, pl. liii). Half way down, at a depth of sixteen feet, lay a complete though broken globular South Spanish amphora, a type which was not imported into Britain after the second century (Callender 1965, Form 11, pp. xxix and 19). Nearby lay a box flue-tile, a small vessel (May 1922, pl. xxxiiB, 211), and the bowl already described above (Fig. 16,4). The bowl bears a label stating that it came from this well. One foot deeper lay the two pieces from a bell-mouth jar or cooking-pot, wrongly reconstructed by May (1922, pl. xxxiiiA, 212), where it is too squat. I asked Mr Gillam for his opinion on this vessel, and he thought that it might be early (i.e. second-century) Derbyshire ware. Unfortunately I could not find the actual sherds. However, all the datable objects in the well belong to the second century, and the filling of the well may mark the end of the occupation of Fort II.

May's Section L—L across the north-eastern defences showed a burnt layer over Fort I, and he also found that the stone granaries were founded in a burnt layer. Fort II is presumably the fort built by the Fourth Cohort of Gauls whose stamped tiles roofed the commandant's house.[1] Post-military use of the fort area is indicated by industrial remains in the commandant's house, and a corn-drying kiln in the western granary. No cross-walls were found in the granaries in 1877, but there are none in the fort granaries at Brecon or Ilkley either. A second fire had damaged the stones about the south gate; the four irregularly spaced columns, which had supported the granaries' porticoes, fell, and one column and the bases were found below the rampart of Fort III. Later walls were found over the colonnade along the side of the granaries, and these are probably part of the post-military occupation.

There seem to have been three successive headquarters buildings at Templebrough. The south-facing *principia* was about 70 by 48 feet. This may be the earliest of the three, and the early double *principia* at Hod Hill, Dorset, was about 85 by 50 feet. The first eastern-facing timber *principia* was about 82 by 70 feet, slightly smaller than that of Agricola's fort in Perthshire at Fendoch (88 by 76 feet) and slightly larger than the Gelligaer *principia* (in South Wales) which was stone-built, possibly about the same time. The third *principia*, of stone, was unfinished, and measures about 90 by 78 feet.

May plotted a series of post-holes for timber barracks, and although none is dated by him, it is interesting that Mr Hartley found similar post-pit structures in the fourth fort at Ilkley. Those belong to the early fourth century (Hartley 1966, p. 40). This does not mean that the Templebrough post-holes are so late, but simply that timber buildings can be put up at almost any period, with any combination of timber, half-timber, or stone principal buildings. There are two other types of barracks shown on May's plan, in the north-east corner of the fort, but these, too, are undated.

The final piece of evidence May records, concerning the sequence of the three forts, is in the road levels at the north gate. He found 2 feet 6 inches of road-metalling in five distinct layers, representing repairs to the original road. Then above this road lay 1 foot 6 inches of sandy loam, which indicates a long period when the fort was not in use. Finally, above it, a 6-inch layer of boulders and gravel formed the road contemporary with Fort III (May 1922, p. 22). An early second-century tombstone, of one Cintusmus, a soldier in the Fourth Cohort of Gauls, was reused partly to line a drain

---

[1] Later in the second century this cohort was at Castlesteads on Hadrian's Wall, then at Risingham beyond it, and then at Castlehill on the Antonine Wall. In the third century the cohort was at Chesterholm (Birley 1931, pp. 191–2; 1939, pp. 215–16).

through the north gate of Fort III, and partly to serve as a drain cover. The same mundane use was accorded to the tombstone of Crotus, veteran of the Gauls. Broken dressed masonry, tiles, and rubbish were the building materials of the free-standing fort wall of Fort III.[1] But however hastily constructed, Fort III, with its stone *principia* and regular plan of four gates and interior roads, is still a military work. It is after this period that the interior was given over to industrial activities, mainly within the former commandant's house.

A very large civil settlement, or *vicus*, extended southwards from the ramparts. This was being excavated by Mr W. V. Wade at the time of his sudden death. He had found a great deal of pottery and other evidence of lengthy occupation, and this should be compared with the coarse pottery from the fort.

The latest pottery from the fort does not include types post-dating A.D. 369. There are a number of late third- to early fourth-century mortaria, especially the hammer-head mortarium in buff ware with a cream-coloured slip, which is also the type found in a group in the fourth-century *principia* at Bewcastle (Richmond *et al.* 1938, p. 221, fig. 22, 9–17). A third-century scale-pattern beaker in Castor ware,[2] was found on the fort site in 1932 by Mr Wakelin, who also recorded the contents of the well in the *principia* already described. A few scraps of Castor ware were with the sherds of coarse pottery in the museum outhouse, and May published one piece (May 1922, pl. xxxv, 244), and a Dr. 45, probably a Trier or Rhineland type, not made before A.D. 180 or after *c.* A.D. 250 (May 1922, pl. xxviii, 168).

Coins of the first and second centuries from within the fort, including a hoard of nineteen *denarii*, closed with coins of Marcus Aurelius as Caesar and two of Faustina the Younger (died A.D. 175). Third-century coins total seven, one of Severus (193–211) now lost, and three of Claudius II (268–70), one of Victorinus (268–270) and two of Carausius (287–93).[3] Two or three coins of Constantine I (306–37) and one Urbs Roma coin (330–7) are the latest recorded, and agree with the latest pottery noted above. The complete absence of late fourth-century objects, noted by May, is un-changed.

In conclusion, it is possible that an early Neronian fort continued in garrison until the time of Agricola's advance into northern Britain. Early in the second century, Fort II, housing at first the Fourth Cohort of Gauls, lasted until some time in the middle Antonine period. Non-occupation, perhaps for a century or more, was suc-

[1] For the latest (early fourth-century) fort wall at Bewcastle, see Richmond *et al.* 1938.
[2] For a similar beaker, see Pryce 1912, p. 208, fig. v, 10.
[3] For the coin lists, see May 1922, pp. 61–71; Freemantle 1913, p. 83; Preston 1950, p. 301.

ceeded by the hastily built defences of Fort III with its incomplete buildings. Finally squatters moved in, perhaps from the *vicus*, and built tanks and kilns within some of the principal buildings which were by then in ruin. It would be interesting to know just when that was. 'But we are moving in a dim land of doubts and shadows. He who wanders here, wanders at his peril . . .' (Haverfield 1923, p. 88).

Bibliography

BIRLEY, E., 1931. 'An introduction to the excavation of Chesterholm-Vindolanda.' *Archaeologia Aeliana*, ser. 4, 8, pp. 182–212. Newcastle.

—, 1939. 'The Beaumont Inscription, the Notitia Dignitatum, and the garrison of Hadrian's Wall.' *Transactions of the Cumberland and Westmorland Antiquarian and Archaeological Society*, ser. 2, 39, pp. 190–226.

BRASSINGTON, M., 1971. 'A Trajanic kiln complex near Little Chester.' *Antiquaries Journal*, 51, pp. 36–69.

BRUTON, F. A. (ed.), 1909. *The Roman Fort at Manchester*. Manchester.

CALLENDER, M. H., 1965. *Roman Amphorae, with Index of Stamps*. Oxford.

DÉCHELETTE, J., 1904. *Les vases céramiques ornés de la Gaule*. Paris. (Abbreviated *D*.)

FREEMANTLE, W. T., 1913. *Templebrough*. Rotherham.

FRERE, S. S., 1967. *Britannia: a History of Roman Britain*. London.

FÖLZER, E., 1913. *Die Bilderschüsseln der Ostgallischen Sigillata-Manufacturen*. Bonn.

GILLAM, J. P., 1939. 'Romano-British Derbyshire Ware.' *Antiquaries Journal*, 19, pp. 429–37.

—, 1951. 'Dales Ware, a distinctive Romano-British cooking-pot.' *Antiquaries Journal*, 31, pp. 154–64.

GREENE, DOROTHY, 1952–5. 'The Ricknild Street.' *Yorkshire Archaeological Journal*, 38, pp. 112–17.

HARTLEY, B. R., 1966. 'The Roman Fort at Ilkley: excavations of 1962.' *Proceedings of the Leeds Philosophical and Literary Society*, 12, pp. 23–72.

HAVERFIELD, F., 1923. *The Romanization of Roman Britain*, 4th edn. Oxford.

HAWKES, C. F. C., 1947. 'Britons, Romans and Saxons round Salisbury and in Cranborne Chase.' *Archaeological Journal*, 104, pp. 27–81.

HAWKES, C. F. C., and HULL, M. R., 1947. *Camulodunum*. Society of Antiquaries of London Research Report, no. 11. Oxford.

HOGG, A. H. A., 1953. 'The Lower Roman fort.' *Archaeologia Cambrensis*, 102, p. 182.

KAY, S. O., 1962. 'The Romano-British pottery kilns at Hazelwood and Holbrook, Derbyshire.' *Derbyshire Archaeological Journal*, 82, pp. 21–42.

KUZSINSKY, B., 1932. *Das Grosse Römische Töpferviertel in Aquincum*. Budapest.

LEADER, J., 1879. 'Roman Rotherham.' In J. Guest (1879), *Historic Notices of Rotherham*, pp. 593–616, with Oliver's excellent plan opp. p. 593.

MACDONALD, Sir GEORGE, 1934. *The Roman Wall in Scotland*, 2nd edn. Oxford.

MAY, T., 1922. *The Roman Forts of Templebrough near Rotherham*. Rotherham.

MILLER, S. N., 1922. *The Roman Fort at Balmuildy*. Glasgow.

MOUNTFORD, A. R., GEE, J., and SIMPSON, GRACE, 1968. 'The excavation of an early Neronian pottery-kiln and workshop at Trent Vale, Stoke-on-Trent.' *North Staffordshire Journal of Field Studies*, 8, pp. 19–38.

NASH-WILLIAMS, V. E., 1930. 'Further excavations at Caerwent Monmouthshire, 1923–5.' *Archaeologia*, 80, pp. 229–88.

OSWALD, F., 1936–7. *Index of Figure-Types on Terra Sigillata*. Liverpool. (Abbreviated *O*.)

PETCH, J. A., 1950–1. 'The northern defences of Roman Manchester.' *Transactions of the Lancashire and Cheshire Antiquarian Society*, 62, pp. 177–95.

PHELPS, J. J., 1912. 'The north wall of the Roman fort at Manchester.' *Transactions of the Lancashire and Cheshire Antiquarian Society*, 30, pp. 195–210.

PITT-RIVERS, A. H. L. F., 1887–98. *Excavations in Cranborne Chase*, 4 vols.

PRESTON, F. L., 1950. 'A field survey of the Roman "Rig" Dyke in south-west Yorkshire.' *Transactions of the Hunter Archaeological Society*, 6, pp. 197–309.

PRYCE, T. D., 1912. 'Margidunum, a Roman fortified post on the Fosse Way, excavations 1910–11.' *Journal of the British Archaeological Association*, ser. 2, 18, pp. 177–210.

RICHMOND, I. A., et al., 1938. 'The Roman fort at Bewcastle.' *Transactions of the Cumberland and Westmorland Antiquarian and Archaeological Society*, ser. 2, 38, pp. 195–237.

RICHMOND, I. A., 1953. 'Excavations on the site of the Roman fort at Lancaster, 1950, with notes upon the pottery by J. P. Gillam.' *Transactions of the Historical Society of Lancashire and Cheshire*, 105, pp. 1–23.

ROEDER, C., 1899. 'Recent discoveries in Deansgate and on Hunt's Bank, and Roman Manchester re-studied (1897–1900).' *Transactions of the Lancashire and Cheshire Antiquarian Society*, 17, pp. 87–212. Reprinted as ROEDER 1900.

ROEDER, C., 1900. *Roman Manchester*. Reprinted from ROEDER 1899.

ROGERS, G., 1966. 'Terra sigillata in Southampton Museums.' In G. Rogers and L. R. Laing, *Gallo-Roman Pottery from Southampton and the Distribution of Terra Nigra in Great Britain*. City Museum Publications, no. 6, Southampton.

SIMPSON, GRACE, 1964. *Britons and the Roman Army*. London.

SIMPSON, GRACE, and ROGERS, G., 1969. 'Cinnamus de Lezoux et quelques potiers contemporains.' *Gallia*, 27, pp. 3–14.

STANFIELD, J. A., and SIMPSON, GRACE, 1958. *Central Gaulish Potters*. Oxford. (Abbreviated *S & S*.)

TODD, M., 1968. 'The commoner late Roman coarse wares of the East Midlands.' *Antiquaries Journal*, 48, pp. 192–209.

WHEELER, R. E. M., 1923. *Segontium and the Roman Occupation of Wales* (= *Y Cymmrodor* 33).

—, 1926. *The Roman Fort near Brecon*. Cymmrodorion Society's Publications, London.

WHITAKER, JOHN, 1771. *History of Manchester*, Book 1.

WOODWARD. A. M., 1925. 'The Roman fort at Ilkley.' *Yorkshire Archaeological Journal*, 28, pp. 136–326.

Commentary 4
Late Roman and Sub-Roman : British Isles and Austria

The account of the Manchester and Templebrough Roman forts, prepared by Grace Simpson from her reviewing of the evidence, has illumined as far as possible their respective earlier phases, from the first occupation of Templebrough through the Flavian and following periods. She gives us the best assessment we can have of their importance each side of the British southern Pennines. Then, when the third century brought a lull, she has shown them passing to the fourth, when Templebrough was never to be refortified, while Manchester, walled in stone, became a regional seat of defence. For the civilian population, left at Templebrough to itself, the seat of defence no doubt was at Doncaster, lower down the Don valley on the road to York from London. On the other side, where the Manchester fort defended it, we need not discount it because it has eluded the archaeology. Forts beyond, starting at Ribchester, guarded the coast and the Pennines too, with the northerly routes across them; and defensive strength was upheld for as long as the Roman record lasts. Yet the northern natives were fated, when garrisons fell or were ordered away, to do their best to persist in the condition which we name Sub-Roman, and which Haverfield before us, as Dr Simpson has recalled, once described as 'a dim land of doubts and shadows'. They did persist, in these hills and dales, although the western coastal plain would lie open to the Irish, and the Vale of York to east was to be a borderland for Angles. For there were Celtic entities here in the Dark Age that followed, Loidis and Elmet, and Rheged away to north, with which the Angles had to struggle before they could isolate and reduce them. But as we know so very little, and even in the South not very much, might we possibly turn elsewhere within Romano-Celtic Europe and find a region with features to compare with ours, which for the fifth century at least allows more knowledge to be gained than Britain?

Rather than 'wander at peril' here further—another of Haverfield's phrases—we are changing the scene, for the rest of this book, from the British Isles to Austria: from the last of Roman Britain to the last of Noricum. In the future fuller comparisons may be hoped for, between our land and that, through the period now before us. But the time for them cannot be yet, because research in either country has till now been so feebly conscious of the other. So it is best for us that Noricum should first introduce itself to English readers. It can claim an interest, furthermore, that is all its own. Johanna Haberl, when working in Oxford under the care of the British Council, passed that interest on to me, and has steadily herself pursued it. With my collaboration latterly in the presenting of her study, she has offered this as a fresh introduction and appraisal of facts and probabilities for the period in her country: above all along the Danube, and in the area of Vienna, where archaeology meets history in the life of a fifth-century saint, St Severinus. Its record, by a disciple who shared the later years of his labours, was written in Italy after his death and completed in A.D. 511. Topographically and historically, and in the opportunities it gives archaeology, it tells much that in Britain we shall never know so directly of situations and events of that time. Dr Haberl has rightly addressed herself to readers strange to her landscape. I have tried the same for strangers to its history and its saint. But an old prehistoric people, protohistorically Celtic, and then moving into community of sentiment with Rome, is something we cannot be strangers to. We have it ourselves in Britain. So here is the change of scene. We pass to Noricum.

The Last of Roman
Noricum:
St Severin on the Danube

BY JOHANNA HABERL, WITH CHRISTOPHER HAWKES

The Danube on its eastward course through Austria, of over 300 kilometres to Hungary from Bavaria, has the bordering hills of Bohemia and Moravia on its northern side, and on its southern the Alps. Between the confluent Inn and Salzach on the west, and the winding Leitha on the east (Fig. 17), the Alps behind stand range upon range, blocking the valley's length from a way through to Italy. Thus to contemplate the territory of Austria today, with its mountains bordered by the Danube corridor, can bring vividly to mind, through its geography's implications, realities from the past that have validity even now, after more than 2,000 years of history.

I. INTRODUCTION TO THE HISTORY (FIG. 17)

Through many pre-Roman centuries, the older inhabitants of Austria, like their western neighbours who in history were the Raeti, were infiltrated from various south-easterly quarters, Venetic or more loosely called Illyrian. Yet the Iron Age could enter by the Danube too, where the Hallstatt civilization, on from the eighth century B.C., had an eastern province, down from about the confluence of the Enns, and a western too, upstream and thus open to Bavaria. From this direction, around the late fifth century B.C., came movement which is attested more plainly as invasion: the culture that it brought was the La Tène, then new, while its leaders (in a new sense also) were Celtic. And when next, through the fourth and third centuries and after, these and further immigrants reduced their precursors—Hallstatt and Veneto-Illyrian or older—into mainly Celtic-dominated tribes, the name given to one became common to them all: Latin made it *Nōrici*, and the country therefore Noricum. By the end of the second century, and on through the first, it was a single Celtic kingdom which passed into Roman clientship: the *Regnum Noricum*—a title not forgotten even a hundred years after Claudius, about A.D. 45, made it a province of the Empire.[1]

Noricum stretched from Venetia in the south to Rome's northern military frontier on the Danube—between the Inn which bounded Raetia (finally *Raetia Secunda*), and the eastern edge of the Alps which bounded the downstream province of Pannonia (Fig. 17). The nearer part of this was finally named *Pannonia Prima*. From Carnuntum, its northern frontier fortress on the Danube, the chief Roman military road ran south, below the Alpine edge, to Poetovio (Ptuj) on the Drave, and on through the mountains south-west into Italy by Aquileia. Inside Noricum, through the inner Alpine mass, crossing was far less easy than there, or again than farther west through Raetia. Under the late Roman system,[2] when Noricum was divided, this inner Alpine part was named *Noricum Mediterraneum*, with capital (in modern Carinthia) Virunum, and later Teurnia. All the more vital became the corridor in front, north of the Tauern range of Alps and along the Danube bank: this 'riparian' part of Noricum became, by the division, the province known finally as *Noricum Ripense*. It is the history of this, Late Roman and Early Christian, that I think should interest the English reader. With archaeology and topography, and Latin texts relating, it deserves a wider notice and comparison, in particular, with the Late and Sub-Roman age in Britain.

First, then, a sketch of the historical events.[3] Beyond the Danube the Suebic German Marcomanni (with the Quadi just to the east and the Sarmatians down in Hungary) outlived their war with Marcus Aurelius (to 180) and always might again menace Italy through Pannonia; the Raetian frontier, from around 230, faced the often sharper threat of the Alamanni. At last, despite reinforcement by Valentinian (to 375), all these Danube frontiers were put in peril from lower down, when the Huns, appearing out of Asia, struck the Goths of Eastern Europe, and went on (from 375–8) to change the whole situation. While the Visigoths fled by thrusting into the south-eastern provinces, and later, through Italy, passed to homes in the south-western, the Ostrogoths behind them were left outside the Empire, threatened, like all the Germans round, with a further Hun advance. In 395, the Pannonian Danube

---

[1] For standard historical surveys of Roman Noricum, encompassing older literature, we have Betz 1956, and for English readers Alföldy 1973; Pannonia in same series, Mócsy 1973.
[2] Jones 1964 will be a sufficient citation, to the English and every reader, for the Late Roman Empire in general, and widely in detail; amongst the older literature, all of it given there, mention is called for here only by Stein 1928 (1949–59).
[3] Professor Hawkes's collaboration begins with this purposely summary section. In those on topography, smoothing my English, he has firmly observed my views; as again in his Conclusion, made from these and from the Life of St Severinus. J. H.

was crossed and its frontier breached; by 400, the Raetian had suffered a similar fate at the hands of the Alamanni; in 401 the road between, through Noricum Ripense, was forced from the east by Vandals allied with Sarmatian Alans; and though assault on Italy southward out of Raetia was checked, yet the Danube road to the west was again forced by Vandals, with Alans and Suebic Germans, in 406. They streamed through Raetia to cross the Rhine into Gaul, where their ravages drew the final Roman army out of Britain; they later moved to Spain, and the Vandals at last crossed over to Africa. To all of this, Noricum Ripense had given the key. Roman power here, then, had got to be re-asserted. And with only a single interval, though against increasing perils, it was maintained for a further eighty years.

Raetia, from Danube up to Alps on the west, was lost. Pannonia, off to the east, could be given away in whole or part to barbarians for settling with Imperial permission. But Noricum was never thus officially conceded. Through most of the fifth century it continued to be held. What were the perils? Among Suebic Germans the Marcomanni, in the previous century still next to the Quadi (on the Peutinger Map: Pl. V), by now supplied the Romans with a force (p. 105) in Pannonia Prima (where archaeology has Suebi afterwards, through to the early sixth century). North of the Danube again, there perhaps survived some of those Celts whom the second-century geographer Ptolemy named *Rakatai*: that they might be known later than this, to Slavs already settled near them, has been held to explain the Czech and Slovak name for all Austrians, Rakoužani, and for Austria, Rakusko, in use even today. Yet such chances are transcended by the main historic fact: Rome's most prized possession here was Noricum itself, along and within the Alps guarding entry into Italy. And the perils now were from neither Celts nor Suebi; they came, first and foremost, from the Huns.

For the years when the Western Roman Emperor was Honorius (395–423), and the frontier here was renewed after the Vandals' last break-through in 406, we can learn of the forces stationed in Noricum Ripense and what remained as Pannonia Prima, from the *Notitia Dignitatum*, the general list of Late Roman garrisons and commands (p. 101, note 1). Imperial taxation levied to support this vital front brought revolt, in 431, amongst the civil populace. But the situation then was truly exceptional. The Huns, from the big encampment that served them as a capital in the Middle Danube plains, were in movement, and their leader was Attila. In 433 the Empire ceded them Pannonia and for nearly twenty years held Noricum alone, while Attila kept the neighbouring Germans, Ostrogoths and others, in a dominion which at last he projected against the west. His host, advancing again through Noricum Ripense, set out on the great invasion into Gaul, which led to his defeat, by Aëtius, in the battle of the Mauriac

Plain (near Châlons-sur-Marne) in 451; he returned by the same route, meaning now to enter Italy. But with his death in 453 his dominion fell apart; and the Romans in Noricum, repairing what they could, passed into what was now to be their frontier's last phase.

The perils soon grew, for with the Hun dominion broken, and the Goths (Ostrogoths) settled on the lower Danube, they and all Germans still hungry for land—Rugii, Heruli, Thuringi, Alamanni—could now take to raiding into Noricum Ripense, and threaten the Roman hold there with ruin. Yet Odovacar (Odoacer), the German potentate in Italy, who in 476 deposed the last Western Roman Emperor, maintained the province for a dozen years more. Only in 488 did he ordain its official evacuation. This last phase of Roman life in Noricum is known to us from the record of the Christian Saint Severinus. I shall call him here, more simply, St Severin.[1] He died in 482; but when the official evacuation came his disciples bore his remains with them from Noricum to Italy. They received land at Naples (Pizzofalcone: estate of Lucullanum Castellum) for his reburial, and then for a fresh monastery where in 511 its abbot, his former pupil Eugippius, completed his Life, the *Vita Sancti Severini*.[2] We have here what is far more a first-hand account, and very much closer to the doings it describes, than are many, even early, lives of missionary saints. And his works were performed, within that century's second half, amongst imperilled but persisting local Roman towns and villages. Addressing 'the tribes of Noricum' and sustaining them as his flock, St Severin declares survival not of population only, but of ways of life such as can have left us opportunity for filling out the history with archaeology. Yet this needs applying with topographical exactness. The places named should all allow identification on the ground; archaeology, thus guided, can spread interpretation of the period out farther. Such work, in its present state, perhaps leaves room for a fresh review.

II. INTRODUCTION TO THE TOPOGRAPHY (FIG. 17)

Of the places named by Eugippius in Noricum, most are among the entries in the *Notitia Dignitatum*. Its list here (pp. 105–6), not seriously confused, represents the

[1] Spelt thus as in German, and stressed as in French 'Saint-Séverin', the form Severin seems as natural for English as Crispin, Martin, Justin or Quintin.
[2] He records this in its final chapter (46, 1–2 and 6) and the date in its prefatory letter to Paschasius, deacon at Rome, whose reply he gives also. The text of the whole, transmitted essentially in Italy, survives in manuscripts of which eight (four in each of two classes) are of the tenth to twelfth century A.D., the oldest (in Rome) being Lateran 79, called *L* (Mommsen 1898; Vetter 1963). The editions, after that of *L* by A. Kerschbaumer (Schaffhausen 1862), are

system held as standard after 395 and no doubt till 433.[1] For it gives us a Noricum Ripense combined in one command with Pannonia Prima east of it, which in that year was passed to Attila. It is after that, when the Norican line of frontier was held alone, and again when Attila was dead, after 453, that we become most indebted to Eugippius. Where his names agree with any in the Notitia, the continuity that he vouches for in general is made specific. Next, for continuity passing back a little farther, into the late fourth century, we have entries in the 'Peutinger Map': that treasure of the Austrian National Library in Vienna, more properly entitled the *Tabula Peuteringiana*, of which the appropriate part is here reproduced (Pl. V).[2] And from the later third century, though thought to be adapting an earlier original, there is the 'Antonine Itinerary' road-book, or *Itinerarium Antonini Augusti*, which gives routes through Noricum complete with place-names and distances.[3] So for starting on exact topography, we are not too badly off for texts. Yet archaeology, pointing to

P. Knöll's in the *Corpus Scriptorum Ecclesiasticorum Latinorum* (IX, 2: Vienna 1886), and H. Sauppe's in the *Monumenta Germaniae Historica, Scriptores*, I (Berlin 1877), revised (for IV, Berlin 1898) and issued ('for schools') as Mommsen 1898, with his introduction and commentary; reprinted without these, Heidelberg 1948; succeeded now by Noll 1963 (with Vetter): translation into English, Bieler and Kristan 1965.

[1] Seeck 1876 (standard edition of the Notitia; includes the Verona and other Roman province-lists) was reprinted (Frankfurt, Minerva) 1962; the old ed. of E. Böcking was 1839–53. Principal disquisitions: Polaschek 1936; Jones 1964, vol. III, Appendix II, pp. 347–80.

[2] The sheets of this famous map (Vienna, Codex Vindobonensis 324), seldom published as a whole, were formerly a single roll, a later medieval copy (obtained 1508 by the collector Peutinger) of an early medieval rendering of a Late Roman original, possibly by one Castorius (both these of course lost). Our Plate V gives quick recognition of the geography's distortion (vertical compression and sideways extension) to make it fit the roll. This required also the zigzags introduced in the lines of the roads. Between the place-names along them, the Roman numerals are mileages; the map is thus a kind of cartographical 'itinerary': hence its appearance in Fortia D'Urban 1845, pp. 238–9; Miller 1916, pp. xxxiiiff., 419ff.; and the refs. to it in Cuntz 1929. On its art and palaeography, see Hermann 1923.

[3] With Cuntz 1929, the standard modern edition of Roman 'Itineraries', see also Miller 1916; Kubitschek 1919; all covering the *Itinerarium Antonini*. The reference-numbering of entries is that instituted by Wesseling, adopted by Parthey and Pinder for their edition of 1848, and maintained ever since. For Noricum, the routes of most importance are those from Pannonia west into Gaul: (i) to Trier, by *Scarabantia* (Sopron)-Lorch-Salzburg-Augsburg (Wess. 231, 8 to 240), Cuntz pp. 33–4; (ii) to Xanten (Lower Rhine), by the Danube to *Carnuntum*-Lorch-*Regina* (Regensburg)-Augsburg (Wess. 241 to 256, 1–3), Cuntz pp. 34–7. On his p. 37, less important here, are (iii) that from Lorch to Salzburg and Innsbruck–Wilten (Wess. 256, 4 to 258, 1), and (iv) from Lorch to Augsburg and on to Bregenz (Wess. 258, 2 to 259, 1). *Carnuntum* is in the north-east corner of modern Austria; Lorch was *Lauriacum*; Augsburg, *Augusta Vindelicum* (or -*orum*). See map, Fig. 17, and further text here following.

presence or absence of material remains, whether in agreed or doubtful places, has of course its part to play; and so has the study of medieval place-names. In 1963 the Austrian Academy of Sciences, in its atlas series for the country, published a Roman-period map entitled *Topographie der Römerzeit* (Egger and Vetters 1963). Through its conservative respect for work by previous writers, it does less to mark the opening of a newer phase of research in site-identifications than to commemorate an older one. For Noricum Ripense, with the Austrian strip of Pannonia, seven of these are accepted here; the rest are re-examined.

Let us look first (with note 3, p. 101) at the Antonine Itinerary. The part of its route (i) that follows the Danube, in Noricum, from Vindobona to Lauriacum, coincides with route (ii), coming along upstream from Carnuntum. It writes in the stages (place-names) with their case-endings various (some seeming in the locative case which in plural names is in *-is*), and the distances in Roman miles (m.p., for *milia passuum*, '1,000 paces'), each in a column. The parts concerning us are as follows (Fig. 17):

On route (*ii*), from
Carnuntum, leg. XIIII GG
248,1 Aequinoctio et
Ala Nova in
medio

On route (*i*), from
Vindobona (mis-spelt
'Vindomona'):

234,1	Comagenis	m.p. XXIIII		2	Vindobona	m.p. XXVII
						leg. X Gem.
2	Cetio	m.p. XXIIII		3	Comagenis	m.p. XX
3	Arlape	m.p. XXII		4	Cetio	m.p. XXX
4	Loco Felicis	m.p. XXVI		5	Arlape	m.p. XX
235,1	Lauriaco	m.p. XX		6	Loco Felicis	m.p. XXV
				249,1	Lauriaco	m.p. XX
						leg. II I
2	Ovilavis	m.p. XXVI		2	Ovilatus	m.p. XVI
3	Laciaco	m.p. XXXII		3	Ioviaco	m.p. XXVII
4	Iovavi	m.p. XXVIII		4	Stanaco	m.p. XVIII

etc., to Augusta Vindelicum (Augsburg), and by Bregenz to Gaul and the Rhine.

5	Boiodoro	m.p. XX
6	Quintianis	m.p. XXIIII
7	Augustis	m.p. XX
250,1	Regino	m.p. XXIIII

etc., to Augusta Vindelicum, as on route (i), to Gaul.

On route (*iii*), from Lauriacum:		On route (*iv*), from Lauriacum:	
256,5 Ovilavis	m.p. XXVI	258,4 Ovilavis	m.p. XXVI
6 Iaciaco	m.p. XXXII	5 Laciaco	m.p. XXXII
7 Iovavi	m.p. XXVIII	6 Iovavi	m.p. XXVIII

On route (*iii*): etc., to Veldidena (Innsbruck-Wilten). Iovavi (locative case) is for Iuvavum

On route (*iv*): etc., to Augusta Vindelicum (and Bregenz).

The mileages are those of the standard edition, Cuntz 1929 (p. 101 n. 3.), omitting manuscript readings there rejected. Its Introduction pp. v–vi explains his critical method. Example: in 248,2 (Vindobona from Carnuntum) Cuntz prefers the XXVII in the oldest complete ms., L (eighth century); XXVIII, in a later hand there, is also in B (but both ninth century); ms. D (tenth) has XXVI; P (seventh) XXXVII, plainly error for XXVII. Yet the Peutinger Map must support XXVIII; and this best fits the actual distance (pp. 125, 134 below).

These stages leave quite a number of places disregarded, which later, in the Notitia, had garrisons in forts. But foremost amongst those it names will be noticed the fortresses occupied by legions. That in Noricum was at Lorch, close to the Danube's confluence with the Enns; its name (correctly spelt) was *Lauriacum*. Here the legion was II Italica (read the text as II. I); there was a civil town besides, municipal in status, from which a road branched to the older civil town at Salzburg, *Iuvavum*. Lauriacum (modern Lorch through having kept continuity of name) is in the plain a little beyond the rivers' confluence. It is quite distinct from the town of Enns which is the medieval Ennsburg, built on a rock at the confluence in the ninth or tenth century; to confuse the two was an error made by Mommsen. The route goes on from here to reach the border of Noricum, on the confluent river Inn, at *Boiodurum*. This is Innstadt, opposite Passau which was the border-fort of Raetia and named *Batavis* from its garrison 'the new cohort of Batavians', brought long before from their home on the lower Rhine (Noll 1963, p. 132). But we find that between Iuvavum, Boiodurum and Lauriacum the topography of intermediate places is confused. One of the reasons—though not the sole one—is variety of mileages, from one place to another, in the Itinerary's various manuscripts.

How the standard editor has handled such (Cuntz 1929) has been seen from the example just given. We shall find, in that and several other cases when we reach them, some further help from inscriptions, notably milestones found *in situ*, besides what our second written source affords.

Our second written source is the *Tabula Peutingeriana*, or Peutinger Map (Plate V; see p. 101 with note 2). Scholars are agreed that its contents point to the later fourth century, perhaps about 370 (Miller 1916). The map as we have it is in twelve segments, I–XII from west to east, reckoned as each divided into five (1–5) for ease of reference, its length being close to 6·5 metres. Along the Danube, Segment IV, 4 includes the last corner of Raetia, from *Regina* east (modern Regensburg, *Regino* in Antonine Itinerary) to the confluence at *Boiodurum* (Innstadt) of the Inn; the Map makes a single river of this and its tributary the Salzach, named *Ivaro* where passing *Iuvavo* (Salzburg). Along a road to this city from the east-north-east, it marks successively xiii (miles) from *Tarnantone*, xiiii from *Laciacis*, xviii from *Tergolape*, and xiiii from *Ovilia*, which though here misspelt (like many other of its names), has a road-junction and certainly stands for *Ovilava* (modern Wels). This, being on the Antonine Itinerary's other route, my (i), going on to Salzburg, yet not far from Boiodurum on route (ii) along the Danube, brings the Map into the problem introduced here already, of the topography between these places and Lauriacum. The place it records between them, with a name spelt *Marinianio*, is unhappily not too helpful since the spelling must be corrupt. But from Lauriacum (misspelt *Blaboriaco*) eastwards on to Segment IV,5, past the two new names *Elegio* (xiii miles) and *Ad Ponte(m) Isis* (xxiii), comes the Antonine route's name Arlape, in the spelling *Arelate* (viii); and then, after three more new ones, *Namare* (vii), *Trigisamo* (xvi, on Segment V,1) and *Piro Torto* (viii), it repeats the Antonine name *Comagenis* (xiiii miles), adds a *Citium* (vii), and repeats Antonine *Vindobona* (vi). What is more, in proceeding still farther downstream (on Segment V,2), past the new *Villa Gai* (x), it repeats *Aequinoctio* at iiii miles on, and gives thence xiiii to reach *Carnuntum*; in all, 28 miles. So the map enters also into the problems we must face in the stretches on either side of Vindobona.

And now we approach our third source, the *Notitia Dignitatum*, which we have seen (p. 101 with note 1) is a general list of commands and garrisons; for the Western Empire (*Occidens*), its chapter XXXIV gives those in Pannonia Prima and Noricum Ripense, combined under a single *Dux* ('Duke') in charge of both, as they were in the period starting in or just after 395 (Jones 1964, pp. 347–80). They shared a fiscal officer (*Rationalis Summarum*) with Valeria and Noricum Mediterraneum (*Occ.* XI,11); and each of these provinces had a civilian governor (*Praeses*), reporting to the Praetorian Prefect of Italy (*Occ.* I, 87–9, 95; II, 31–3, 25). The Dux, like his British counterpart and the West's ten others, was a frontier general under the high command of the Master of Infantry (*Occ.* I, 40, 138). Among the arsenals supplying him, under the Master of the Offices, Lauriacum had a factory for shields (*Occ.* IX, 21). He had thirty-two units under him, each in a fixed location or fort, besides that of the 'tribune of the tribe of Marcomanni' (unlocated: p. 99 above), and his own *officium* or staff (*Occ.* XXXIV, 13–55). Subtracting those in Pannonia beyond Carnuntum, so not here relevant, we have twenty-two units: ten under prefects, four under tribunes, and eight with commander's rank not stated, all of cavalry, *equites*: either 'Dalmatian' (*eq. Dalmatae*) or mounted archers (*eq. sagittarii*), or fast light horsemen (*eq.promoti*). Of the infantry, cohorts were commanded each by a tribune; prefects had units formed from parts of them, four of which were of soldiers serving in the river-fleet, and called *liburnarii* from their 'Liburnian' type of galley; the other three prefects each had a squadron of the fleet called *classis*. In Noricum it was named adjectivally from its station; in Pannonia, where the Danube was known as the Hister, *classis Histrica*.

The Notitia list of these units' locations seems seldom to regard topographical propinquity. Vindobona and Carnuntum indeed appear adjacently (list nos. 25–6; and 28 names both), but Ala Nova and Aequinoctium, which the Itinerary puts between them, are seven lines higher (nos. 18 and 19). The Boiodurum entry, which ought to be the last, is the last but two. Only once, downstream from it, are there three names together which other sources show to have been adjacent: Ioviacum (*-o*), *Lentia* (modern Linz) and Lauriacum, the list's 37–8–9. So of topography as such it reveals distinctly less than do the Peutinger Map and Antonine Itinerary. The table here given follows it simply for convenience; its great value lies in its information on the garrisons.

Number in Notitia list (*Occ.* XXXIV)	Location in list (some spellings corrected)	Name of unit (abbreviations etc. explained above)
18	Ala Nova	*Eq. Dalmatae*
19	Aequinoctiae	*Eq. Dalmatae*
25	Vindomarae (=Vindobonae)	Leg. X *Gemina*
26	Carnunto	*Liburnarii*, Cohort of Leg. XIIII superior part
28	Arrunto (= Carnunto), or transferred from there to Vindobonae	*Classis Histrica*
29	Arrianis	Cohort

31	Ad Mauros	*Eq. promoti*
32	Lentiae	*Eq. sagittarii*
33	Lacu (= Loco) Felicis	*Eq. sagittarii*
34	Arlape	*Eq. Dalmatae*
35	August(i)anis, perhaps same place as Peut. Map's *Trigisamo* (see p. 121)	*Eq. Dalmatae*
36	Comagenis	*Eq. promoti*
37	Ioviaco	*Liburnarii* of Leg. II *Italica*
38	Lentiae	Leg. II *Italica* inferior part
39	Lauriaco	Leg. II *Italica* (the original unit)
40	Adiuvense	*Liburnarii*, Cohort v of Leg. I *Norica* (written *primae Noricorum*)
41	Fafianae (in manuscript *C*, Fasiane), see pp. 127ff.: *Favianis* in Eugippius	*Liburnarii* of Leg. I *Norica* (written *primorum Noricorum*)
42	Presumably Arlape and/or (Co)magenis	Squadron of *classis, Arlapensis et Comagenensis* (ed. Böcking's emendation for text's *maginensis*)
43	Presumably Lauriacum	Squadron of *classis, Lauriacensis*
44	Boiodoro	Cohort
45	Austuris (= *Asturis* in Eugippius)	Cohort
46	Cannabiaca	Cohort

Lastly we have the place-names mentioned by Eugippius in the *Vita Sancti Severini*. Besides Noricum Ripense and Noricum more widely, the neighbouring Pannonian and Raetian provinces, the Alps, and the rivers Danube and Inn, the places in or

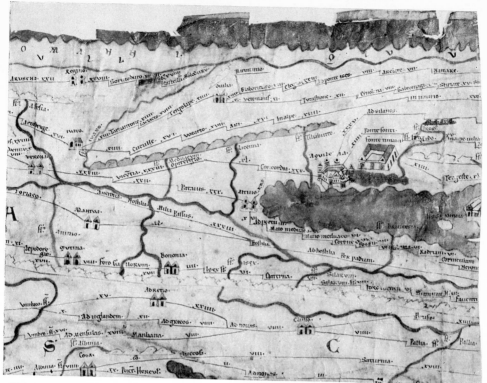

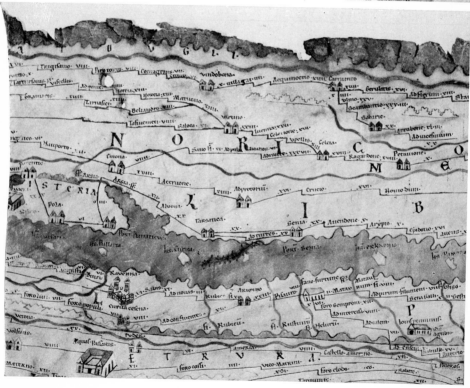

PLATE V *TABULA PEUTINGERIANA* (THE 'PEUTINGER MAP'): UPPER
PART (HERE BISECTED) OF SEGMENTS IV, 4 TO V, 2, WITH NORICUM
ABOVE THE ALPS AND ADRIATIC (pp. 101, 104, and 109 ff.).
From the original in the Austrian National Library, Vienna.
Haberl, 'The Last of Roman Noricum'.

Ph.: Austrian National Library Photo-Atelier

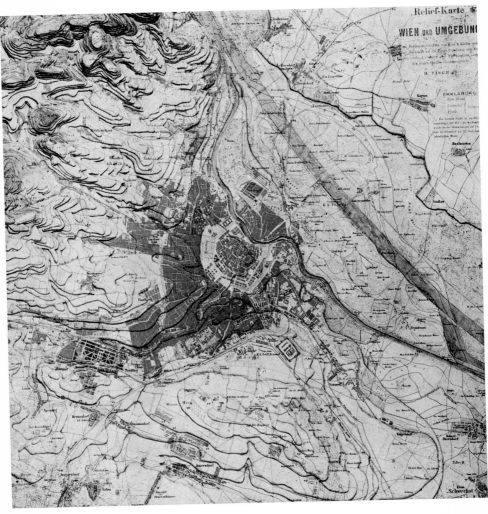

PLATE VI   H. FISCHER'S MAP, 1869, OF VIENNA AND SURROUNDINGS WITH
ADDED STRESS TO GROUND-RELIEF LINES (pp. 127–34). From copy in the Karten-
sammlung, Austrian National Library, Vienna.   *Ph.: Austrian National Library Photo-Atelier*

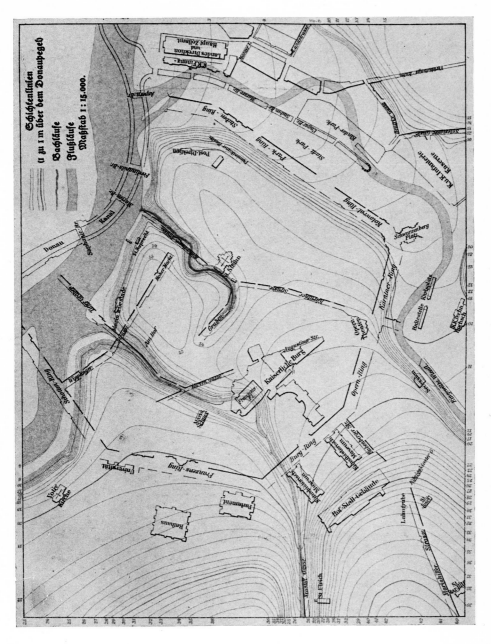

PLATE VII MAP OF THE PHYSIOGRAPHY OF CENTRAL VIENNA (pp. 131–8, 138–42) Scale 1:18,750, SHOWING THE RISE TO WEST AND TO EAST (IIIrd DISTRICT), THE DANUBE JOINED BY THE WIEN-FLUSS, AND THE RING AND INNER CITY (1st DISTRICT). From M. Eisler, *Historischer Atlas des Wiener Stadtbildes* (Vienna, 1919), Map A1.

Ph.: Austrian National Library Photo-Atelier

PLATE VIII FROM THE VIEW OF VIENNA BY J. HOUFNAGL, 1609, LOOKING
SOUTH-WEST
A (above): EASTERN UPPER PORTION (pp. 132–4) B: CENTRAL UPPER PORTION
(pp. 132, 136–8, 143). From copy in the Austrian National Library, Vienna.

Ph.: Austrian National Library Photo-Atelier

adjacent to Noricum are the following, with their references to chapter and paragraph in the *Vita*.

Asturis 1, 1 & 5

Batavis 19, 1; 20, 1; 22, 1 & 4; 24, 1; 27, 1 & 3

Boiotrum (= Boiodurum) 22, 1; 36, 1

Comagenis 1, 3; 3, 1; 33, 1

Cucullis 11, 2; 12, 1

Favianis 3, 1; 4, 7; 8, 2; 10, 1; 22, 4; 23, 1; 31, 1 & 6; 42, 1

Ioviaco 24, 1 (for Ioviacum)

Iuva(v)o 13, 1 (for Iuvavum)

Lauriacum 18, 1; 27, 2; 28, 1; 30, 1; 31, 1 & 6

Ad Vineas 4, 6

Quintanis 15, 1 & 2; 24, 2; 27, 1 (in Itinerary 'Quintianis': in Raetia near the Danube 24 miles above Boiodurum).

Tiburnia (= Teurnia, capital of Noricum Mediterraneum) 17, 4; 21, 2.

Some names recall earlier garrisons brought from other Roman provinces, as of Astures (Spain), Batavi (Rhine mouth) or Commageni (Syria), but their traces will long have been merged now in the Norican population. Twelve in number, these places and what is said of them, in those more than forty passages, will connect our topography with the history of St Severin's time in the later fifth century.

III. PLACES AND EVENTS, TO THE TIME OF ST SEVERIN AND EUGIPPIUS

St Severin arrived on the Danube at a date probably closer to 455 than to 470. His repute was already drawing visitors including soldiery, Germans bound for Italy seeking mercenary service there, at a time when the future king Odovacar could have been among them, still young and unknown (*Vita*, 7). As he led his revolution there in 476, and the saint could have come to Noricum over ten or even twenty years before, being at first here quite unknown himself (1, 4), this agrees sufficiently well with Eugippius's prior statement (1, 1) that when he came, the Pannonian and other Danube lands were in confusion following Attila's death in 453. If he arrived towards 460, and started to preach a little after, he would have twenty or twenty-five years before he died, in 482, for his labours (42–3). He made for Noricum Ripense near its border with Pannonia, settling first in a 'small town' called *Asturis*—still identified by nothing more than guesswork (p. 124). Regular in church here, and in time asked for a sermon, he gave one that warned of an imminent enemy attack; this was disbelieved, and before it eventuated—that same day—he had decamped to the nearby town of Comagenis (1,2–2,2). Living inside, and guarding it by a treaty they had made with the Romans, was a force of barbarian 'federates'; despite this the inhabitants feared for their safety, and only accepted the saint's call to assure it by repentance when they learned that Asturis had been destroyed. Thus began Severin's ministry; and a nocturnal scare of earthquake, which the federates mistook for a besieging enemy and thereupon fled, only to fall into fight with each other in error, augmented his successes. He was invited next to move over to *Favianis*, and by prayer to rescue it from famine (3, 1–3). There his wrath with a rich widow who had been hoarding food compelled her hastily to part with it, and all were saved by the timely arrival, down the Danube, of a fleet of food-ships from Raetia: the frozen Inn, which had been holding them up, having thawed to let them pass downstream in time to effect the miracle for him. His third success (4, 1–5) was against barbarian raiders, who were sweeping livestock and captives from the countryside. Finding the local tribune short of arms and soldiers, he nonetheless made him take the field, with the result that, two miles from the town, by the Tiguntia river, the raiders were surprised and either fled, leaving their arms, or were captured and brought in fetters to the saint. His commination, setting them free, was so forceful that the township—seemingly still Favianis—never suffered raiders again. The tribune later was made a bishop, Mamertinus (4, 2).

Altogether, then, this eastern area of the province, beside the troubled Pannonian border to which the saint had come first, can be seen as brought by his preaching, and his way of getting things done, into a state much nearer to tranquillity. Though he made himself first a cell, in a sequestered place *Ad Vineas*, meditation showed him his need of a larger base. So he founded a monastery, close to Favianis itself, and brought into his scheme for it everyone he could. The cell he now made for himself was 'only a mile away', in a 'burgus' (presumably a former Roman fortlet), and his work for his people was both spiritual and temporal (4, 6–12). On the far side of the Danube here was the kingdom of the Rugii (Fig. 17), barbarian North Germans; he worked among them too, and had continual dealings with their king and his son and his wicked queen. Eugippius's tales of these (5–6, 8ff., etc.) need not concern us here in detail. But the relationship served his own flock in good stead, and seems wholly in accord with our believing that his first field, the easterly part of Noricum, now had a new lease of life, due in great measure to his personality and efforts. And with this as a base behind him he could look farther west, to Lauriacum and the country up to the Inn, or even farther. Eugippius starts including this with his chapter 11 and onwards. The interest of his record is still similar in general, but the place-names now brought in have the effect of changing the scene. And here we have to recall those topographical problems which our reference-texts have posed, and Eugippius ought to help to solve. The rest of this section will thus be a brief four-part survey, arranged topographically and starting here in the west. The standard modern authors, besides Egger and Vetters 1963, are Pascher 1949 and Noll 1958, whence often Noll 1963. Less often needed here will be Ertl 1965; also Reitinger 1969. The maps to accompany it are Figs. 18–20; in certain parts also Fig. 17.

IV. SURVEY, PART 1: RAETIA-LAURIACUM (Fig. 18)

The Roman town and border-fort of Raetia, on the Danube road, has been seen (p. 103) to have been *Batavis*, in the modern Bavarian frontier town of Passau. Opposite on the Austrian (east) bank of the Inn (Roman *Aenus*) which here joins the Danube, there is equally no doubt about the placing of *Boiodurum*, at modern Innstadt (Noll 1958, p. 28), whence finds of Roman material are attested. The name should imply an earlier, pre-Roman occupation by the Celtic Boii, who seem to have once stretched their dominion thus far (Strabo, *Geogr.* IV, 6, 8; VII, 1, 5, with 3, 11 and 5, 2).

The Roman crossing of the Inn at this place, on what became the boundary of Noricum, will have made it a station for collecting tolls on traffic, and in the Late imperial system a fort, held (p. 106) by a cohort of infantry under a tribune. Its appearing in the Peutinger Map on the wrong side of the Inn (Pl. V), instead of Batavis (p. 103), is of course a mere mistake. In St Severin's time (*Vita* 22, 1–2), the town at Batavis had still its fortification walls, though the other forts on this stretch of the upper Danube (*cetera superiora castella*), abandoned by their occupants, stood deserted. To hold Batavis then was enough, and the saint's few monks established at 'Boiotrum' (Eugippius' spelling of Boiodurum) had on their own side of the Inn no defence. How he insisted on removing them and the townsfolk too, and refused to intercede for the place with the king of the German Rugii, I recall below (p. 145); that, however, was as late as about the 470s. Before its abandonment (possibly 451/3), it guarded the Norican side, as Batavis did the Raetian side, of the passage of the Inn by the route up the Danube to *Regina* at Regensburg (my route (ii); see above, p. 101, with note 3, and the text p. 102). The fork between that and route (i) was lower down, at (or close to) *Lauriacum* (Lorch), to which I shortly shall return. Turning to the map (Fig. 17) we find that route (i), bending west-south-west, makes for *Iuvavum* at Salzburg; it is followed past there by route (iii) and also (iv). And Lauriacum, Iuvavum and Boiodurum mark the corners of the area I have warned of (p. 103) as containing topographical confusion. Yet on the Salzburg route, Lauriacum to Iuva-

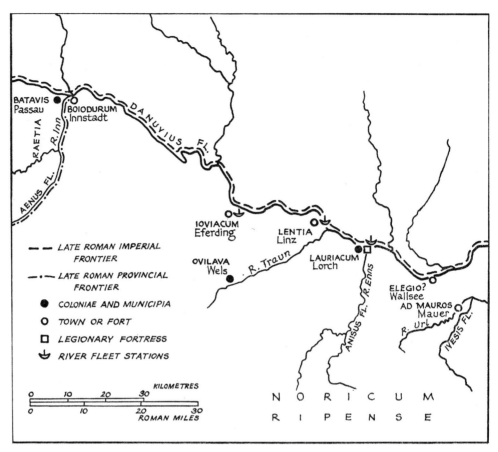

FIG. 18 MAP FOR THE AUTHOR'S SURVEY OF LATE ROMAN NORICUM
RIPENSE, PART I (pp. 109–14). *Drawn by Marion Cox after Architekt Norbert Ullreich.*
ANISUS (river Enns) may be better spelt ANESUS.

vum, one location is in any event certain: *Ovilava* (texts have *-is*, Oviliavis, Ovilabis),
at the crossing of the river Traun at modern Wels. This was the region's chief
civilian town, with the status of Roman *colonia* since the time of Caracalla (211–17),
and centre for civil administration since his father, Septimius Severus, confirmed the
province's governorship to the commander of its legion, at Lauriacum, which required
the civil departments to be close to him. (Brief summary, Reitinger 1969, I, pp. 253–
256.) The two places are distant only some 35 km., or exactly the 26 Roman miles
which the Itinerary, routes (i)-(iii)-(iv), assigns them. As Iuvavum is certain, 60
miles beyond Ovilava, and as the place half way between, *Laciaco*, has an obvious
marker in the lake now called the Attersee, this and the points each side of it on the
Peutinger Map, *Tergolape* and *Tarnantone*, need not here concern us further, nor
those on the route south from Wels into the Alps. The difficulty arises on the Antonine
route (ii), and the answering Peutinger road from Lauriacum to Boiodurum.

Eugippius (*Vita* 24) tells how the warnings of St Severin failed to save, from sacking by the German Heruli (Fig. 17), the town named *Ioviacum*. Its distance from Batavis, which he states was 'twenty miles and more' (*viginti et amplius milibus*), was back along this Boiodurum road beside the Danube, for we already know Ioviacum from its place in the Notitia, where its garrison (above, p. 106) is a cohort of *liburnarii*, in other words a unit of the river-fleet. The Antonine route (ii), along the same road, names it also. The distance between it and Boiodurum there, however, is 38 miles. What the text puts at 20 miles is an intermediate station, *Stanago* (for Stanaco) which I do not map (possibly at or near modern Oberanna). Searching 'more than' this (*amplius*) for Ioviacum, therefore, many have thought to find it a little farther downstream where the Danube turns to the left in a very sharp 'hairpin bend': namely at Schlögen, which has remains of a small Late Roman fort, or fortlet (Novotny 1925, pp. 93–4; Noll 1958, p. 43; mapped by Egger and Vetters 1963). Yet not only should this be too small for a cohort, but the 'hairpin bend' is the start of a course through narrow rocky canyons where the river, twisting and racing, is quite unsuited to *liburnae*: these boats, light and fast, were meant for rowing in quiet waters (Pauly, XIII, 1927, cols. 143–5). And the Roman place-name at Schlögen was very likely *Saloatum* (Kubitschek 1906, on etymology). So to find Ioviacum and the quiet waters, required for its *liburnae*, which the Danube provides once again beyond the canyons, will need much more than 20 miles from Batavis: the required distance will in fact be over 30. Did Eugippius and the monks remember so well, in Italy, mileages in distant Noricum? The Antonine Itinerary, for Ioviacum–Boiodurum, has it firmly as 38 miles. Suiting this, then (at roughly 50 km. from Innstadt), and beside a quiet Danube, I would put the place at Eferding, where I mark Ioviacum on my maps (Figs. 17, 18).

Nevertheless, there remains a problem. The Itinerary distance, on route (ii) up to Ioviacum from Lorch, makes the total of miles 43, whereas, if direct, it is much less, being barely over 36 km., or 25 to 26 Roman miles. Yet 26 miles on route (i)—and (iii) and (iv)—is the distance from Lauriacum (Lorch) to Ovilava (Wels). Our Ioviacum route, (ii), is often given the same road, Ovilava being assumed as the one place that is named between. Yet its mileage to this place is not 26 but 16, and for the place itself the name is not Ovilava but Ovilatus. Lastly its distance on thence to Ioviacum, which is 27 miles, is not only too much to fit the 38 miles Ioviacum–Boiodurum, but is also too much for a road to Eferding straight from Wels, which (at 17 km.) is barely 10 miles. If one emends the text, from 27 (xxvii) miles, the figure instead should be surely 17 (xvii); and this would mean a journey somewhat back along the Traun to a fork for Ioviacum lower down it. If this be accepted it could fit the 16 miles (xvi)—instead of the 26 (xxvi) Lauriacum–Ovilava—which this route from Lauriacum gives to the place spelt 'Ovilatus'. For were that not just a mis-spelling of Ovilava, but the name of a different place altogether, this place could be at the fork; Ovilava at Wels, moreover, could fall out of the route entirely. 'Ovilatus' would fit the text's 16 miles from Lauriacum, and also its 27 on to Ioviacum, at Eferding as already here proposed. This solution has been argued for by Ertl 1965. Although ingenious, yet its acceptance of the text's 'xvi' from Lauriacum to 'Ovilatus', when the route (ii) text, and the (iii) and (iv), have 'xxvi' to Ovilava, which is the actual distance to Wels where Ovilava has got to be, seems equally naïve with its acceptance of 'Ovilatus' as a truly different place. Both ideas neglect the fact of the Itinerary's propensities to textual error both in mileages and spellings. The varieties in the present case seem probably irreducible till we get more facts about roads and sites—including that named *Marinianio* on the Peutinger Map, near to Lorch on our route (ii)—from more field archaeology. At Eferding itself, on the other hand, extensive Roman remains have been found (Novotny 1925, p. 90; Noll 1958, p. 31; mapped by Egger and Vetters 1963). When these authors make it not Ioviacum, however, but the Notitia fort *Ad Mauros*, which was held by *equites promoti*, light cavalry (p. 116 below), they overlook Eferding's fitting so well the Notitia's *liburnarii* who were stationed at Ioviacum, and—though the Danube has shifted course a mile from it now—here would have had waters suited to their craft.

Two names, Lentia and Lauriacum, now remain for completing this portion of my survey. *Lentia*, where the Notitia places mounted archers and also a part of the legion II Italica (p. 106), is unquestionably located in the centre of the modern city of Linz. Roman remains are discovered here in plenty (Noll 1958, p. 31; Reitinger 1969, II, under 'Linz'). Both the hills and the plain each side of it will have suited patrols of the mounted archers on guard against cross-river infiltration. Moreover, in an early medieval ordinance for Danube tolls, the 'Raffelstettner Zollordnung' of A.D. 906, it is named as *Ad Lyntzam*, which links the Roman Lentia with its modern name and implies its having kept an urban identity throughout.[1]

Finally, a few words on *Lauriacum*. The links between its name and the modern one, Lorch, are medieval forms such as those found entered as glosses in manuscripts of the *Vita S. Severini*: 'Loroch' (at 18, 1) in the Vindobonensis 444, and 'Lorach' there in the Vindobonensis 1064, which also (at 30, 1) has 'Loroche';[2] other such

---

[1] Noll 1958, pp. 50ff., with literature. This Raffelstetten ordinance is in *Monumenta Germaniae Historica, Capitularia* II (1896), p. 249, no. 253.

[2] Manuscripts not in Italy, as most (p. 100, note 2), but in Austria like these, would have such glosses, giving locations, for the Latin text's place-names (as here Lauriacum), in the country's vernacular of the glossators' own time.

forms (Loriacha, Laoriaha, Lorache, Larich) are cited by Noll 1963, p. 132, with literature on the Early Christian side besides the Roman (from Noll 1958, pp. 46ff.). To the smaller earlier Roman fort, with its *vicus* on the west, there succeeded under Septimius Severus at the latest (A.D. 205) the primary fortress of the Legion II Italica (p. 103), and its civil town which was made a *municipium* by Caracalla (211–17). A short summary, with excavation-plan of the fortress, is in Reitinger 1969, I, pp. 252–5, following Betz 1956 (*municipium* p. 9, n. 37); two important late cemeteries, Kloiber 1957, 1962. Thus the error made by Mommsen in locating the place at Enns, when introducing (p. v) his edition of Eugippius (p. 101, notes line 3), has outside Austria obtained more credence than it merited: we have seen that Enns, at the Ennsburg where its river joins the Danube, was founded around A.D. 900 as a defence mainly against Magyars. Even after that, Lorch kept its rank as an ecclesiastical centre: its early church has now been excavated under the medieval one, on Roman foundations of what is held to have been a temple (Eckhart 1966). That in St Severin's time it was the see of a bishop, as were all such leading provincial towns when the Empire embraced Christianity, is known from the account by Eugippius (*Vita*, 30: p. 146 below) of the town's being saved from a barbarian night-attack through the saint's guiding the bishop in his conduct of its defence. This bishop, an uncle of St Antony of Lérins (the famous monastic centre in southern Gaul) by name Constantius, is here called the *pontifex*—a synonym for *episcopus*, just as the city is called synonymously *civitas* and *urbs*; neither word implies a metropolitan or archbishop, and the claim for this attempted five centuries later, by bishop Pilgrim of Passau (971–91), as a precedent in support of similar status for his own see, used forgeries of Papal letters which have long since been exposed.[1] The modern excavations in both civil town and fortress have traced sub-Roman buildings (Reitinger 1969, I, p. 332 with references), spreading progressively on to streets and open spaces—of course to save repair of collapsing Roman ones, as in similar cases in Britain, which ought to invite comparative study in detail. So here is the continuity, as of name, so of occupation. It will have lasted at least till the eighth century A.D., when the place was sacked by the Avars, who at that time were engaged on extending their dominion towards the Enns river from its centres in Pannonia. That was in 737; and in 791, when Avar rule was about to be extinguished there by Charlemagne, he halted his eastward march at Lauriacum, still

---

[1] These are the 'Lorch' or 'Passau Forgeries', of letters declared as Papal (Popes Symmachus, 498–514, and Eugenius II, 824–7); much literature has been given to their exposure and significance, summarized most conveniently by Lehr 1909. Bishop Pilgrim, claiming his see's direct succession to Lauriacum, might possibly have made Eugippius's words the start for his pretence that it had been archiepiscopal throughout. Covered in modern literature too is the sack by the Avars which the town yet survived.

then a town, to hold three days of celebration of the Mass there for his army.[1]

To summarize then: from the junction of the Danube with the Inn at *Batavis* (Passau), to that at Ennsburg with the Enns, continuity with antiquity has been kept at three places, all towns and each showing a continuity in name: Wels = *Ovilava*, Linz = *Lentia*, and Lorch = *Lauriacum*. Of the others in our texts, all places less important, we can identify two: *Boiodurum* at Innstadt certainly, and *Ioviacum*, I believe highly probably, at Eferding. The rest, till as far as Salzburg = *Iuvavum*, elude us, and can only be identified afresh through archaeology, with whatever probability this and the texts (if of use) may allow.

V. SURVEY, PART 2: LAURIACUM–CETIUM (FIG. 19)

The Itinerary, 20 miles east of Lauriacum, on its routes (i) and (ii) alike (p. 102), has a station *Loco Felicis*. *Locus* is a well-known word for a place with a Celtic religious sanctuary, but this one enters our period through its naming in the Notitia (above, p. 106), like Linz, with a garrison of mounted archers. The Peutinger Map (p. 104), on what must have been the same road, has nothing for this place, but instead marks *Elegio*, distant from Lauriacum 13 miles. That would be approximately 20 km.; and Roman remains at about this distance have been found at a place called Wallsee (Pascher 1949, col. 160). As against any different site with remains, such as Engel-bachmühle (Pascher 1949, col. 32), the distance makes Elegio at Wallsee likely; Egger and Vetters, however, map the place as the fort of Locus Felicis, rejecting thus the Itinerary's 20 miles from Lauriacum. Ertl 1965, pp. 57–8, sees at Wallsee both a civil site, namely Elegio, and a fort as well, beneath the middle of the town towards the river: not, however, Locus Felicis, but the Notitia's *Ad Iuvense*, on the river because garrisoned again by *liburnarii* (p. 106). This identification (see below) seems doubtful; yet the idea of a joint location, for civilian settlement (Peutinger) and fort (Notitia) had occurred already to Kenner (1868-9, p. 179, with map). Kenner's fort to go with Elegio, however, was Locus Felicis; this meant rejecting Elegio's 13 miles from Lauriacum, and using only the Loco Felicis distance, namely 20 miles. But this ought to negative the joint location at Wallsee. That the German name's first element is from Walch-, standing for Celtic (romanized) natives, like English names with *Weala*- ('Welsh'), is consistent with Elegio as a civil settlement only; and there need have

---

[1] The Avars' entry into Pannonia in 567, and Charlemagne's destruction of them in the late eighth century, need no documenting here; his army's halt in 791 for worship at Lauriacum is recorded by Eginhard (Einhard): *Einhardi Annales* in *Monumenta Germaniae Historica, Scriptores*, I (Berlin, 1876), p. 177.

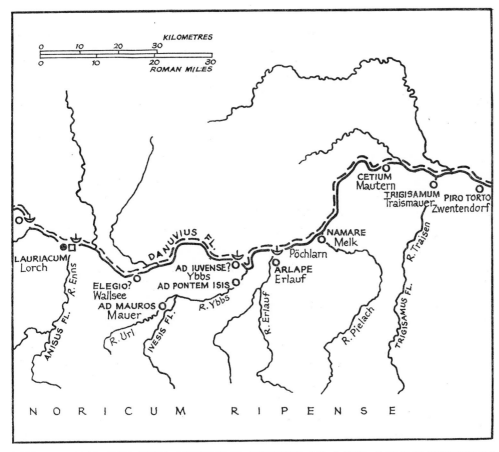

FIG. 19 MAP FOR THE AUTHOR'S SURVEY OF LATE ROMAN NORICUM RIPENSE, PART 2 (pp. 114–19; for symbols see Fig. 18). *Drawn by Marion Cox after Architekt Norbert Ullreich.*
ANISUS (river Enns) may be better spelt ANESUS.

been no fort there, unless one is proved by future excavation. Following Kenner, now, and the distance of 20 miles from Lauriacum, means bending away from the Danube and reaching Mauer on the Url. For remains of a fort are well known here since the early nineteenth century, discovered through the river's washing half of the site away (Pascher 1949, cols. 82–3; originally, Hormayr 1823, I, 2, p. 180). Kenner's Locus Felicis here requires a bend of the road to south; we have to satisfy the Itinerary's distance from its next point eastward, which is *Arlape*—on the Danube once more, for the Notitia, besides assigning it *equites Dalmatae*—Dalmatian horsemen— has a *classis Arlapensis*, namely a river-fleet unit too: here above, p. 106. I shall shortly come to the solution which appears required by that; meanwhile, we have still to deal with Locus Felicis. As there is nothing in the Itinerary's texts to suggest that its distances are wrong here, it seems that the site may still be waiting for discovery, on the

line that one expects for the road (Fig. 17), running straight between Ybbs and Danube, east and west. Mauer on the Url, requiring a bend in it to south, is not only awk-
ward (in spite of Kenner and of Ertl 1965, p. 83), but has an altogether superior claim
as the Notitia's fort *Ad Mauros*. Some have removed this from hereabouts entirely:
Ertl to a point between Lauriacum and Ovilava, in the course of his 'Ovilatus' argument (above, p. 111–12), and Egger and Vetters 1963 to the location at Eferding, preferred here already for Ioviacum. Its garrison was of *equites promoti*, fast light cavalry,
and their purpose thus far south towards the Alps would be patrolling of the ways,
beside the Url and the Ybbs higher up, towards the Alpine crossings into 'Mediterranean' Noricum, which the main road approached from Ovilava across the Enns.
And in a medieval document of date 1030 (Hormayr 1823, I, 2, p. 180), we find that
the *curtis* ('court' of the manor) of the Markgraf Adalbert, on the eastern bank of the
Url just here, is named *Ad Murum*, thus suggesting assimilation, to the common
murum (Mauer, 'wall'), of a name deformed from *Ad Mauros* as the original Roman
place-name.

Thus far, we have found all the other names lost, and of Locus Felicis the site lost
also. *Ad Iuvense*, with its river-fleet unit in the Notitia, doubted as at Wallsee (p.
114), is generally identified with the site of modern Ybbs, where the river so named
joins the Danube (Figs. 17, 19). For the Roman remains here found, see Pascher 1949,
col. 182 (Egger and Vetters 1963 are in agreement); they include stamped tiles of
Legio I Norica—the mother unit of the river-fleet garrison of *liburnarii*—and an
inscription naming *milites Lauriacenses* of A.D. 370 (thus prior to the Notitia). The
medieval spelling was 'Ipsburk' (Hormayr 1823, I, 2, p. 145, n. 26), and both this
and the Roman adjectival form 'Iuvense' can relate to the river's Romano-Celtic
name, *Ivĕsis*. My doubts (for I still retain some) arise only from the fact that at Ipfdorf,
a place near the Danube west from Lorch and upriver towards Linz, Roman finds
have included tiles of stamped *figulinae Ivensianae*: 'of the Ivensian tile-works'
(Kubitschek 1906, cols. 41 ff.). Ipfdorf (Hormayr 1823, I, p. XIX, no. XLVI), in 1137
'Ippha', was a Danube port that lost its function through late-medieval change of the
river-bed—in this like Raffelstetten (p. 112 with n. 1)—and certainly the Danube
in its natural state would suit *liburnarii* there. I do not press this suggestion very far;
I have marked *Ad Iuvense* at Ybbs, but with a question-mark. A little way up the
river Ybbs from here, the Roman road crossed it by a bridge, where there was a settlement, *Ad Pontem Isis* (contracted form of *Ivesis*), put by the Peutinger Map as 8 miles
west of Arlape, the next place here to be considered. Earlier confused with *Ad Iuvense*
(Kenner 1868–9, p. 149, with map), it is now placed at a site (between Neumarkt and
Blindenmarkt) where Roman finds indicate the river-crossing (Pascher 1949, col.

196; 'Ibisivelt' (Ibisi-field) in 1137: Hormayr 1823, I, 1, p. 145; I, 2, p. 20). River-names are recognized as capable of strong persistence, and this is plainly a case in point.

Arlape, named already in the Geography of Ptolemy (2, 13, 3), but spelt in its manu-scripts *Aredate* or *Arelate*, has the latter spelling in the Peutinger Map, but is Arlape in both routes (i) and (ii) of the Itinerary; likewise in the Notitia, where, as seen above (p. 106), there was a force of *equites Dalmatae* there, and also—unlocated—a river-fleet unit called the *classis Arlapensis*. The Peutinger Map mileage 'Arelate'—Ad Pontem Isis being 8, and this, east of the Ybbs, being the distance to modern Pöchlarn, the place has been located almost unanimously there (Egger and Vetters agreeing as expected). Roman remains, both there and thereabouts, are very plentiful (Pascher 1949, col. 111). Pöchlarn certainly suits the river-fleet, being right on the Danube; and as a tributary that joins it here has the German name of Erlauf, a clear etymological derivative from Arlape, the location may seem quite well enough sup-ported by this instance of a strongly persisting river-name. But Erlauf is also the name of a place, 3·5 km. south from Pöchlarn, up this same river; the 'Erlapha' or 'Erlaffa' of medieval documents is equally a place, and plainly this one.[1] Between it and the nearby village of Harlanden, Roman remains have been found in addition to those at Pöchlarn (Kubitschek 1906, pp. 34ff.). From this and from the aggregate abundance of these finds, we may surely infer two forts; and thus explain, in the Notitia, the *classis Arlapensis* fleet unit, at Pöchlarn on the Danube at the Erlauf's confluence, and the cavalry unit of *equites Dalmatae* at Arlape itself, a couple of miles to the south. This also suits the road on which Arlape appears, as we have seen, in both the Map and the Itinerary. The name surviving as Erlauf, then, was not so much the river's as that of Arlape itself. It only remains to note that the Map's next name, 7 miles east-ward and written as *Namare*, is normally sited at the town of Melk, where Roman remains occur (Pascher 1949, col. 90, whence Egger and Vetters, map), but do not yet include specific evidence for a fort: the inscriptions mentioned by Pascher are in the collection of Melk Abbey, but none certainly came from Melk itself.

So we reach the question of *Cetium*. Its name, as we shall see, is Celtic; made muni-cipal no doubt by Hadrian (117–38) it had the title *Aelium*, taken from his family name. The Itinerary's mileage between this place and Arlape is, in route (i) 22, in route (ii) 20. From *Vindobona* (in Vienna) west, by way of a place *Comagenis*, it is 48 miles in (i) and 50 in (ii). On the Peutinger Map its name and a distance for it are missing:

---

[1] e.g. used in the tenth century by Bishop Pilgrim's forgers (above, p. 113 with note 1) in listing the genuine names of the many places which they pretended the bishopric had received from Louis the Pious: Böhmer 1908, p. 308; Hormayr 1823, II, 5, p. 49; Hansiz 1727, vol, I, p. 71.

the Map's '16 miles' to Namare from the place beyond again, named as *Trigisamum*, is 8 or 10 miles short. The Map's miles to Trigisamum from the next place farther (*Piro Torto*) being 8, one might insert the 'viii' a second time, and Cetium along with it, so restoring the original thus supposed (so Ertl 1965, p. 24, table, and p. 80 placing Trigisamum near Kapelln); or what I myself would prefer, correct the '16 miles' from there to Namare (xvi) to xxvi, making the error due to Cetium's being omitted in between. But there is also a Roman milestone, reading XXVI M.P. A C(etio), found *in situ* at a place called Nietzing (some 7 km. south-east of Tulln, Fig. 20; Kubitschek 1894, see further here below). This is a fixed point for our checking the texts by the actual distances. From it, Cetium emerges not where modern writers have wished, at St Pölten (Egger and Vetters, map; Pascher 1949, cols. 129–30). Named from St Hippolytus, its tenth-century monastic founder (Werner 1858; p. 121 below), St Pölten has no definite claim to be a Roman site at all.

Nor is its distance from Nietzing 26 Roman miles (some 39 km.), but barely 24. The place with Roman remains that fits the 26 is Mautern, on the Danube. Mautern is therefore Cetium on my maps, Figs. 19–20, and Fig. 17 (with its title, Aelium Cetium). Its distance from our Arlape locations (Pöchlarn-Erlauf) must favour the Itinerary's route (i) figure—it actually somewhat exceeds the 22 miles—so Cuntz 1929 was right to discount the 20 in (ii). With its distance from Vindobona I deal below (pp. 122, 134). Although its placing at St Pölten was first proposed a century earlier (Schönwisner 1780), the Mautern identification was generally accepted in the period after that (Fortia d'Urban 1845, p. 72) until claimed to be wrong by Kenner, before and after 1880. And Kenner's reason for doing so will concern us much below: he preferred this site for the principal place recorded by Eugippius, as chosen for his chief monastic centre by St Severin—the place Eugippius names as *Favianis*.[1] Kenner's adopted theory had a great success. K. Miller (1916, col. 419, fig. 119) has been the only independent twentieth-century scholar to maintain the old belief in Mautern. Kubitschek (1894), when publishing the Nietzing milestone, being confronted with Kenner's theory had to put Cetium at St Pölten, though this was really belied by the mileage. The longer-known inscriptions, giving Cetium its title, come all from the

[1] Kenner in 1868–9, p. 146, had no Roman name for Mautern because he followed his teacher Aschbach, 1860, in taking Favianis for the same place as Trigisamum, at Traismauer, and Cetium as an older name for the same place again. Later, however, Kenner (first 1878, pp. 312, 317; next 1880, then 1882) turned to follow Huber (1875, p. 313) in adopting the location of Favianis at Mautern, first launched—against the evidence pointing really farther east—in 1849 by F. Blumberger. The earlier nineteenth-century view that Cetium was at Mautern, which as late as 1873 was still maintained by Mommsen (*Corpus Inscript. Latinarum*, III, 1, p. 683), was abandoned by him later for the sake of Kenner, as we shall see.

general neighbourhood of Mautern, east of Melk and north of St Pölten.[1] Abundant finds occurring and excavated in Mautern, mostly east and south of the medieval town walls (Pascher 1949, col. 85; Stiglitz-Thaller 1963), point to the Roman occupation's having been ruined by Danube floods, in the later fourth century and so well before St Severin. The latest context in which Cetium's name is given is the martyrdom here of St Florian—the Austrian patron saint—in A.D. 303, commemorated in the *Passio Sancti Floriani* (Zibermayr 1956, pp. 17–30). The exposure of the site to floods led at last to its replacement, as a Danube harbour, by Krems, on the left bank opposite (Güttenberger 1924, pp. 127–8). Medieval Mautern, mentioned first in the Annals of Fulda for 899 (as 'Mutarin'), was a new foundation near but unconnected with the Roman site. Roman Cetium, however, left bequests in etymology. Its district or *pagus*, in the early Middle Ages, had still the name of 'pagus Cetiensis'; a forest stretching to Erlauf was the 'silva Cetiensis'; and when Bishop Altmann, in 1083, gave his Benedictine abbey near Mautern the name which is today spelt Göttweig, the documents show the forms were then Chotwig, Kotwig, Ketwein (Slavic God-vice): their adjectives in Latin are 'Kotwigensis' and 'Cetvicensis'. Texts here are in Hormayr 1823, I, 1, pp. VII–XII, no. IV: 'in monte Kotwigensis monasterium . . . extruens'; Klein 1781, II, pp. 53, 113. Both editors already discussed the element Cet-, perceiving it rightly as Celtic *cet-*, 'wood, forest'; we shall meet it for the mountain range *Mons Cetius* soon again. But if Cetium had its name from that, the -wig or -wein or -vic (in 'Cetvicensis') stands for Latin *vicus* (village, township): it was the *vicus* of Cetium that had started the town's civilian life, so that *Cetium Vicus* lies behind the medieval 'Cetvicensis'.[2]

In this survey's second part, then, we have signs of continuity, from Celtic and Roman through Sub-Roman to medieval times, in names not only of hills and rivers but also of places and districts or tracts of land. Not often, certainly: others have perished. Wherever this has happened, and topographers are puzzled, we are left with modern theories which I have tried to treat with brevity—just as in part 1, where the confusion was somewhat worse. Whereas signs of continuity in the stretch from the Inn to the Enns seem restricted to Wels, Lorch and Linz, here in the middle stretch they partly affect the country. We shall later be comparing this idea with what we learn from Eugippius about St Severin. Archaeology, from the ground and in the field, should give us more to learn; of as much as it has given to date, in both these parts, I have tried to make the best. But the next part awaits us.

[1] *Corpus Inscript. Lat.*, III, 5630, 5652, 5663, etc.
[2] Finsterwalder 1966, pp. 33ff., has rightly repulsed the 'Germanist' view (Göttweig = Gotti-weig, 'God's home' in Langobardic!) proffered tendentiously by Rungg (1963, p. 80).

VI. SURVEY, PART 3: CETIUM–CARNUNTUM, WITH FIRST INTRODUCTION TO VIENNA (FIG. 20)

East of Mautern, our Cetium, by about a dozen kilometres, the Danube is joined from the south by the river Traisen (Figs. 17, 19, 20: *Tragisa* or *Trigisamus*). And hereabouts the Peutinger Map, though with mileage defective (above, p. 118) has *Trigisamum* as a place. Its next place eastward, by 8 Roman miles, has the name *Piro Torto*; its next again, 8 miles beyond, is *Comagenis*. Of the three this last is the only one to appear in the Antonine Itinerary; I shall deal with its mileages here below. Comagenis is in the Notitia too, with a light cavalry unit which I shall be placing south of Tulln, though not forgetting what ought to be near this too: another river-fleet unit. For

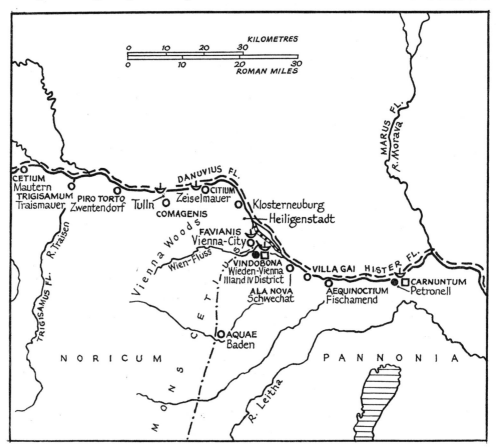

FIG. 20 MAP FOR THE AUTHOR'S SURVEY OF LATE ROMAN NORICUM RIPENSE, WITH PORTION OF PANNONIA PRIMA, PARTS 3 AND 4 (pp. 120–7, 127–44; for symbols see Fig. 18). *Drawn by Marion Cox after Architekt Norbert Ullreich.*

Piro Torto the location now accepted, at Zwentendorf, fits both the Map's 8 miles from Comagenis, and its further 8 miles to a Trigisamum at Traismauer. I prefer at present to hold that this is the best site for Trigisamum, following Pascher 1949 (col. 150), Polaschek 1939 (cols. 132ff.), and Polaschek and Ladenbauer 1948 on the fort there, with walls beneath the medieval town walls.[1]

It is true that the Notitia has no name Trigisamum, but does have an unlocated name *Augustianis*, mis-spelt for 'Augustanis'. This is commonly thought to be due to the Roman unit of Thracian cavalry, the 1st Augusta, here or hereabouts at least in the second century, whose title might have made a name to replace Trigisamum officially, though ignored in the Peutinger Map. (See the *Corpus Inscriptionum Latinarum*, III (1873), pp. 684–5, with no. 5654, dated A.D. 140/4; hence Seeck 1876 (1962), p. 198, n. 10.) The Notitia at 'Augustanis' again has cavalry, now Dalmatian (here p. 106), but its location remains in doubt unless the replacement theory is held. Egger and Vetters, even though holding it, map the place elsewhere, namely north of St Pölten; Ertl (1965, p. 80), though also holding it, gives another location (Kapelln) suiting a theory of his own, whereby the Notitia's river-stations are here distinct from road-stations. Yet both require Cetium not at Mautern but at St Pölten, and this we do not want (p. 118 and here), because it cannot be fitted to the mileages.

Reverting then to Trigisamum, and preferring it at Traismauer, on account of the fort discovered there and the mileages which suit it, we lastly turn to questions about its name. It stands on the river Traisen downstream from St Pölten, which is 16 km. south from it and was founded by St Hippolytus (p. 118 above) in the tenth century. Now a document of 985 gives *civitas Traisima* as the name used before the saint's arrival at this place; from it or near, moreover, came a Roman altar to Neptune, which Hormayr records as reading D. NEPTVNO . . . TRAGISA . . .[2] But whatever the god of the waters may have signified here, we shall shortly find *Tragisa* as the name of the river Traisen. Precious indeed for this, the name cannot make St Pölten, by itself, a Roman fort or a Roman town; while as for the mention in 985 of *civitas Traisima*, it shows that this was the town-district chosen for the saint's foundation, 'in civitate Traisima', but not that the site was its town. No writer about Trigisamum, in fact, has located it at St Pölten. We can therefore pass now to its preferred location, Traismauer. Spelt as in Peutinger with -i-, not -a-, Trigisamum has been

[1] Unlike those of medieval Mautern (p. 119), which have measurements not in Roman feet but in Austrian 'Wiener Klafter' (125 by 115 of these), these walls measure just 800 by 575 Roman feet, giving an area of 16 *jugera*: Novotny 1925, p. 115.

[2] Document of 985: *Monumentorum Boicorum Liber XXVIII*, Tom. II, pp. 208–9. Altar to Neptune: Hormayr 1823, I, Heft 2, Anmerkungen p. 138, which I believe to be its sole printed record.

viewed (as by Aschbach 1860) as a mis-spelt rendering of *tricesimum*, Latin for '30th'. Yet this does not assist the location: if '30th mile', then measured from whence? To guess from Arlape (p. 117–18) would again need Cetium at St Pölten. It is better to begin with the inscription just noticed, and compare its word TRAGISA . . . with the river's name, the Traisen. Should not the German form point back, through medieval loss of -g-, to this very word 'Tragisa', for the river and thence the place? 'Traismauer' is the same with a suffix -mauer denoting its walls; and in a donation of 1112 (Hormayr 1813, p. 105) we have answering forms in Latin, 'Trasamurus' and 'Trasamura'. Without it, one of the tenth-century Passau bishop's documents (p. 113, note 1) gives us 'Trasma(m)'. The donation, again for the river, indeed has also the name 'Trigisama(m)'; yet just as the form with 'Tragi-' was already Roman, in the inscription, so was that with 'Trigi-' in the Peutinger Map. The inscription is plainly earlier Roman than the Map, and the river-name forms with 'Tra-' support its 'Tragi-' through their recurrence. The Peutinger 'Trigi-', due or not to confusion with *tricesimum*, was thus a secondary spelling which has never ousted the primary one. I have used 'Trigisamum' for Traismauer in all my maps, as they answer to the Peutinger so closely in their period, and in Figs. 19–20 have matched it with 'Trigisamus' for the river; but in the general map Fig. 17 I have spelt the river-name 'Tragisa', affirming thus my etymological case.

My placing of *Piro Torto*, 8 miles to east on the Map, follows the finding of this fort-site by the late K. Hetzer, exactly where the mileage points, 1 km. west of Zwentendorf, and the excavations ensuing (Stiglitz 1961). These showed that in the later fourth century the site became flooded, but was partly re-used in the early Middle Ages, first for a Slav and then for a German cemetery.[1]

As for *Comagenis*, on the Map 8 miles farther, it is of course what the Itinerary writes as *Comagena*, distant from Cetium as stated above (p. 117), and from Vindobona, within Vienna, 24 miles in route (i) or (by seemingly different road) 20 miles in route (ii).[2] These and the Nietzing milestone (p. 118 above) should bring the road (by now united) across some 2–3 km. south of Tulln. Roman finds, absent from this

---

[1] Native inhabitants still, in between the two periods, are indicated by the German place-name element in Zwentendorf, 'ze-winden', referring to natives (in English 'Wends'; Latin 'Vinidi', as in the seventh-century chronicle of Fredegar, 'ac Vinidos': *Monum. Germ. Hist., Script. Rerum Merovingicarum* II, 1888, 48 and 68). See further p. 138, with note 1.

[2] The Peutinger Map, where the distances make 21 or 23 miles (according as whether corrected by adding 8 miles or 10: p. 118 above), may have meant a road from Vienna partly different again. One of three roads will have passed through Klosterneuburg and Zeiselmauer, as shown on Fig. 17, a second south of it over the Vienna Woods (the Wienerwald; and on through Nietzing which this map could not mark), and the third using the Wien-Fluss valley, south again. At the edge of the Vienna Woods, approaching the plain of Tulln (the Tullner Feld) the roads

medieval town itself, have occurred here south of it, but the fort *Comagenis* named in the Notitia, with light cavalry garrison (*equites promoti*), is not yet revealed by archaeology. It is likely to lie to east of south, on the west edge of the Vienna Woods ridge. The usual medieval Latin name for this was 'Mons Comagenus', and the German (with many variants) 'Cumeoberg'. It looks as if the German forms began from the ancient name, or in whatever form retained by Late and Sub-Roman natives; but the Latin use of the ancient name unaltered (beyond the mere grammatical termination) is by some suspected as spread by medieval readers of Eugippius. His *Vita S. Severini* mentions the name three times: at 1, 3, *Comagenis . . . oppidum* ('town'); at 3, 1, *ex . . . oppido Comagenis* again, and at 33, 1, *. . . oppidanis Comagenensibus*. The 'town' can be seen from these as fairly far east in Noricum, and also quite near the Danube; any reader knowing that the 'Cumeoberg' had a centre of old habitation, with a German name now much like its own, could guess the identification. Thus when Charlemagne was here in 791 (cf. p. 113), and Eginhard then names a 'iuxta Comagenos civitatem [town] in monte Cumeoberg', the name implying native survival is the German one, as showing the ancient name deformed through time. And if 'Comagenos', here, or in texts from the tenth century on, might be really from Eugippius, this does not, as some have held, rule the native survival out: the 'Cumeoberg' name and its variants make the case for it, and all the better because the Vienna Woods ridge, in antiquity, was reckoned part of the much longer chain, *Mons Cetius*, stretching down to end here northwards out of the Alps (Fig. 17). Thus 'Cumeoberg' for Vienna Woods in the late eighth century (Eginhard) will have come from *Comagenis* locally; and the native habitation-centre carrying the name will have been somewhere on their slope, overlooking the expected Roman site south-east or south of Tulln.[1]

Three further points remain in this sector (Fig. 20). First, on the Danube bank, at the farther side of Tulln, there could well have been a river-fleet station. The Notitia's *classis Arlapensis* (mentioned pp. 115, 117 in connection with Arlape) had a name in fact double; and its second component has no meaning unless (with the old editor Böcking, at his p. 750) we supply two absent letters, and read it as (*Co*)*magenensis*. If this unit had then two stations under the same command (*praefectus*), one being at

---

would become united: on my Figs. 17, 19, a little east of the circle that indicates Comagena. Nothing points to Roman occupation of the site of medieval Tulln, in spite of Pascher 1949 cols. 153–5, and the Egger and Vetters map; these and others followed Schönwisner 1780, pp. 133–40.
[1] The Eginhard passage is *Monum. Hist. Germ., Script.* I (1876), p. 177. Vienna Woods as ancient Mons Cetius: Kenner 1878, pp. 289–92; the same, with medieval change to Mons Comagenus, Zibermayr 1956, p. 295; Koller 1963, again rehearsing charters, re-asserts (like Rungg 1963) Comagenis spread from Eugippius; against, always Hormayr 1823, I, 1, Heft 2, p. 132: he did not like it.

Arlape, the other can have been here. Secondly, the Peutinger Map's next station, 7 miles east, is *Citium*. We need not hesitate to place it at Zeiselmauer (Figs. 17, 20), though Egger and Vetters (map) took this place for the Notitia fort *Cannabiaca*, the location of which is really still unknown. Like Cetium (p. 119), and like the Mons Cetius here, the name no doubt has the Celtic element *cet-* (wood, forest), plainly from the Vienna Woods adjacent. It is apparent still in early medieval forms of Zeiselmauer, as modern 'Zeizinmurus' and Hungarian 'Cezumaur' (Hormayr 1823, I, 1, no. XI, p. 134; Kalt 1867, pl. VIII); the town was a leading Danube port, till it suffered too heavily from floods. And as Tulln, upstream from it, had never been Roman, it will have kept a life of its own beside the Vienna Woods community of natives, providing a boat-harbour for them, just as it also kept its name. Recognition of it as Citium is due to Güttenberger (1924, p. 153); on the site itself, recognition of the fort was followed by excavations there in 1910 (Kaschnitz-Weinberg 1910-11; Pascher 1949, cols. 184–6). Lastly, if we turn now back to Comagenis, and consider its distance from Vindobona on the Peutinger Map, we find this is 10 miles short of the reality; our copy must have lost that 10-mile figure somehow, and with it the name of the station it referred to. The mileage total to Citium must in fact be 16, instead of the 6 which is all that our copy gives; 6 miles along on the Vienna side of Zeiselmauer (Fig. 20) bring us down to Klosterneuburg, where Roman remains have been found in some plenty. Further to Pascher (cols. 63–4), and from excavations in the 1950s, we have amongst those (near the present abbey) the remains of a Christian monastic establishment: see Egger 1957. The name of the place being plainly not ancient, we can only guess that one of those in the Notitia, unlocated (pp. 105–6), may have been its name in Roman times. Of these, rather than *Arrianis* or *Cannabiaca*, the most usual guess has been *Asturis* (Egger and Vetters, Astura): Pascher 1949, col. 63; Noll 1963, p. 18. This name, in the Notitia '*Austuris*' through mis-copying, is of high significance in the life of St Severin. *Asturis* was the 'small town' (Eugippius 1, 1 and 5) where he first arrived and afterwards first preached (pp. 107–8).

From above the Danube here, on the tip of the Vienna Woods, one can look down east over the great modern city, where the Wien-Fluss bends north-east to join the Danube between the Inner City's circuit and the Prater. Beyond it rises the terrace-flank of Vienna's IIIrd district; and around the Arsenal and the Aspang railway station here one has the point where the distance required from Klosterneuburg, 10 Roman miles, ought to place Vindobona. I should add that at Klosterneuburg was found the Roman milestone, *Corpus Inscript. Lat.* III, 5753, on which the damaged mileage figure might be V or might be X; reading it as X, we can see the same 10 miles. The IIIrd district has duly yielded Roman remains. In conventional belief they are those of the civilian Roman town, the *municipium Vindobonensis* (Kenner 1908/ 1910). The same belief places the legionary fortress, of Legio X Gemina, within the Inner City area down on the west bank of the Wien-Fluss, overlooked from the *municipium* on the east (see in general Neumann 1961). This location fails by 2 to 3 kilometres to suit the 10 Roman miles that we require to Klosterneuburg: it is that much too far west, so must leave us to suppose that the miles were measured from the *municipium*. Yet the Antonine Itinerary, with its own still-relevant mileages (pp. 102, 117–18), which habitually names the resident legion when reaching any fortress, does so here just as at Lauriacum and Carnuntum. One would expect then that the fortress, as there and indeed quite normally, would be the point from which all official mileages were measured. We find ourselves introduced, in fact, to a peculiar problem. Where were Vindobona's fortress and its civil town in fact? For the first time, I believe, the present article endeavours to examine and re-assess this problem, and to answer it. It is for this that I reserve the fourth part of my survey. Its importance, while of course topographical, is more than that. With the Vindobona question there arises a further one, of the location of St Severin's monastery: the question of *Favianis*. I have touched on it once already (p. 118), in connection with Mautern. Kenner, deciding to pull the two questions apart, placed *Favianis* there. But far more waits to be said. Our survey must first have its present part completed: down the Danube to Carnuntum.

To begin with, I have to recall that the eastern boundary of Noricum, wherever it ought to be drawn, had Vindobona outside it: that is, already in Pannonia. This holds, of course, for both the *municipium* and the fortress: X Gemina was a legion of the Pannonian command no less than was XIV at Carnuntum. Noricum, when it got one (in the years towards 200: above, p. 113), had its legion at Lauriacum, Legion II. Somewhere, then, we have passed the border and entered Pannonia: under the Late Roman system, Pannonia Prima. The Notitia, in the time of which the two formed one command, that of the 'Duke' entitled *Dux Pannoniae Primae et Norici Ripensis* (p. 104), does not locate the border. But its list includes two of the three more forts which we know, on other grounds, were between Carnuntum and Vindobona. One is *Ala Nova*, where it puts Dalmatian horse. The Itinerary names this too, as one of its route (ii) stations *in medio* along this road (p. 102). With the help of the XXI M.P. A KAR, '21 miles from Karnuntum', inscribed on four extant milestones (*Corpus Inscript. Lat.* III, 4642, pp. 464–6), leaving thus 7 miles of the Itinerary's 28, we can place the site in Schwechat, where Roman remains (Pascher 1949, cols. 137–9) are on record from the village, now much built around. The Peutinger Map, instead of this, has a station *Villa Gai* 3 miles farther east (being 10 from Vindobona), which brings one (nowadays in Schwechat still) near to Vienna Airport: probably north of it near the Danube, but apparently no remains have been found. *Aequinoctium*, the Itinerary's other intermediate station, is located on the Peutinger Map at 14 miles from Carnuntum, and (at 4 from Villa Gai) 14 also from Vindobona; hence its name which the Notitia spells *Aequinoctiae*, assigning it again Dalmatian horse (p. 105). Roman remains have long been known from just here, round the Danube-side village of Fischamend (Pascher 1949, cols. 33–5); the more modern of these discoveries attest the fort's civilian *vicus*, but ruins of the fort itself (so it seems) were seen in 1737 by Pococke ('Pockocius') and Milles, two English travellers (Kubitschek 1929, pp. 76–7). This 28-mile stretch, like the rest of the land behind it, appears bare of ancient place-name elements. It was right in the path of the invasions, across and beside the Danube, summarized above (p. 99), and causing the confusion described by Eugippius (p. 107) as prevailing when St Severin first arrived: *rebus turbabantur ambiguis* (1, 1). And it has plainly nothing to tell of any native survival later, through the succession here of Suebi, Rugii, Longobards, and Avars, the Moravian Empire and at the last the Magyars.

Carnuntum itself, pre-Roman Norican at first, but a great Roman stronghold from the time of Augustus onward, had its maintenance later increasingly interrupted by invasions. Not long before the likely date of the Peutinger Map's original, Ammianus had been calling it a *squalens et desertum oppidum Illyriorum* (book 29, 6: middle fourth century, under Constantius II); and by the time of the Notitia, the legion was represented only by its river-fleet cohort, *liburnarii* for patrolling its many channels of the Danube, while the main fleet was reported as transferred to Vindobona.[1] Carnuntum's name in Roman history, indeed, could not fail to stay remembered; Eginhard, as a well-read cleric under Charlemagne, used it when narrating his doings in 805 (Koller 1963, p. 244), and it passed into scholastic knowledge of geography, as is shown by the famous world map of 1285 at Hereford (Crone 1954). Not surprisingly, for its massive Roman ruins, at least when Magyar Hungary became pacified and Christian (around 1000), were bound to attract attention from intelligent travellers; so they did in

---

[1] Carnuntum as Norican (Celtic) before becoming Roman, Velleius Paterculus 2, 109; compare Zosimus 2, 10 (sixth century): how much did he know? Carnuntum in Roman history and archaeology altogether, Swoboda 1964; in Notitia, here above, p. 105: *liburnarii* of old Legion XIV under *praefectus*. The main fleet, *Classis Histrica*, was officially still here too (Carnunto only by mistake spelt Arrunto), but the alternative recorded, 'or else at Vindobona' (by mistake spelt Vindomana) 'transferred *from* Carnuntum', shows what certainly had happened. The fleet was *Histrica* because the Danube, on reaching Pannonia, began to exchange its Celtic name Danuvius for *Hister*, its name throughout south-east Europe (in Greek spelt 'Istros'). On this change of name, at the Norican border, in regard to *Favianis*, see pp. 128–9 below, with note 2.

Renaissance times (e.g. Lazius 1546, II, pp. 7–8), and after the retreat of the Turks again from some in the eighteenth century, as Marsigli 1726 (pp. 232–3, with fig. 1), and in 1737 the English Pococke and Milles (Kubitschek 1929, p. 37). The site is really two: the legionary fortress, discovered between two villages (near the modern Hungarian frontier), Deutsch-Altenburg and Petronell, and the civil town, which was made the *Colonia Carnuntina*, two Roman miles to west, within Petronell itself (Pascher 1949, cols. 21–5; Swoboda 1964). Both, through the invasions ensuing, became deserted. Only in the tenth century, when the Magyar Hungarians had met defeat from the German empire and would soon be turning Christian, was the frontier against them here given a fortress of another kind. This was the town and castle of Hainburg; looking east from higher ground, right above the Hungarian borderland, it might perhaps cover a pre-Roman Norican hill-fort (note 1 opposite),[1] and anyhow stands for a new regime, a millennium from that time. But the events of the millennium's second half had broken all local links with the first. And since the East Roman Empire had reckoned Pannonia as a province to be bestowed (as it could not be held) by treaty, and had conceded it so to a series of peoples from the Huns to the Hungarians, we must see the provincial boundary, which divided it from Noricum, as in great part explaining what appears such a contrast: Noricum, as I said before, was never given away. It was left—and by no emperor, but Odovacar—to itself. Rather like Roman Britain, in fact. But its boundaries were inland ones; which brings us back to the question where to trace its eastern boundary, and so to the Roman—and Eugippian—topography of what today is Great Vienna.

VII. SURVEY, PART 4: VINDOBONA AND FAVIANIS (FIG. 20)

Vienna today, as an extended modern city, covers even more ground than does my map Plate VI, which shows its extent and surroundings a hundred years ago. This presents H. Fischer's map of 1869, a 'Relief Map' with contours (5 Klafter = approx. 10 metres) stressed to bring out the gradients and height of the rising ground, and showing also how the Danube, formerly winding and branching, has been canalized to an even course, with its branch nearest the city made into a canal. At the south-east corner, Schwechat (the Roman *Ala Nova*) shows the road that leads in here from Carnuntum; and at the top, west of the Danube, the clustering contours mark the

[1] This German folk-name, meaning Hunn-burg, 'burg of the Huns', suggests something prior to the castle, seeming ancient (so vaguely 'Hunnic') to German settlers strange to the land. (Deutsch-) Altenburg itself, 'burg of the old [the ancient] people', taken usually thus to refer to the ruins of Carnuntum, leaves one wondering why there were two such names. But I leave this to conjecture.

steepening slopes of the Wienerwald, the Vienna Woods ridge, to be crossed for reaching *Comagenis*. In the middle, the river entering from the west is the Wien-Fluss, joining the canalized Danube close to the east of the Inner City; the contour-lines from the Wienerwald side spread down to it, and the three lines opposite show the terraces up to the Arsenal and adjacent railway-station, noticed above (p. 124) in connection with *Vindobona*. The whole displays what geographers call the 'Vienna Basin' (*Wiener Becken*). Between *Ala Nova* and *Asturis*—if this was really Klosterneu-burg (see p. 124) on its spur of the Vienna Woods, north of the map—we have more than one Roman name to accommodate. Besides Vindobona, there is *Favianis*.

The Notitia tells us that Legio I Norica (or *Noricorum*: Seeck 1876 (1962), p. 198, 40–1; my p. 106) was now a river-fleet unit. Its *liburnarii* had a cohort (*quinta*, the fifth) at *Ad Iuvense*: that of the *partis superioris*, up-river and supposed at Ybbs (p. 116 above, with Fig. 19). But the prefect of the legion's main or primary force of *liburnarii* had his station 'at Fafiana' (*Fafianae*). This name, with the ending plural and v for the f, is the Favianae (Jones 1964, III, p. 372) which Eugippius, using its locative undeclined, calls Favianis—the place that figures so much in his *Vita Severini*. And the force's being not of the 'superior' part, but therefore lower down the river eastwards,[1] agrees with his record that the saint arrived, to settle at first Asturis, next Comagenis, and then Favianis, 'in the borderland of Noricum Ripense and the Pan-nonians' (1, 1; echoed in the prefatory letters: his own at para. 10 and Paschasius's at para. 2: p. 100, n. 2). The same was later known to the historian of the Lombards, who came into Pannonia in 526/7: namely Paul the Deacon, who says that in his *Noricorum finibus* had been the monastery of Blessed Severin, now entombed at Naples (*Historia Longobardorum* 1, 19). The monastery, states Eugippius (4, 6), was *haud procul*, 'not far' from Favianis. And not only was it near the Danube, as the Notitia requires, but near the Danube at a place where its names, Danuvius and Hister, were close together; they were the upstream and downstream names respectively (p. 126 here, note 1), and the former's use (Celtic) ran at least to Vindobona.[2] For Eugippius tells (10, 1–2)

---

[1] Similarly in Pannonia the XIVth legion's *liburnarii* had their 'superior part' cohort at Car-nuntum, their main force at *Arrabona*, down the river at Györ (Raab) in modern Hungary.

[2] For the placing of the change of name, see *Geographi Graeci Minores*, ed. C. Müller, II (Paris 1861), p. 496, on §9 of the anonymous compendium called the Hypotypōsis, where the place's name is written corrupted to a meaningless οὐδούνου. The editor Tennulius (Amsterdam 1671; never mind that he was wrong in thinking the author was Agathemerus: Müller pp. xli–xliv) emended this to οὐινδοβούνης (= Vindobonae). Müller's note cites Strabo, Joannes Lydus and Ptolemy for the change as at places lower down, in Pannonia or farther (himself conjec-turing 'Noviodunum' near the Black Sea!), but Pliny for its coming 'where [the river] reaches Illyricum'. This could loosely include Pannonia (as p. 126 here, Ammianus), where Celts had mixed with 'Illyrians' and so will have caused the names to overlap. But in Noricum and higher,

how the monastery porter, one Maurus (earlier ransomed by Severin from barbarian captivity), on a day when the saint had warned him of danger if he went anywhere outside, let a 'worldly man' take him off fruit-picking, at midday, to the second milestone out from Favianis. Barbarians soon appeared and bore them away across the Danuvius. At that same hour the saint in his cell, shutting the book he was reading, called 'Fetch me Maurus at once!' When the porter could not be found anywhere, Severin himself instantly took boat, and pursued the brigands (*scamaras*) with all speed, 'wending along the river-channels of the Hister': *Histri fluenta praetermeans*. Presenting himself, he cowed them with awe and they gave their captives up. This is the only place where Eugippius writes 'Hister', as against 17 places where he writes 'Danuvius': at or near Favianis 9; at Comagenis 1; for Noricum upstream, or Raetia, 5; vaguer mentions, 2. Did he write 'Hister' here because he remembered—his tale is so vivid—that the saint on this occasion had boated downstream, to some spot where he was sure he could cross and take the brigands by surprise? Can we see the winding channels, if we look at Plate VI again, as those of the river from opposite Vindobona downwards? Anyhow, it looks as if Favianis was close above that. Just where, however, has been a long-debated question.

Its placing at Mautern by Kenner (1880; above, pp. 118–21), followed by many like Egger and Vetters, at Zwentendorf now by Ertl (1965, pp. 104–16) and earlier at Traismauer by Aschbach (1860) and at Mauer on the Url by Pallmann (1864, p. 398), had certainly each one reason besides the wish to reserve all Vienna for Vindobona. This was also used by Mommsen, supporting Pallmann, in the *Corpus Inscript. Lat.*, III, p. 687. It was that Eugippius (22, 4) gives the distance to Favianis from *Batavis* (Passau) as '100 miles and more than that' (*centum et ultra milibus*). Pallmann was indeed not the right man to support, for the distance to Mauer is only about 75 miles. But the distance to anywhere in Vienna (around 220 km.) is more than 150 miles, and Mommsen thought Eugippius should be taken to mean less. His memory, however, should really not be trusted on such matters; Noll, though believing in Mautern, does agree with this in general (1963, pp. 121, 134), and here we have seen the same (p. 111) on Ioviacum. His '100 miles and more', then, cannot invalidate other evidence. Pursuing this, we must next revert to Klosterneuburg.

The book of Kramert and Winter, 1959, followed the then still new discovery of an early Christian tomb beneath the eleventh-century church that stands at Heiligenstadt,

---

where Celts had been fully dominant, the Istros or 'Hister' name ceases to be claimed and only 'Danuvius' prevails. So Tennulius may have emended better than he knew; and Eugippius, our only author with a resident's local knowledge, can have marked the change quite rightly at the Pannonian-Noric boundary.

not far from Klosterneuburg, guessed to be Severin's *Asturis* (p. 124), on a hill standing out from the Vienna Woods and in the city's XIXth district. Excavation of this
tomb in 1952 had found it constructed within a Roman building, with the present
church standing over it. It was empty. Heiligenstadt was medieval Heylegenstatt
(place where holy one has been laid) and has a twelfth-century record of being known
as 'Locus Sanctus'; the traditional explanation, as connected with St Severin, even
if due to later guessing, appeared yet likely to be right. For the tomb could have been
that built for him at his death in 482 (8th January: Eugippius 43, 9), and empty because
of his translation to Italy by his monastery's brethren six years afterwards (44, 6–7).
That belief, formed in consequence of the discovery and then made known, was met
with doubt and quickly with ridicule and rejection: the sequence showing this is that
of Neumann 1952 a-b; Thaller 1953; Neumann 1954 a-b; Noll 1954 pp. 53, 80–1;
Lechner 1954; Egger 1957 (delivered 1954); Neumann 1956 and finally 1962, treating
of both the discovery and an ensuing excavation, in an account written as final and
published in Germany. Kramert and Winter meantime, however, in their book of
1959, gave their own reflections on the affair thus far; and Winter 1959 (pp. 44–5)
declared his conviction that Heiligenstadt itself was Favianis. While Aigen (1959,
1963) supported the contrary opinion, I myself upheld the two authors, in a book-
review (Haberl 1960). I showed how impossible it was to continue with placing Favianis at Mautern—insistence on which had been a principal reason for the views of
the prevailing opposition. In a further one (Haberl 1964), which covered the account
put out from Germany, I had to notice weaknesses it showed over facts disclosed by
the excavation (p. 144 below); yet by then, and already in 1960, I was looking at a
problem that remained beyond it. Favianis and Asturis had both been in Noricum.
Taking Noricum's border as along the Vienna Woods, Klosterneuburg could be just
inside it, Heiligenstadt hardly. This was a factor influencing the identifications.
But had it really run there? The question must be reopened.

The authority is the *Geography* (second century) of Ptolemy. Noricum and Pannonia had their boundary, he tells us (2, 13–14) along 'the Ketian range of mountains':
τὸ κέτιον ὄρος, in Latin the Mons Cetius. Renaissance and subsequent geographers
therefore drew it (Ortelius 1579, p. 50; Mannert 1818, p. 152) along the crest of the
range of the Vienna Woods, cut by the upper Wien-Fluss but stretching to the Danube, broadly northwards, from Baden (the Roman *Aquae*: Fig. 20). Kenner 1870 drew
it on the range's western side; thence Polaschek 1939 (col. 977), Zibermayr 1956 (p.
295), Egger and Vetters 1963, and general belief. To include Klosterneuburg and
Heiligenstadt, of course, it has to be shifted, nearing the Danube, to the eastern side
instead. But in any case, making the 'Ketian range' the Vienna Woods only (as on the

Egger-Vetters map) is against Ptolemy's intentions. See my Fig. 17: the range bounds Noricum altogether, right over southward to the Drave and the Save; even *Celeia*, now Celje in Yugoslavia, was just within Noricum, and this full length for the Mons Cetius has been well recognized (Klein 1781, pp. 116–17; Kubitschek 1934, pp. 52–53). In contrast stands the case (my pp. 122–3) for expecting the final northern appendix to the range, the Vienna Woods (Fig. 20), to have been called the Mons Comagenus, as a local name taken from the nearby Comagenis, and deformed into German 'Cumeoberg' or its other medieval variants. Fig. 17 hence marks this name in Latin, Mons Comagenus, with that of the Woods in modern German: the well-known Wienerwald. The full-length Mons Cetius was well remarked by Graf (1936, pp. 23–24) to be virtually as long as two degrees of latitude (some 270 km.) and as wide as one degree of longitude (some 80 km.): it was a general name for the multitude of mountains and hills stretching from Celje (and the Kolos mountains) up towards the Danube. More than a hundred years ago the Styrian Knabl (1866) published a study of this borderline, between Noricum and Pannonia, based already on good material: Roman military inscriptions, and tile-stamps. His result was to draw the line not along the crest of Mons Cetius, but rather by its eastward skirts, at the start of the plains that pass into Hungary. He further opined that rivers, flowing south-east from it or north-east, might in certain places mark parts of the border (his pp. 76–7) more conveniently than hill-slopes. So can archaeological topography explain how a text, here Ptolemy's, ought to be interpreted. The border along the crest has been in general an error; still more so is any on the westward side: it was the eastward skirts that counted, with parts of rivers at times assisting. Knabl has been undeservedly forgotten. But if, with our map (Fig. 20), we now look again at Plate VI, we must wonder where the province's border could be drawn when the skirts are sloping to the Vienna Basin. The slopes of Vienna Woods fall right down into it: they are disguised where getting lower and gentler, of course, by the buildings of the extended modern city, yet towards it from Heiligenstadt and Klosterneuburg they hardly let a provincial boundary make sense till they reach the bottom: at the river Wien-Fluss. To draw the boundary beyond Vienna Woods, west and north, e.g. with Egger and Vetters, takes Favianis and St Severin over-far from Vindobona; we have seen that already. So what other course is left? Is this not a place for assistance from a river, from the Wien-Fluss, in its course through the city to join the Danube?

The stream (its ancient name unknown: p. 136) has its natural course shown in the map on Plate VII. This is from Eisler 1919, and gives the natural physiography of Vienna's Inner City (seen in the centre on Plate VI) on a convenient larger scale (1:18,750 as here reproduced, with contour-lines at 1-metre intervals). The principal modern buildings and streets superimposed, show its relation to the Ring, where stood the latest line of former fortifications. Its winding course is heading north-east where it enters the map; it is piped underground till it emerges at the Stadt-Park, where it is canalized as an ornamental water through the park, between the Kinder-Park and the Park-Ring, to reach the Danube Canal, just beside its former mouth to the nearest channel of the natural river. How it looked in former days, when the fortifications were standing, with their moat filled with water, is strikingly displayed by the bird's-eye view reproduced as Plate VIII A. This is the eastern portion, as Plate VIII B is the central, of the view (from north-east) over Vienna done in 1609 by Houfnagl. It shows how the stream (marked WIEN FL. in foreground) had cut into the flank of the terrace-ground rising, on the left, to what is now the IIIrd district, then open country still. Between this and the Inner City (Plate VIII B, with the Cathedral of St Stephen, and the curve to the Graben on the right of it: compare Plate VII), the Wien-Fluss had only a quite narrow trough to flow through. When its waters at any time rose, the constriction could thus cause flooding. And such was the occasion, in the Roman third century, of the votive dedication of an altar to all divinities, naming especially those of the waters, to appease them and forfend the river's floods. The inscription was found *in situ*, in 1899, during the work of the river's modern canalization, on its right bank near the Kleine Marxerbrücke bridge: on Plate VII, the fourth of the small bridges (marked *Marxer Br.*) on its canalized course just opposite the Stuben-Ring, and the Marxer Gasse leading in from the east (the IIIrd district). This, as we shall see, was lower down its course than its expected point of crossing by the main Roman road, yet still within the narrows that would cause it to flood. The year is 233, and the dedicants were two: high officers acting jointly, each the commander of a legion. One was Marcus Atilius Regulus, Legate of Legio I Norica; the other, Marcus Rufinus, Legate of Legio X Gemina Pia Fidelis, the legion at Vindobona.[1] Vindobona being Pannonian, why was the Norican legate joining him, if the river had not harmed them both alike, because its course was where their provinces met?

We have already begun to see where the Vindobona fortress was: on the right bank of the Wien-Fluss, where in Plate VIII A there are fields, above the scarp in its terrace-slope and somewhat to south, from the Arsenal and railway-station beside it (Plate

---

[1] *Corpus Inscript. Lat.* III, Supplement II (1902), p. 2328[41], no. 14359[27], gave this often difficult inscription only its first publication, with reading by von Domaszewski and Kubitschek. Revising it, and permitting thus my interpretation here, the stone was re-published by Neumann 1967, pp. 20–1; his 'Wien-Fluss-Valley-regulating' (*Wienflusstalregulierung*) must be seen to refer to 1899: more effective than the Roman *comprecatio* of divinities. See p. 156.

VI) to the botanic garden amidst the buildings north from that, which surrounds the Belvedere Palace. Both these Plates display the advantages of position, typical of the choice of site for Roman fortresses, which this plateau situation in Vienna's IIIrd district would provide for a fortress just here: overlooking the whole Basin, with the Danube and its farther bank, commanding the Wien-Fluss crossing and well placed for communications, with Carnuntum and also with Pannonia farther south. Here the Turks, for the Siege of Vienna in 1683, placed their camp, around the place of the later Belvedere (itself a revealing name); its suitability to Romans was long ago perceived: Prandau 1789, p. 9; Weiss 1872, p. 16, Note (based on work by the Surveyor von Hauslab and by A. Camesina, an expert on the city's development famous in his time; on the Turks here, Camesina 1865, pp. 96–7); Süss 1897, pp. 11ff. Eisler 1919, plate A1, is my Plate VII. Nonetheless, from the days of F. Kenner, active from 1865 to 1919, this has been seen as the site of the civilian town, *municipium Vindobonense* (Kenner 1897, pp. 107ff., 1910; Neumann 1961, cols. 73ff.). Yet what are the principal finds here? Stamped tiles do include the mark of a civilian tilery, of Antonius Tiberius of Vindobona (no. 18, p. 586 in *Corpus* III, 1), but also (pp. 579–80) of the Tenth Legion Gemina Pia Fidelis, in garrison here till the times of the Notitia (p. 105 above) from the end of the Dacian wars or the death of Trajan (Mócsy 1962, col. 616). On its way to those wars (101–8), the Thirteenth Gemina was here, beginning to build the fortress and leaving stamped tiles and building-stones, to be followed perhaps by the Fourteenth before it settled at Carnuntum (Mócsy cols. 614–15). Among the finds referred to by Neumann and assembled first by Pascher (cols. 167–72: as from the supposed *municipium*), are Vienna's only known inscriptions to Mithras, favourite deity of soldiers; tombstones are military, epitaphs again are of soldiers (Neumann 1967, pp. 21–4); and the large trenches recorded as 'rubbish-pits' by Kenner (1897, p. 120), containing swords and other military objects with human skeletons, should be recognized now as mass graves of soldiers who had died in battle, like those at the Vindonissa fortress in Switzerland, determined by Ettlinger (1961, col. 103). Besides some large coin-hoards and more various material, arched tunnels on the first terrace up from the Wien-Fluss (aqueducts?), and remains of Roman buildings near the Belvedere in the gardens (Kenner 1897, pp. 107ff.), the more recent discovery of two defensive ditches, parallel and 284–5 metres apart, under the Klimschgasse and Keilgasse (streets near the Rudolf Hospital), was referred by Neumann 1961 (cols. 61–2), to an auxiliary cavalry fort for the Flavian regiment of Britons, *Ala Prima Flavia Britannica*. This should have been prior to any legionary fortress; and its presence, in Inner Vienna, is attested by inscriptions (*Corpus Inscript. Lat.* III, nos. 4575–6 and 15197). They are on tombstones, and I shall come to them below. But whether these ditches belonged to that or another early auxiliary fort, one would hardly expect its site to pass (as Neumann still believed) to the civil *municipium*, letting the fortress follow in the Inner City on a site supposedly virgin. Besides what I shall soon be saying on that, there is a general point to be noticed. Such civil towns by a fortress were usually placed on its safer side, as in Britain at Caerleon on the south (Nash-Williams 1952, with map) and in Austria on the west at Lauriacum and Carnuntum. Here it would be the contrary, with the fortress behind the Wien-Fluss, safe on the low Inner City peninsula (Plate VII), and the civil town up on the open plateau to the east (Plates VIII A and VI). Lastly, here by the railway past the north-west corner of the Arsenal, early this century, was found the track of a Roman road (Kenner 1910, col. 130). Ten metres wide, it was traced for 100 metres; and answered neither to the course usually assumed for the main frontier-road, on the *Landstrasse* well beyond the Arsenal's eastern side (Plate VI, running due north-west, and thence Plate VII, ending opposite the Park-Ring), nor to any alignments offered within the circuit of the Inner City. For Roman topography, this is strange.

Let us look once again at the distances, by road to or from Vindobona, which our written evidence gives: pp. 103–4, 118, 122, 124–5. The Antonine Itinerary puts the legionary fortress, of Legio X Gemina, 27 miles (corrected to 28) west of Carnuntum; onwards to Cetium (past Comagenis) it has 48 and a better figure, 50 miles. On the Peutinger Map, the stages from Carnuntum add up to 28; the distance west to Citium (on the way to Comagenis) we have seen we have to correct, from the 6 that it gives, to 16. In addition to these, we have several Roman milestones, found *in situ*, which state their mileage from Vindobona. That of Klosterneuburg (p. 124), read as X M.P. A VIND, '10 miles from Vindobona'—5(V) would be far too little—gives more than the real mileage from the Inner City of Vienna, but the right one from the IIIrd-district plateau east of the Wien-Fluss. On the south, where a road led away from the Danube, to *Scarabantia* (Fig. 17: Hungarian Sopron), five Roman milestones are extant from Inzersdorf (Plate VI lower edge). The earliest is of A.D. 143, the rest ensue in the third century: *Corpus Inscript. Lat.* III, 4649–53. Four of them give IIII M.P. from Vindobona, and the 4 miles are too little here if we start from the Inner City: only the IIIrd-district site will fit them. Next, on the Carnuntum road, we have four more stones, from Schwechat: *Corpus* 4642 and 4644–6. They give their miles from Carnuntum: XXI, leaving 7 or 6 (from the 28 or 27) to Vindobona. Even 7 brings us hardly past the IIIrd-district railway-station (Aspangbahnhof), short of the Inner City thus by 2 miles. Finally, on the south-east edge of the IIIrd district itself, near its boundary with the IVth, but in the sixteenth century, the stone *Corpus* 4647 was found, *in situ* and giving Vindobona II miles. The 2 miles take us near to the edge above the Wien-

Fluss, but cannot be stretched to reach the Inner City.[1] The location in the IIIrd (or IIIrd/IVth) district, therefore, seems certainly that from which Roman distances were measured; in other words, as normally, the legionary fortress.

This part of Vienna, where the Landstrasse enters, so now known as 'Landstrasse' itself, had a medieval name of its own which we know from the thirteenth century. This was 'Widem'. It is attested in a grant dated 1211, and printed by Hormayr 1823 (I, 2, Heft 3, p. 185), of lands which are defined by perambulation of their bounds. Having proceeded 'towards the east below the bridge of Wyenn', these pass 'to the high bank' (*ad litus altum*, high river-bank), and thus complete the stated bounds 'of Widem' (*iam dicti quod vulgariter WIDEM dicitur*). This of course locates 'Widem' up east beyond the Wien-Fluss. In the seventeenth century the topographer Georg Mathäus Visscher, in his 'Eastern Prospect of Vienna', shows the name extended between Landstrasse on the east and the whole course of the Wien-Fluss from south-west to north-east: Visscher 1672 (1920), print no. 2. This carried it farther down, over the modern IVth district (originally called Bernhardstal). Fuhrmann 1765 (p. 351) spells it 'Wieden', and these lower quarters 'Neu-Wieden'; but as its primary area came to be more generally known as 'Landstrasse', the lower quarters captured the name of Wieden for themselves. Thus it is those (between the Wien-Fluss and the Favoritenstrasse) that are alone called Wieden today. Though the district's common seal was given the canting device of a pasture (*Weide*), remarked by Fuhrmann, this is not the name's origin (as Egli 1893, p. 999; Müller 1897, p. 178). It comes neither from 'Widmer', which was the Old City quarter round the Witmarkt,[2] where the 'Witmer Tor' was later replaced by the inner gate of the Burg (imperial palace), nor again from 'Diu Widem', Old German for 'donation' (Müller 1897, p. 178; Grienberger 1894, p. 24); all these old etymologies are fanciful. For in the Slav languages, Czech and Slovak (with Polish also), the name for Vienna is Vidēn. It has been seen since the days of Müllenhoff (1882, editing Jordanes' *Getica*: at 166[b]) and Wessely 1893 (pp. 174–6), that this will have to be a derivative, Slav or already Avar, of the Roman name Vindobona. When Pannonia was held by the Avars, and then by the Slavs of Great Moravia (Graf 1936, p. 13; Bekker 1890, p. 175), they naturally knew its boundaries; this name can be no more recent than that. Slav 'Baschova' from

---

[1] Its exact position was still known to Prandau 1789 (p. 115), and before him to Schönwisner 1780, who observed (p. 128) that from here the distance to the Stubentor (the Inner City's nearest gate) was 72 Klafter (or 140 metres) short. For the supposed Roman fortress site protected by the Graben (middle of my Plate VII) it would be nearer 1,000 metres short: almost three-quarters of a Roman mile.
[2] Afterwards, as still today, called the Kohl Markt (charcoal market); I suggest that *Wid* meant 'wood'.

Batavis, whence the German Passau, Celje from *Celeia* and Ptuj from *Poetovio* (my map Fig. 17) are similar formations, comparable with (German) Augst from *Augusta*, and the well-known many others; although Neumann 1961 (col. 53) seems unclear on this, the interval for deformation is not too long. The buildings in the 'Widem' or Landstrasse district, too, referred to as late as 1398 as visible ruins,[1] will through that interval have still been monument enough: can we really imagine they were nameless? It is true that for the Wien-Fluss to be fancied as named 'Vidunia', on a constructed stem for Wien as if derived from Vindobona (Öttinger 1951, p. 74), is a theory lacking all direct ancient authority, despite its adoption on the Egger and Vetters map. But the Viden-Widem-Wieden chain of genuine names transcends this. Can its meaning be fancy too? I hardly think so.

The Slav Viden of course has meant Vienna altogether. It confronts us, then, again with the question of a Vindobona inside the Inner City. The conventional belief has been that the legionary fortress, established around A.D. 100 (p. 133), was built on virgin soil in the city's northern-central portion. My Plate VII shows how the street called the Tiefer Graben ('Deep-ditch Street') passes from the filled-in Danube bank south-west up a cleft in the natural relief, till it reaches the diagonal Herren-Gasse. The fortress's west front is supposed to have stretched along that cleft, turning for a south front in line with the Graben: Plate VII and also Plate VIII B, where this is the broad street that crosses the middle from the right, curving forward by the cathedral. The turn to an east front (by the Kramergasse and Rotgasse, making for a north front facing the river by the Salzgriess) need not detain us here; defences on all these sides indeed there were, but the outline's being Roman is a notion that grew up from the fact that these defences were medieval.[2] They were the city's walls before its enlargement to the size presented in my plates; 'oppidan' and castle quarters antedating any enlargement were in the late thirteenth century still inside them.[3] That their outline was one of Roman walls was an eighteenth-century theory (Fischer 1764, p. 55; Fuhrmann 1765, pp. 59, 67). And in spite of the unmilitary choice of

[1] List of properties then held by Vienna's Irish (Scottic) monastery: 'Auf der Stetten [regular German for a place with old ruins] in summitate custodie et in principio circa Rusten circa Rennweg incipiendo et versus Lantstrass transeundo': Hormayr 1823 I, 1, p. LX, document xxi.
[2] For the eastern front, the wall described by Kenner 1897, p. 56, note 2, which gives the original excavation-report, had bricks of a shape and size (the measurements stated) which in my experience declare them medieval; so in the Heiligenstadt 1961–3 excavations (here pp. 130, 144, and Haberl 1962).
[3] Thus in the treatise on the Translation of St Deliciana, by Gutolf of Heiligenkreuz (1281–7), fugitives flee within the walls of the city in its main and other mentioned portions also: . . . 'fugerunt . . . . pars intra moenia urbis Wienne [the main walls], pars in oppidis, pars in castellis . . .': ed. Redlich and Schönbach 1907/8, p. 12.

situation, remarked on above (p. 134), the Vindobona of this theory was the fortress. The discrepancies with likelihood, or with facts such as those of the mileages, have some of them occasionally had some notice, from some scholars: Pascher 1949, cols. 175–6, must be mentioned here with due respect.

What really Roman finds, then, has the Inner City given us? Some inscriptions of Flavian auxiliaries, we have seen (p. 133), but those are prior to any legion. Tombstones, if legionary (p. 133 again), go to the other site; on this one, they are civilian, wives with husbands: Neumann 1967, pp. 20, 25–7, nos. 17, 29, 33. Behind his belief in the fortress here (Neumann 1961, cols. 62–75), we have Polaschek 1944 (pp. 95ff.), Novotny 1923, and behind them all, Kenner 1897. Kenner did think (see below: his pl. III) that there had also been a smaller fort. But the walls claimed for that have been today pronounced medieval: by Neumann himself (1961), when repeating, with plan (cols. 67–9), the accepted legionary fortress. The western half of the site appears quite bare of Roman finds, but for remains of conduit-drainage on the edge of the Tiefer Graben, directed at its rivulet (Plate VII), the former Ottakringer Bach. And these can have belonged to the smaller fort, discounted now by Neumann but claimed, as just noticed, by Kenner 1897 (pl. II: his pp. 86–7) from walls reported in four places.[1] It is between the lines of these walls only, I believe, that Roman finds have occurred in any amount. Against the face of the northern wall was built the church of St Ruprecht (excavations here, Schmeller 1951):[2] Vienna's second oldest church. The oldest, St Peter's, is somewhat farther outside the area, and was built on virgin soil; this was quite clear from excavations on the spot (later than Neumann 1961) which I myself inspected. That both these oldest churches should have been built outside those walls, while of course within the area supposed for a larger fortress, can suggest that in Carolingian times the smaller area only, not any larger one, seemed Roman to their builders. Building churches outside walled towns that had been pagan, rather than inside, was a custom that of course they knew. Thus the smaller area's Roman use, though no doubt begun early, might also perhaps last late.

We can take this notion further. On the city map Plate VII, where St Ruprecht's church is marked close to the filled-in Danube channel, there appears below it the Hoher Markt; on Plate VIII B this is right in the foreground. Sites along its northern side, when cleared in 1965, disclosed what had been the headquarters building of an

[1] Wipplingerstrasse 6, Lazzenhof, Gundelhof, Steindlgasse; to Neumann 'impossible to recognize' for a fort-plan.
[2] Unaware, it must seem, that in the fifteenth century this church had collapsed, and had had to be rebuilt from its foundations by Georg von Auersperg in 1436: Hormayr 1823 II, 1, p. 110 (from Lazius 1546).

early Roman fort: Ladenbauer 1966, p. 42, first-century (Flavian) in age. Believers in the legionary fortress, including Ladenbauer herself, were surprised, for this had been Neumann's place for the legionary baths. Moreover the fort of that Flavian regiment of Britons, placed by him (p. 133) away up in the IIIrd district, was now to be seen as the fort that had had the newly found headquarters. For the regiment was the one that had left the three military tombstones, known as found within the Inner City before (p. 133): there would of course be plenty of room in it for the regimental cemetery, outside a fort of auxiliary-unit size. So far, so good; but there follows more. The headquarters building's remains (disclosed in cellars after war-time bombing) were built up into modern and fifteenth-century walls, but none Late Roman. On this site as a whole, however, we have medieval record of a structure called in thirteenth-century German the 'Vinidenburch'. In this name, the '-burch' (for 'Burg') explains the forms mis-spelt with e, 'Berghof' and 'Perckhof', here later applied to this, which was reputed the oldest dwelling in Vienna. The 'Viniden' stands for 'Wenden', showing again, as on p. 122 (n. 1), this name in medieval German for pre-German natives, to be credited with any strange old work. Such could be really Roman; and if built of stone, like a 'Burg', might have been Late Roman, renewing the place of the former early headquarters, and standing here by the time of the Notitia. There is a plan, too, that marks this place in Latin as 'Castellum'; authenticated today for the year 1137, but having long been thought to be forged, I place its evidence in a footnote.[1]

We may now go back, before turning again to this 'smaller fort' in the Inner City, to the walls and gates adduced for belief in its legionary fortress. The topography above explained, with my Plates VII and VIII B, has shown us that before the enlargement they present, Vienna had been walled to give a quadrilateral outline. As late as 1386 (Fischer 1764, p. 90) it could thus be called 'Wienn, die stat auf dem hoff': its castle (Hof, Hofburg) and 'oppidan' part were still not external (p. 136 with note 3

---

[1] A. Mayer, in a long article on the growth of Old Vienna, in the *Blätter des Vereines für Landeskunde von Niederösterreich* for 1877/8, documents the Vinidenburch p. 394, n. 3; but he decried the plan with 'Castellum' as a forgery. Its ill repute had followed its publication by G. Zappert, in the Academy of Sciences' *Sitzungsberichte* (*Phil.-historische Klasse*) for 1857, pp. 399–444, as of the city estates of the See of Passau in 1137; hence its name of 'Passauer Rentplan'. Accepted when Zappert had first discovered it, the change of opinion against it, which made him out its forger, must be ascribed to his race: he was thus a victim of antisemitism. But it is now among the manuscripts in the Austrian National Library, where expert scrutiny and ultra-violet radiography, performed at my request, have shown the plan to be authentic. So 1137 holds good for 'Castellum'. Was this 'Burg' then (partly or entirely) of Roman stonework? And if so, would it not have belonged to a small Late Roman fortified town or fort, resuming the site of the early fort with this as a new headquarters? Such a building would have been standing in the time of the Notitia; I return to the idea on p. 142.

for the 1280s). That the outline first was Roman, walling the legionary fortress, is the belief that has grown by stages from the eighteenth century onwards: medieval walls and gates would have been preceded thus by Roman ones. Lines could be drawn straightened to conform with Roman practice, but could start from a known medieval gate if standing over a Roman one. On the south, where the line is set by the major medieval gate, the triple-arched Peiler Tor, still standing in the seventeenth century,[1] it is drawn to pass in front of the church of St Peter, in the Graben (Plate VII). A wall was indeed revealed here in 1964, but it was found, when I inspected it myself, to be medieval. Moreover, it was off the line prolonged for the Roman direction westwards (Neumann 1961, cols. 68–9 and notes 160–1). For a Roman south gate, the fortress's 'Porta Decumana', what he takes as a left-hand tower coincides with structure left by the Peiler Tor. It is clear that for Vienna, to prove any Roman walls and gates, as against medieval work that is anyhow known to have existed, calls for the greatest care alike in excavation and in measurement. There have been further opportunities now through sewer-trench excavations. On the east front (p. 136: from the Graben towards the river), in a trench some 12 metres deep at the crossing of the Kramergasse and Ertlgasse, there was lately disclosed a portion of wall that was slanting from the trench south-eastwards, 2 metres thick, and viewed as part of the projecting outer northern tower of a gate. A main east gate here, or 'Porta Principalis Dextra', would suit the line commonly expected for a road across the fortress, its 'Via Principalis', south of the Hoher Markt and Wipplingergasse, to the west front drawn along the Tiefer Graben (Plate VII, with p. 136 already). Where the line meets this, there has been supposed a Roman west gate, the fortress's 'Porta Principalis Sinistra', but the state of the evidence noticed above (p. 134) is hardly encouraging. The brief general sketch including the sewer-trench discovery (Langmann 1971) leaves the literature still without distinctions, clearly defined, between acceptably Roman and medieval stonework. Two-metre wall-width, in itself, scarcely suffices; as for bricks, see p. 136 with note 2. The subject of bricks, however, brings us on to the bricks or tiles, famous in Roman studies because impressed with lettered stamps. The number of these from Vienna and relevant other Roman centres, besides inscriptions on stone, is what does most to allow the movements and locations of the legions, each from its own tile-stamps, to be charted by historians. And for the opening of the reign of Trajan, the turn of the first and second centuries, such tiles have brought them to confidence that fortress-building here, where no legion had been before, was done by two in quick succession: the XIII Gemina starting and the XIV

[1] See Eisler 1919, plate IV, reproducing Bonifaz Wohlmut's map of 1547, and plate XVII, reproducing W. A. Steinhausen's of 1710.

Gemina completing it. Trajan's wars away in Dacia, taking them off, then followed; and from their end (say towards 110) the garrison was X Gemina, which remained a long time and is well attested (Mócsy 1962, cols. 614–16). Can anything, in the light of this, be advanced about the topography?

The first of these legions came here from Poetovio: Ptuj on the Drave (Fig. 17). The building-tiles it made there may be stamped LEG XIII only, but begin the fuller series soon plentiful at Vienna, adding letters for its title (G, GE, GEM) and others following. Mommsen, discussing them in 1873 (*Corpus Inscript. Lat.*, III, 1, pp. 580–581, under the general number 4660), found already one (his 12*b*) read earlier by Lazius (1546, I, p. 41) as LEG XIII GE POT or POET, which can suggest it had been made at Poetovio. The legion then marched to the Dacian wars, yet has a tile-stamp (Mommsen's 20) reading LEG XIII GE CAR, suggesting some manufacture at Carnuntum. So although the Vienna tile-stamps include a fair number where the letters following the title stand for names not of places but persons, or other official nomenclatures, yet some can be place-names still. And no. 7 in Mommsen's series, which he cited in three examples, follows the title with FA (or in one of them, possibly FAB: this was an old find, read by Lazius). These like many of the rest are from Vienna Inner City.

Was it the supposed fortress here that Legion XIII started, XIV completing it, as in general belief? Yet the tile-finds known are in the 'smaller fort' area. It is normal for tiles at auxiliary forts to be those of the relevant legion; might the finds be explained by this? Or by the legion's having its tile-works here? We have viewed already the independent case for a fortress elsewhere, namely at a Vindobona on the IIIrd-district plateau. If Vindobona was the Inner City, why the tiles that end in *FA(B)*? Of the only similar ending known in an inscription here on stone (*Corpus Inscript. Lat.* III, 1, p. 565, 4557), a civilian's, whose list of his civic offices ends with PRAEF. CO..FAB., the accepted meaning is 'prefect of a *collegium fabrorum*': of a craftsmen's guild, not of soldiers, and neither a personal nor a place-name. Mommsen in the *Corpus*, using Renaissance scholars' transcripts—the stone was found in the sixteenth century and lost by the end of the seventeenth—picked *FABR* from Augustino's, and took the previous word as *CO(LL)*. Yet accepting this (with note on it by Stiglitz 1963) still leaves the tile-stamps facing us. The 'prefect' was a citizen of civilian Vindobona, the municipal town that grew beside the fortress later on (p. 133). Our tiles of course are military, of Legion XIII, and the first for a possible fortress here at all. But unlike perhaps Poetovio and more probably Carnuntum, Vindobona has never in any form appeared on them. Certainly their final letters may stand for place-names only seldom, yet its absence calls for remark; and so, on a few, does the presence of *FA*.

Let us move to the second century after Trajan's wars were over. The fortress-garrison now becomes the Tenth Legion Gemina. Its tiles may have LEG.X.G. for this, or LEG.X.G.P.F. for its full title, Gemina Pia Fidelis. They are *Corpus* III, 1, 1459 (at p. 579), and no. 6 has final letters in six varieties (*a-f*). Variety *e* ends PR·V· A·F.; variety *b*, to give it in full, reads LEG·X·G·FAB. This is one from Lazius (1546, p. 671, 1161), found in Vienna. On the city's modern outskirts, at Oberlaa, has been found a tile that I myself have inspected; it reads LEG X G P F FA*J*. So FAB or FA*J* or FA or F can point to a name recurring, in stamps of both the legions. Might it then have been a place-name, and be Fab- or Fav-ianis? We know Favianis was on Norican ground, on the west of the Wien-Fluss, yet near to Vindobona. We are not quite sure, at this point, about locating it. But neither are we, now, about locating the *municipium*: the civilian Vindobona mentioned above. Where was it? We want the IIIrd-district site for the Vindobona fortress. Still less can we be sure about the municipal *territorium*. An inscription from Maria-Lanzendorf, to south but from a Norican direction, recorded in the eighteenth century but lost, was read as FABIANA COHORS VINDOBON(ensis) MVN(icipium). And the milestones considered above, from Norican situations, take their distances from Vindobona fortress, although this was Pannonian. Was this because the Vindobona municipal territory took an enclave out of Noricum, within which there stood these milestones? In that case, or in any, legionary tiles produced at Favianis, as those here adduced may now seem to have been, can have been used on either side of the Wien-Fluss here alike, without upsetting the provincial border as such, and without confusing the two distinct primary locations, Vindobona on the east and Favianis on the west. The fact seems to be, that so much expenditure of learning has still not obtained a better topography than we have: in part from lack of sufficient facts from archaeology, in part from weakness in interpreting those available. One sign of this has been the eagerness to remove, away from the city, the name of Favianis; and this despite the pointers towards its really being at home there, including those afforded by Eugippius.

Why has this been? Why a Vindobona in the Inner City? In 1669 Peter Lambeck of Hamburg, Petrus Lambeccius Hamburgensis as he wrote himself, dedicated to the emperor his Commentary on the Imperial Library. He himself was the Librarian. He declares he has made much study of the numerous names which scholarship had proposed for Vienna in Roman antiquity. He has come to the conclusion that Vindobona is the right one; fifteen other names he has found he has to reject, two of them being *Faviana* (Favianis) and *Fafiana* (the same in its Notitia spelling). It is therefore not unjustly, he declares, that his Library, the most august library of the Caesar who is his emperor, should have been named by him Bibliotheca Vindobonensis. His grandiose baroque Latin merits quoting below in full.[1] With each of the Library's manuscripts thus made a 'Codex Vindobonensis', and with the name used on every Vienna book in printed Latin, it was hailed wherever Latin was used, confirming all those who had been using it so already, and was honoured by the world of scholarship thus until the time, towards a century later, when scholarship began its embracing of topography, and a Fischer or a Fuhrmann in the Vienna of Maria Theresia felt that its Inner City had got to enclose Vindobona as a Roman fortress. In short, Vindobona has had the greatest prestige. Favianis, by comparison, though sanctified by St Severin, has been a name of small account—and even uncertain in its grammar. I do suggest, nevertheless, that we take it now more seriously.

There seems a good case for believing Favianis to have been the ancient name of all the site on the west of the Wien-Fluss, with the Flavian auxiliary fort garrisoned by Britons, and with somewhere or other soon a military tile-works; afterwards, in relation still unclear with the civil *municipium*, and in Late Roman times with the Legio Prima Norica, the name of a fort, or a small walled town little different from a fort (as in those times so frequently). This garrisoned town or fort of Late Roman times will have followed the first-century fort in the lines of its defences. It will be the place named in the Notitia with the spelling *Fafiana*, and held then by the legion as a river-fleet force with galleys. Finally, we will find it as *Favianis* where St Severin, after his earlier deeds, came to build his monastery near by. Vindobona, by then probably little but Roman ruins, had a name to pass to barbarian tongues, but is never named by Eugippius. And though its name as later deformed could cling again to its old location, to spread thence farther, or more loosely over the whole, there is a companion problem still in the transmission of this other name, Favianis. We have two

[1] Lambeccius 1669, p. 34: 'Wiennam Austriae nec Viennam, nec Biennam, nec Vianam, nec Vendum, nec Galbiana, nec Flavium, nec Flavianum, nec Ala Flaviana, nec Aras Flavias, nec castra Flaviana, nec Flavabim, nec Faviam, nec Faviana, nec Fafiana a Romanis olim appellatam fuisse, superest ut porro demonstrem, eam vero ab iis genuino nomine suo ab iis vocatam fuisse Vindobonam, ideoque Augustissimam Bibliothecam Caesaream haud injuria Vindobonensem a me cognominari.' From the Peutinger Map (p. 101, n. 2), new found in the sixteenth century, Vindobona had to be seen as Roman Vienna's only name; the Hamburger Lambeccius, like Philipp Cluverius (*Introductio in universam geographiam tam veterem quam novam*, Brunswick 1678, p. 287), had received this as a point assured by the best Renaissance scholars: Ortelius, 1579 (p. 50) and before him Beatus Rhenanus (*Rerum Germanicarum Lib. I*, Strasburg 1530, p. 103). Arrived in Vienna itself, and strange to beliefs retained in Austria, he could put these into eclipse. Yet in the light of modern etymology (Müller 1879, p. 181) Vindobona and Wien are names quite unrelated—a position confirmed by the study 'Der Name Wiens' in 1912 (author anonymous: *Berichte und Mitteilungen des Altertumsvereins zu Wien*, XLV, pp. 5ff., p. 12). (To write Vindobona into Pliny, *Hist. Nat.* III, 146 (written no later than A.D. 79), in his list of 'towns' in Noricum, could never be a sound emendation of the text's 'Vianiomina'. What it should really mean, I hope to show on another occasion. J. H.)

sets of medieval forms, one with Fa- and one without (-Viana or -Wienne). The first
set might be ascribed to medieval knowledge of Eugippius's Favianis (compare the
Comagenis case, p. 123): certainly none seem earlier than the first claims of Passau
(tenth century, p. 113; later also of Freising) to authority as 'episcopus Favianensis'
here. Yet that at least shows that the location had then been recognized; was it wrong? [1]
In the second set, Byzantines used 'Biana', so did Arabic and Turkish: independent
of Eugippius, yet ignoring Slavic 'Viden' names, its use recalls the Geographer of
Ravenna (seventh century), in whose text we have *Cliena*, no doubt mis-copied for
'Biena'.[2] Somehow, then, a name without Fa-, and never with -d-, will lie behind the
German forms that have given modern *Wien*. To make it nowadays a monosyllable
(rhyming English *queen*) follows the false derivation claimed by Lambeccius 1669
(his p. 57) from the Vin- of Vindobona, against the two-syllable Wienn (see Plate
VIII B) or Wian, with spoken stress (Wiénn, Wián, Vĭān) on the second syllable, as
in Austrian dialect everywhere still ('Wiān') to the present day. But it is time that
from etymology we should return to archaeology.

Besides his monastery near the walls of Favianis, St Severin made himself a hermitage in a 'more remote' spot which local people called the 'Burgus' (Eugippius 4, 7):
presumably a disused Late Roman fortlet. It was 'one mile' from Favianis, say the
manuscripts (4.7): all but the Vienna codex 1064, a twelfth-century manuscript (R^s)
from Salzburg. This has 'five'; says local people *call* (not 'called') it the *Purgus*
('Burg' with a P being frequent medieval German spelling); and lastly, over 'Favianis', has written in *Wiena*. Mommsen 1898 (pp. XXIV–v), following Kenner 1880,
declared that the Salzburg scribe had changed the text here on purpose, to indicate a
spot known to be 5 miles from Vienna, and thus equate the city with Favianis arti-

[1] That it was invented by the Freising bishop Otto von Babenberg (1109–58; see his *Gesta
Frederici*, printed Basel 1619, p. 213), was the belief declared by Lambeccius 1669 (see note
1, p. 142), whence Kenner 1880, pp. 62–3, 75, and 1882, pp. 30–3. On Passau (with p. 113) see
Hormayr 1823, I, 2, Heft 3, pp. 73–4. Later documents using 'Favianis' or 'Favia': Hormayr I,
1/2, p. xxi, doc. no. VI, of 1159; p. xv, doc. v, of 1158, ducal charter for the Irish (Scottic)
monastery in Vienna; its presence, and home connections, will explain the form *Fafna* (from
Irish) which must account for the 'Fatna' in the Hereford Map of 1285 (see p. 126 here): Crone
1954, p. 14, from Miller 1895, p. 15. The Arab Idrisi's map, which could use Western sources,
while giving 'Ubiana' in Idrisi Oxford 1, has in an Arabic copy (Leningrad) 'Vaviana', or
some form similar: Miller 1926, pp. 43ff.; Jaubert 1836/40, pp. 357ff.
[2] Ravenna: Schnetz 1940, pp. 58–9. Byzantine: Müller 1897, I, with p. 166; Lelewel 1851, pl.
XIV, map drawn from Idrisi, again with 'Biana'. Arabic and Turkish: the forms as passed
to the nineteenth century were given me, verbally, by the Vienna University Oriental Institute;
the Old Arabic forms were at my request carefully read to me in the Austrian National Library,
by Mr S. Balič of its Oriental Department, from the photograph-reproductions in Miller 1926.
From the bibliography in Öttinger 1951, however, it can be found how much theorizing has
confused and transcended what can only be these two basic sets of forms.

ficially—like the Freising bishop and the rest (p. 143, n. 1). Marcus Welser in his edition (Augsburg 1595), based especially on the eleventh-century manuscript from Regensburg St Emmeran (R^m, now Munich 14031), has also 'five miles'. But need this make the equation wrong? Was Eugippius's 'one mile' right? We have found cause already (pp. 111, 129) to question his memory for mileages. Heiligenstadt, where the empty tomb was discovered as I previously have explained (p. 130), would be 5 miles measured from the Vindobona site, from the Vienna Inner City site less, though more than one. But the measurement seems less important than the fact, already here mentioned, that the tomb was in a Roman building, older than itself and much resembling such a *burgus* as that at St Margarethen in the Burgenland, south-east of Vienna, excavated in the 1930s by A. Barb, and published by him after the war (Barb 1948). Neumann 1962 (pp. 480–2), took the Heiligenstadt building for a 'granary': an unexpected feature of an exposed situation, not far above the Danube in a place where it was fordable, and one not at all so consonant with the facts of the excavation as a *burgus*, which the comparison with Barb's site suggests. I pointed this out in my review in *Die Furche* (Haberl 1964); also that his 'empty grave of a child', next to the tomb, was no doubt a place of baptism. The excavation report, by my friend G. Mazanetz, was generously made available to me for closer study.[1] I judge it as possible, then, with a fair degree of likelihood, that the grave was not only that of St Severin himself (p. 130), but was purposely placed in the 'Burgus' which he had taken for his hermitage, and where 'the quiet of his little cell delighted him'.

VIII. CONCLUSION

When the saint passed away, in January 482, with his monks around him and Eugippius himself amongst them (43, 8–9), an outrage against the monastery was committed by a prince of the Rugii, the Germans over the Danube with whom he had so often had dealings, though space forbids my narrating them fully here (p. 108). This (44) was Ferderuch, the brother of the Rugian king Feva; he arrived to seize the clothes that were kept for dispensing to the poor, and terrified a soldier called Avitianus into looting for him the altar plate, with its chalice of silver. He then pillaged everything and left the bare walls only, taking all his spoils away beyond the Danube. Within a month, indeed, he was murdered by his nephew Frederic, the king's own son; but these doings moved Odovacar, still ruling as king in Italy, to reply by making war. The Rugii were defeated, and Feva and his evil queen were taken prisoner. But

[1] Unpublished at the time of my writing this (1971), it has been held by the Wissenschaftliche Arbeitsgemeinschaft of the Brotherhood of St Severin, Vienna XIX, since 1962.

Frederic, who had fled, soon returned; a stronger expedition came, under Hunwulf Odovacar's brother, so that Frederic fled again, to the Goths far down the Danube. But Hunwulf then declared, in the name of Odovacar, that all 'Romani' must migrate out of Noricum to Italy. Thus came about the removal of St Severin's body, in 488, when the monks left their monastery and presently reburied him where they built their new one at Naples. The evacuation has to be viewed as the end of a truly Roman Noricum. Odovacar's war certainly wrecked the power of the Rugii. But his purpose in quitting the Danube none the less was to concentrate in Italy on defence against the east. For the Goths from there were soon setting out to invade him, by the head of the Adriatic (Fig. 17). Their king was Theoderic, through whom the Eastern emperor Zeno meant to ruin him, making in his stead an Italian realm (besides Pannonian and Illyrian) for the Goths. In the bloodstained years 488–93, it was done; and only when Theoderic had died, in 526, did the Longobards or Lombards start, from the north, to enter Pannonia—later to pass to Italy in their turn. But Noricum, our subject here, lay aside from these events; and likewise now, on the west, from the Alamanni. It was Baiowari, after retreating from Bohemia into Bavaria, who later began the infiltration here down the Danube. Natives would thus have an interval of time, still unknown to us directly, to aid the saving of their remnants. The 'Romani' had gone. But what of the natives not so classed? Cannot our survey, helped by Eugippius, give an idea of what to expect of them?

Its part 1, the highest up the Danube, led us to judge (p. 114) that native continuity, although too slender to leave much light for us on countryside topography, could anyhow keep the town-names of Wels (Ovilava), Linz (Lentia) and Lorch (Lauriacum). And if country life at all near the river had been ravaged, by the raids for loot and captives, there were always the hills behind, southward up to the skirts and valleys of the Alps. Over the Inn in Raetia, Eugippius tells how Alamanni (19, 1; 25, 3; and with Thuringi, 27, 1–3 and 31, 4) were in Severin's time such ravagers that he advised and prompted flight: from Quintanis (Künzing, Fig. 17) to Batavis, and thence into Noricum (24–7). Yet the country was not devoid of all chances of escape; and the time of the final flight, hardly before 470–5, came late enough to have assisted the survival which the three towns' names imply. At Boiodurum, across the Inn from Batavis, when the saint foretold its destruction, and saw no use in trying to beg for it (22; p. 109 above), Eugippius shows us the people as accustomed still to commerce, and even as led by worldly motives to go for Christian saints' relics (22, 1–2); yet they were also used to work in the fields. For when the German Hunumund attacked them, his party (*comitatus*) could be small, because almost all of them were busy with the harvest, leaving only forty men to guard the town (22, 4). Thus town-dwellers were living off the land around them. These in Boiodurum, indeed, had angered St Severin through having disdained him and his warnings, just like those in Ioviacum, which then was surprised and sacked by the German Heruli (24). Such towns indeed, or forts (if small, there was not much practical difference: e.g. 17, 1, 'oppida vel castella'), had their class of poor, and of captives, whom an economy like this kept hungry. Yet at the saint's example many could afford them tithes of their own foodstuffs; and though inuring himself to cold, he arranged to hand them out clothing, even possibly from Noricum Mediterraneum. From its capital Teurnia (Fig. 17; by Eugippius spelt Tiburnia), he got a combined gift promised, but warned its citizens that they too might soon be needing it, to help to appease needy barbarians. Not long after, when Gothic raiders appeared from the east and besieged them, they used it to assist in buying them off (17, 1–4). So the Alpine and sub-Alpine lands had corn and also sheep, whence the saint tried for supplies, both of food and of woollens, to help his Danube lands.

Rural economy in general, then, was not by any means ruined; and the Germans' raids may be explained in good part as for snatching its produce, and its labourers, for themselves. One raid into inner Noricum (25), by Alamanni, even ravaged the country and left the forts intact. Though our part 1 of Noricum Ripense, like the Raetian lands adjacent, grew in Severin's time too exposed to let its former life go on, yet the farther into the hills it stretched, the better the chance for remnants. Eugippius and our survey show only the gradation's open side. Even at Linz, the Danube cuts through hills; at Wels, Ovilava was too big to be forgotten, though its remnant folk would be safer up the Traun, or moved to Lorch. To Lauriacum, here, came all the refugees from the destruction of walled places farther west (28). Trade was still bringing goods; and though the hardest to get was olive-oil—of course brought from Italy—the saint distributed even that: all the poor people brought their vessels to receive it in, and the capacity of his jug appeared miraculous. As for woollens from Alpine Noricum, a party bringing them was caught by snow (29), but got across through following a bear—again apparently a miracle. Lauriacum itself was large, and for its protection had patrols (30) to warn it of any enemy force approaching. A time came when St Severin, knowing better, spent four days urging the poor countryfolk outside to bring themselves and their possessions within the walls, which he insisted, through the bishop, should be manned the next night. Enemies had come, with ladders, and were waiting hidden in woods; but a townsman's torch, setting fire to a haystack, scared them into staying there till morning, when they departed with only the animals of one man who had defied the instructions, while the populace praised the saint for averting its ruin and captivity. Thus even after the withdrawal from fortified places farther west, Lauriacum—at least when St Severin was in it—could maintain both its urban and its suburban rural life.

In our part 2, from Lauriacum east as far as Cetium, we surveyed a region that let us guess a survival somewhat stronger (p. 119). Untraceable sites were fewer; place-name hints were less few; and mountain communications to south could again be seen as viable (pp. 116–19). Now, reading Eugippius further, we reach his important chapter 31: Lauriacum, with its refugees from the west and all its people, is approached in arms, from the east, by the king of the Rugii. This Feva (or Feletheus) has long had dealings with St Severin, whom the people therefore beseech to go and appease him. Going 20 miles through the night on foot, he meets him at morning—probably at or near the unlocated Loco Felicis (pp. 114–16). From the narrative and the speeches that Eugippius makes them utter, the issue between the saint and the king is clear. The king wants to empty Lauriacum of its inhabitants, to save them further risk of attacks from the west by Alamanni and Thuringi, and remove them to towns opposite his own stretch of the Danube, which rendered him tribute—one of these being Favianis. The saint is agreeable to this, but will not stand for brute force; if accepted as an agent, under God, he will promise to get the removal made as a peaceful migration. Mollified thus, the king at once retires with his army; the saint arranges the peaceful migration, and distribution among the tribute-paying towns, of the people at Lauriacum whom he had taken under his protection (31, 6: 'in sua fide susceperat'). They live thereafter in the friendliness of allies with the Rugii, while the saint, back at Favianis in his own old monastery, keeps prophesying to the people of the towns that they all, one day, shall freely migrate to a Roman province. Those that later did so, as we have seen, were the 'Romani'; and the saint's Lauriacum emigrants are likewise called 'Romani' here.

The region to which they went, where towns paid tribute to the Rugii, close across the Danube (31, 1), was quite far to east of Lorch and the Enns: to get within 20 miles, Feva had had to march some way, since the news of his starting well preceded him. It will hardly have stretched any nearer than the bend of the Danube northward, from Melk to Mautern (Fig. 19), so that the towns would be those surviving from here to the east. And this way there rise, beyond Tulln, the Vienna Woods; this is already our Part 3 (pp. 120 onward, with Fig. 20). By Comagenis, and round the end of the Woods where the Danube turns south again, past Klosterneuburg and the Woods' south-eastern flank, the region runs to the Wien-Fluss, which (pp. 130–2) we have seen as the boundary of Pannonia. Hereabouts was where St Severin's mission had begun; and here was where his dealings with the Rugii and their royalties had so helped—as we can now perceive—to procure a situation in which regular tribute took the place of desultory raiding, and the Rugian king's protection that of local deals with 'federates'. He might fail to control his men at times, as in the case (p. 129) of the fruit-picking porter. And of how the saint dealt, Eugippius has further stories, such as that (8, 1–6) of the prince and the royal family's goldsmiths. We may pass by these to observe that the 'Romani', being several times mentioned as having 'captives' of their own, might themselves practise raiding against Germans. But in St Severin's activities, once this region was more secure and had his monastery as his base, in going to the dangerous lands upstream, and gradually evacuating all who would heed his warnings, till he finally accomplished this at Lauriacum itself, we can see a consistent policy, philanthropic but also prudent, of strengthening his primary region and thus the Rugii as well. That Odovacar, himself too distant in Italy, appreciated this—and not only for the saint's having prophesied his greatness (p. 107)—is plain from his letter to the saint (32, 1) after Lauriacum had been cleared, promising to fulfil any wish he might declare. As at the same time or near it, to 'nobles' praising Odovacar, he foretold that his kingdom would last another thirteen to fourteen years (32, 2, where Eugippius of course is aware that his destruction by Theoderic came in the years around 490), the Lauriacum clearance will have been about 475, some seven years before St Severin's death.

Those were then the final years of peace for this region, in a prosperity enough to supply the Rugian tribute which assured it. His prophecy of eventual migration to a Roman province (31, 6) shows him sure that it would not last: at his death in 482, as we have seen, the Rugii set about destroying it. But since this brought them their own destruction, through Odovacar's war of punishment, the Noricans left behind when the 'Romani' retired to Italy—amongst them Severin's monks with his coffin (44, 7) on a horse-drawn waggon—could find themselves sequestered, with the hope that they could still continue. That they were numerous enough, with even some 'Romani' still amongst them, has long been a thesis in Austrian handling of the so-called 'continuity problem'. Reviewing this at large would exceed the purpose of the present study. That the garrisons of the Notitia, back before the days of Attila, had left their mark on the land's demography, will be obvious. Its soldiers included Germans; and the events of the fifth century, with armies marching through and local raids from German quarters, can have widened this element in the Romano-Noric mixture. But the greatest part in family and cultural continuity is of course played by mothers. We hear little of German women. For the traditionally strongest elements, we should look to the old population, varied no more and probably less than in bigger frontier provinces, and varied least in the country folk whose life was closest to the land. Nobody doubts this for Noricum Mediterraneum; and in Ripense, the first signs of German settlers from Bavaria, archaeologically speaking, come from the end of the sixth century. Their cemeteries, which provide the signs, are all west of the Enns; thus the interval there, for native recuperation, had been a century. East of it, where we have viewed native survival as growing stronger, even quite near the Danube, and notably around the Vienna Woods, through St Severin's primary region where so much of its strength was due to him, the interval might be hazardous past the border of Pannonia, with its Suebi and afterwards Longobards (pp. 99, 126), but on Noric ground could endure at least to the coming of neighbour Slavs, and of the Avars (in Pannonia only from 568). Neither need have affected that primary region greatly.

What has been written of it here above requires little final summary. On the Comagenis neighbourhood, the Vienna Woods and their riverside, and the Vienna Basin itself, with the tale of research within the City (pp. 120–5, 127–31, and 131–44), this study has aimed above all to show that good historical thinking—just as in Upper Austria, but here with a greater intensity—needs an archaeology closely judged in topographical framing: side by side with the ancient texts, inscriptions and lastly place-names. This is the apologia for so much argument from detail. And if further excuse is needed, it lies surely in Eugippius: studied with the same topography, but illumined throughout his narratives—by no means here exhausted—with his saint's personality and character. St Severin's Favianis, and in consequence his grave, do seem to call for placing within his primary region's heart. Thus to the problems posed by Vienna, by Favianis and Vindobona, the claims here advanced for a solution gain strength, as our study has gained refreshment, from the *Vita Severini*. Archaeology, with St Severin, enters deeper into history.

Bibliography

AIGEN, A., 1959. 'Favianis und der Heilige Severin.' *Passauer Jahrbuch* 3, pp. 168ff.

—, 1963. 'Favianis und der Heilige Severin.' *Passauer Jahrbuch*, 6, pp. 5ff.

ALFÖLDY, G., 1973. *Noricum*. History of the Provinces of the Roman Empire, ed. D. Dudley and others. London.

ASCHBACH, J., 1860. 'Über die römischen Militärstationen in Ufernoricum zwischen Lauriacum und Vindobona, neben einer Untersuchung über die Lage der norischen Stadt Faviana.' *Sitzungsberichte der Akademie der Wissenschaften, philosoph.-hist. Klasse*, 35, pp. 3–32. Vienna.

BARB, A., 1948. 'Ein spätrömischer "Burgus" bei St. Margarethen im Burgenland.' *Österreichische-Archäologische Jahreshefte* 37, cols. 263–86. Vienna.

BEKKER, J. 1890. Edition of Constantine Porphyrogenitus, *De Thematibus et administrando Imperio*, in *Corpus Script. Hist. Byzantinorum* III. Bonn.

BETZ, A., 1956. *Aus Österreichs römischer Vergangenheit*. Vienna.

BIELER, L., with collab. KRISTAN, L., 1965. *Eugippius: The Life of Saint Severin* (trans. into English). 'Fathers of the Church' series, vol. 55. Washington.

BLUMBERGER, F., 1849. 'Bedenken gegen die gewöhnliche Ansicht von Wiens Identität mit Favianis.' *Archiv für Österreichische Geschichtsquellen*, 2, pp. 355 ff.

BÖCKING, E., 1839–53. *Notitia Dignitatum*, Occident chapter XXXIV, pp. 98–100. Bonn.

BÖHMER J. F. 1908. *Die Regesten des Kaiserreiches unter den Karolingern*, being vol. I of his *Regesta Imperii*. 2nd edn., E. Mühlbacher, Innsbruck.

CAMESINA, A., 1865. 'Wien und seine Bewohner während der Türkenbelagerung 1683.' *Mitteilungen des Altertum-Vereines zu Wien*, 8.

CRONE, C. R., 1954. *The World Map of Richard of Haldringham in Hereford*. Royal Geographical Society, London.

CUNTZ, O. (ed.), 1929. *Itineraria Romana, I*. Leipzig.

ECKHART, L., 1966. 'Die Arbeiten des Jahres 1965 in der Laurentiuskirche zu Lorch/ Enns,' *Jahrbuch des Oberösterreichischen Musealvereines* 3, pp. 295ff. Linz.

EGGER, R., 1957. 'Berichte über die altchristlichen Funde in Österreich.' *Actes du 5me. Congrès International d'Archéologie chrétienne, Aix-en-Provence 1954*, pp. 73ff. Rome/Paris.

EGGER, RUDOLF, and VETTERS, H., 1963. *Atlas der Österreichischen Alpenländer, V.3, Topographie der Römerzeit.* Österr. Akad. der Wissenschaften, Vienna.

EGLI, J. J., 1893. *Nomina Geographica.* Leipzig.

EISLER, M., 1919. *Historischer Atlas des Wiener Stadtbildes.* Vienna.

ERTL, F., 1965. *Topographia Norici.* Kremsmünster.

ETTLINGER, ELISABETH, 1961. 'Vindonissa.' In PAULY, IXA, 1, cols. 82–105.

FINSTERWALDER, K., 1966. *Romanische Vulgärsprache in Rätien und Norikum.* Innsbrucker Beiträge zur Kulturwissenschaft, 12. Innsbruck.

FISCHER, L., 1764. *Brevis notitia urbis veteris Vindobonae.* Vienna.

FORTIA D'URBAN, Marquis de, 1845. *Recueil des Itinéraires anciens.* Paris.

FUHRMANN, M., 1765. *Alt- und Neu-Wien: Historische Beschreibung . . . von Wien und seinen Vorstädten*, I. Vienna.

GRAF, A., 1936. *Übersicht der antiken Geographie von Pannonien.* Dissertationes Pannonicae I, 5. Budapest.

GRIENBERGER, TH., 1894. 'Vindobona-Wienne: eine etymologische Untersuchung.' *Sitzungsberichte der Akad. der Wissenschaften, philosoph.-hist. Klasse* 131. Vienna.

GÜTTENBERGER, H., 1924. *Die Donaustädte in Nieder-Österreich als geographische Erscheinung.* Vienna.

HABERL, JOHANNA, 1960. 'Severins Grab und die Anfänge Wiens.' *Archiv für Kulturberichte* 62, Heft 3, pp. 348-56.

—, 1962. On the Heiligenstadt excavations, in *Die Furche*, 12, p. 8. Vienna. *See also* 1964.

—, 1964. 'Immer noch St Severins Grab.' *Die Furche*, 35, p. 9. Vienna.

HANSIZ, MARCUS, 1727. *Germania Sacra.* Augsburg.

HERMANN, H. J., 1923. *Die frühmittelalterlichen Handschriften des Abendlandes.* Leipzig.

HORMAYR, J. VON, 1813. *Taschenbuch, Diplomatarien und Scriptorum.* Vienna.

—, 1823. *Wien, seine Geschicke und seine Denkwürdigkeiten.* I, 1/2, and II; each vol. divided into numbered parts (*Hefte*). Vienna.

HOUFNAGL, JACOBUS, ANTVERPIENSIS, 1609. *Viennam descriptam . . .* (engraving). Vienna.

HUBER, A., 1875. *Geschichte der Einführung und Verbreitung des Christentums in Südostdeutschland.* Salzburg.

JAUBERT, A., 1836/40. *Géographie d'Idrisi: Receuil des Voyages*, tomes V–VI, 1836, 1840. Paris.

JONES, A. H. M., 1964. *The Later Roman Empire, 284–602;* 3 vols. and maps. Oxford.

KALT, M. VON, 1867. Edition of the *Chronica de Gestis Hungarorum ab origine gentis*. Budapest.

KASCHNITZ-WEINBERG, G., 1910, 1911. *Mitteilungen der Zentral-Kommission*, 3 ser., 9 (1910), pp. 343ff.; and *Jahrbuch des Altertum-Vereines in Wien*, 5 (1911), pp. 31ff.; both on his excavations at the Roman fort at Zeiselmauer.

KENNER, F., 1868–9. *Römerorte in Nieder-Österreich*. Vienna.

—, 1870. 'Noricum und Pannonien.' *Berichte und Mitteilungen des Altertum-Vereines zu Wien*, 9, pp. 1ff.

—, 1878. 'Zur Topographie der Römerorte in Niederösterreich.' *Berichte und Mitteilungen des Altertum-Vereines zu Wien*, 17, pp. 277ff.

—, 1880. 'Favianis, eine Darstellung des Streites um diesen Ort und seine Lage.' *Berichte und Mitteilungen des Altertum-Vereines zu Wien*, 19, pp. 49ff.

—, 1882. 'Favianis, Mautern und Wien.' *Blätter des Vereines für Landeskunde von Niederösterreich*, n.s. 16, pp. 9ff.

—, 1897. 'Wien zur Römerzeit.' In *Geschichte der Stadt Wien*, vol. I, pp. 107ff.

—, 1908/1910. 'Die Zivilstadt von Vindobona. *Monatsblatt des Altertum-Vereines zu Wien*, 9, pp. 139ff.

—, 1910. 'Die Zivilstadt von Vindobona.' *Mitteilungsblatt des Altertum-Vereines zu Wien*, 27, pp. 129ff.

KLEIN, M., 1781. *Notitia Austriae Antiquae et Mediae*. Monasterium Tegernseensis (Tegernsee).

KLOIBER, Ä., 1957, 1962. *Das Gräberfeld von Lauriacum Ziegelfeld* and . . . *Espelmayrfeld*. Forschungen in Lauriacum 4/5 and 8. Landesmuseum, Linz.

KNABL, R., 1866. 'Der Cetius als Grenze zwischen Noricum und Pannonien.' *Mitteilungen des historischen Vereines für Steiermark*, 14, pp. 72ff. Graz.

KOLLER, H., 1963. *Mitteilungen des Instituts für Österreichische Geschichte*, 71, pp. 237ff.

KRAMERT, K., and WINTER, K. K., 1959. *St. Severin, Der Heilige zwischen Ost und West*. Klosterneuburg.

KUBITSCHEK, W., 1894. On the Nietzing Roman milestone, in *Archäologisch-Epigraphische Mitteilungen*, 17, pp. 149–51.

—, 1906. 'Vom norischen Donau-Ufer.' *Mitt. Zentral-Komm. f. Denkmalpflege*, 3 ser., 5, cols. 41ff. Vienna.

—, 1919. 'Itinerarstudien.' *Abhandlungen der Österreichischen Akademie der Wissenschaften, phil.-hist. Klasse*, 61, 3, pp. 1ff. Vienna.

KUBITSCHEK, W., 1929. 'Ältere Berichte über den römischen Limes in Pannonien. *Sitzungsberichte der Akad. der Wissenschaften, Wien*, 209, art. 1 of Heft 1, pp. 35ff. Vienna.

—, 1934. 'Studien zur Geographie des Ptolemäus, I: Die Landesgrenzen.' *Akademie der Wissenschaften in Wien, Sitzungsberichte*, 215, no. 5. Vienna.

LADENBAUER-OREL, H., 1966. 'Archäologische Stadtkernforschung in Wien.' In *Jahrbuch des Vereins für Geschichte der Stadt Wien*, 21/22 (1965/6).

LAMBECCIUS, PETRUS HAMBURGENSIS, 1669. *Commentariorum de Augustissima Bibliotheca Caesarea Vindobonensi Liber I*. Vindobonae (Vienna).

LANGMANN, G., 1971. 'Haupttor von Vindobona entdeckt.' *Antike Welt: Zeitschrift für Archäologie und Urgeschichte*, 2, Heft 3, p. 56. Zürich.

LAZIUS, W., 1546. *Rerum Viennensium Libri*, I, II. Vienna.

LECHNER, K., 1954. On the Heiligenstadt tomb discovery, etc., in *Wiener Geschichtsblätter*, 69, pp. 31ff.

LEHR, W., 1909. *Pilgrim, Bischof von Passau*. (Dissertation.) Berlin.

LELEWEL, J., 1851. *La Géographie du Moyen Âge*. Breslau.

MANNERT, K., 1818. *Kurzer Entwurf der alten Geographie*. Leipzig.

MARSIGLI, A., Graf, 1726. *De Antiquitatibus Romanorum ad ripas Danubii*. Vol. II of his Danubius Pannonico-Mysicus. The Hague.

MILLER, K., 1895. *Die ältesten Weltkarten*. Stuttgart.

— (ed.), 1916. *Itineraria Romana*. Stuttgart.

—, 1926. *Mappae Arabicae*. Stuttgart.

MÓCSY, A., 1962. 'Pannonia.' In PAULY. Supplement IX, cols. 515–776.

—, 1973. *Pannonia*. History of the Provinces of the Roman Empire, ed. D. Dudley and others. London.

MOMMSEN, TH. (ed.), 1898. *Eugippii Vita Severini: Scriptores Rerum Germanicorum in usum scholarum ex Monumentis Germaniae Historicis recussi*. Berlin.

MÜLLENHOFF, K., 1882. Edition of Jordanes, *Getica*, in *Monumenta Germanicae Historiae, Auctores Antiquissimi* V, 1. Berlin.

MÜLLER, R., 1897. 'Der Name Wiens.' In *Geschichte der Stadt Wien*. Vienna.

NASH-WILLIAMS, V. E., 1952. *The Roman Legionary Fortress at Caerleon, Monmouthshire*. National Museum of Wales, Cardiff.

NEUMANN, A., 1952a. On the Heiligenstadt tomb discovery, in *Amtsblatt der Stadt Wien*, no. 89.

—, 1952b. On the Heiligenstadt tomb discovery, in *Pro Austria Romana*, no. 11/12 (December).

—, 1954a. In *Pro Austria Romana*, no. 5/6 (June).

NEUMANN, 1954*b*. On the Heiligenstadt tomb discovery, in *Amtsblatt der Stadt Wien*, no. 59.

—, 1956. On the Heiligenstadt tomb discovery, in *Carinthia*, pp. 461–2.

—, 1961. 'Vindobona.' In PAULY, IXA, 1, cols. 53–80, esp. 75ff.

—, 1962. 'Die Ausgrabungen in der Jakobskirche von Wien-Heiligenstadt 1952/53.' *Bonner Jahrbücher* 162, pp. 480–506. (For 1962, issued 1963.)

—, 1967. *Die Skulpturen des Stadtgebietes von Vindobona*. Corpus der Skulpturen der Römischen Welt: Österreich Band I. Vienna.

—, 1967–8 and 1971. See p. 156 below.

NOLL, R., 1954. *Frühes Christentum in Österreich*. Vienna.

—, 1958. *Römische Siedlungen und Strassen im Limesgebiet zwischen Inn und Enns (Oberösterreich)*. Der Römische Limes in Österreich (RLiÖ), no. XXI. Vienna.

— (ed.), 1963. *Eugippius, Das Leben des Heiligen Severin*. Schriften und Quellen der Alten Welt, vol. 11, Deutsche Akademie der Wissenschaften zu Berlin. Text with author's translation, introduction, notes and map; bibliography (pp. 36–8) includes previous translations, all German.

NOVOTNY, E., 1923. 'Das römische Wien und seine Fortleben.' *Mitteil. des Vereines für Geschichte der Stadt Wien*, 4, pp. 5ff.

—, 1925. 'Vom Donau-Limes.' *Anzeiger der Akademie der Wissenschaften, phil.-hist. Klasse*, 62. Vienna.

ORTELIUS, A., 1579. *Teatrum Orbis Terrarum*. Antwerp.

ÖTTINGER, K., 1951. *Das Werden Wiens*. Vienna.

PALLMANN, R., 1864. *Die Geschichte der Völkerwanderungen*, II. Gotha.

PASCHER, G., 1949. *Römische Siedlungen und Strassen im Limesgebiet zwischen Enns und Leitha (Niederösterreich)*. Der Römische Limes in Österreich (RLiÖ), no. XIX. Vienna.

PAULY, A. F. von, *et al.*, 1839–52. *Real-Enzyklopädie der Klassischen Altertumswissenschaft*. Stuttgart. New edition, ed. G. Wissowa, 1894–1912; from 1912 ed. successively W. Kroll, K. Mittelhaus, K. Ziegler, vols. I–XVIII. 1; Supplement vols. I– (1903–), in progress likewise; and 2nd series, vols. IA, IIA, etc., in progress 1914– , edd. now K. Ziegler, W. Johm.

POLASCHEK, E., 1936. 'Notitia Dignitatum.' In PAULY, XVII 1, cols. 1077–115.

—, 1939. 'Trigisamo.' In PAULY, VIIA, 1, cols. 132–4.

—, 1944. On Roman Vienna, in R. Donin, *Geschichte der Bildenden Kunst in Wien*, pp. 95ff. Vienna.

POLASCHEK, E., and LADENBAUER, H., 1948. 'Das römische Kastell von Traismauer.' *Österreichische Archäologische Jahresschrift* 37, cols. 199ff.

PRANDAU, Freiherr von, 1789. *Kritische Geschichte der Stadt Wien.* Vienna.

REDLICH, O., and SCHÖNBACH, A. E. (edd.), 1907/8. 'Des Gutolf von Heiligenkreuz Translatio S. Delicianae.' *Sitzungsberichte der K. u. K. Akademie der Wissenschaften, philosoph.-hist. Klasse,* 159, II Abhandlung. Vienna.

REITINGER, J., 1969. *Ur- und Frühgeschichte Oberösterreichs.* 2 vols.: I (narrative) *Oberösterreich in ur- und frühgeschichtlicher Zeit;* II (descriptive catalogue of finds) *Die ur- und frühgeschichtlichen Funde Oberösterreichs.* Linz.

RLiÖ. Der Römische Limes in Österreich (series) (various authors), vols. in progress 1900– . (Vienna, Akad. der Wissenschaften). *See also* NOLL 1958, PASCHER 1949, and p. 156 below (NEUMANN).

RUNGG, J., 1963. *Ortsnamen der Goten, Römer und Franken in Rätien, Noricum, besonders Tirol.* Innsbruck.

SCHMELLER, A., 1951. Reporting his excavations at St. Ruprecht's church, Vienna. In ÖTTINGER 1951, pp. 227ff.

SCHNETZ, A., 1940. *Anonymus Ravennas.* Tübingen.

SCHÖNWISNER, S., 1780. *Commentarium Geographicum in Romanorum Iter per Pannoniae ripam.* Budae.

SEECK, O. (ed.), 1876 (1962). *Notitia Dignitatum, Orientis et Occidentis,* pp. 196–9, with 121, 145, Berlin, 1876. Reprinted photographically, Frankfurt, 1962.

STEIN, E., 1928. *Geschichte des spätrömischen Reiches.* 2 vols. Vienna. Revised as *Histoire du Bas-Empire,* Paris 1949, 1959.

STIGLITZ (THALLER), H., 1961. 'Das römische Kastell Piro-Torto bei Zwentendorf, an der Donau.' *Kulturberichte aus Niederösterreich, Beilage der amtlichen Nachrichten,* 3 ser., 1, 3.

—, 1963. *Führer durch das römische Mautern an der Donau.* Österreichisches Archäologisches Institut, Vienna.

SÜSS, E., 1897. 'Der Boden der Stadt und sein Relief.' In *Geschichte der Stadt Wien,* vol. I, pp. 11ff.

SWOBODA, E., 1964. *Carnuntum, seine Geschichte und seine Denkmäler.* Römische Forschungen in Niederösterreich, I. Vienna.

THALLER, H., 1953. On the Heiligenstadt tomb discovery, in *Carinthia,* pp. 76–8. (Thaller later = STIGLITZ.)

VETTER, EMIL, 1963. 'Handschriftliche Grundlage und Textgestaltung' (der *Vita Severini*). In NOLL 1963, pp. 27–35, 39.

VISSCHER, G. M., 1672 (1920). *Topographie von Ober- und Nieder-Österreich.* Vienna. Ed. M. Vansca, 1920, *Nr. 2: Prospectus Orientalis Viennae Metropolis Austriae.*

WEISS, C., 1872. *Geschichte der Stadt Wien.* Vienna.

WERNER, F., 1858. 'Der Heilige Hyppolytus.' *Theologische Monatschrift der Diöcese St Pölten*, 1, using *Liber Monumentorum Boicorum* XXVIII, tom. II, pp. 208–9 (for document of 985).

WESSELY, C., 1893. 'Wien und die Goten.' *Blätter des Vereines für Landeskunde von Niederösterreich*, n.s. 27.

WINTER, E. K., 1959. *Studien zum Severinsproblem.* Klosterneuburg.

ZIBERMAYR, J., 1956. *Noricum, Bayern und Österreich.* Linz.

Of the works by A. NEUMANN, pp. 153–4 above, relating otherwise all to the Heiligenstadt tomb discovery, those on Roman Vienna are 1961 (article in PAULY) and 1967 (Corpus of Sculptures). His further two volumes, 1967–8, nos. XXIII and XXIV of RLiÖ, add detail but conserve his main position on the topography, as set out in the article of 1961. References to this have been judged sufficient in the text (and p. 132, n.1, to the 1967 Corpus), to avoid overloading it for the reader. But the four works were followed by a fifth, in 1971, addressed to a wider public: *Vindobona* (Vienna, Böhlau). This, which puts his position much as before, appeared after our present work was written.

J.H., C.F.C.H., October 1972.

Index